WOODY GUTHRIE

Woody Guthrie

AN INTIMATE LIFE

GUSTAVUS STADLER

BEACON PRESS
BOSTON

BEACON PRESS
Boston, Massachusetts
www.beacon.org

Beacon Press books
are published under the auspices of
the Unitarian Universalist Association of Congregations.

23 22 21 20   8 7 6 5 4 3 2 1

This book is printed on acid-free paper that meets the uncoated paper
ANSI/NISO specifications for permanence as revised in 1992.

Text design and composition by Kim Arney

Library of Congress Cataloging-in-Publication Data

Names: Stadler, Gustavus, author.
Title: Woody Guthrie : an intimate life / Gustavus Stadler.
Description: Boston : Beacon Press, 2020. | Includes bibliographical
references and index.
Identifiers: LCCN 2020010984 (print) | LCCN 2020010985 (ebook) |
ISBN 9780807018910 (hardcover) | ISBN 9780807019092 (ebook)
Subjects: LCSH: Guthrie, Woody, 1912-1967. | Folk singers—
United States—Biography.
Classification: LCC ML410.G978 S73 2020 (print) | LCC ML410.G978 (ebook) |
DDC 782.42162/130092 [B]—dc23
LC record available at https://lccn.loc.gov/2020010984
LC ebook record available at https://lccn.loc.gov/2020010985

For my parents

CONTENTS

Introduction

WHEN TO BE PERSONAL

O NE EVENING IN MARCH 1942, Woody Guthrie strolled into a small
New York dance studio and sat down on a folding chair. As he
pulled the strings of his guitar into tune, he watched a small group of
dancers—eight women and two men—stretching and twisting themselves
effortlessly, bringing home the contrast with his own broken-down physical state: the stiffness in his joints, the smoke-tarred inside of his lungs.
The group chatted casually with an ease that belied the bandages and
gauze pads covering their knees and ankles.

He knew two of the group before him. One was the ensemble's leader,
Sophie Maslow, who was surveying the room and getting ready to start
the rehearsal. Sophie was the one who had invited him here, just a few
days ago. It wasn't the type of thing he'd ever done, but the decision to
participate was a fairly easy one. She'd already choreographed a couple
of solo pieces based on his *Dust Bowl Ballads* recording from 1940. Her
previous works as a choreographer were tributes to the Soviet Union, a
nation whose social and political structure both she and he were given to
describing in idealistic, utopian terms. And her idea for this piece sounded
good to him: dances, based on folk forms, to traditional American songs,
along with excerpts from the earthy poetry of Carl Sandburg. She wanted
Guthrie's guitar to accompany the group she'd assembled, made up of
dancers moonlighting from established companies; Sophie herself, for
instance, danced in the illustrious, artistically groundbreaking Martha
Graham Dance Company. In between dance numbers, the plan was for
Guthrie and another musician to act out comic dialogues and sketches,

highlighting the folksy wit and wisdom with which he'd built a following on both radio and records, first in Los Angeles in the late 1930s, and now in New York and beyond.

Sophie called everyone to order and nodded at him. The first number in the piece, titled *Folksay*, was the traditional "I Ride an Old Paint," a staple of his repertoire, of everyone's repertoire. He started to strum the simple chord progression. The dancers, dressed in denim, plaid shirts, and cowboy hats, began to move, directed by some graceful, invisible muse. Then something in the atmosphere changed. One young woman hesitated, then quickly recovered. But a couple of seconds later, another girl got stuck waiting for Guthrie to deliver a beat that arrived just a split second late. She tripped, cursed, giggled a little along with the others. Maslow, worried about time, suppressing annoyance at the guitarist's sloppiness, called them back into order.

He began to run through the chords again, wondering if the cocky grin he'd summoned had succeeded in hiding that he was "nervous and scared."[1] Things started out better. It was such a simple song. He'd played it hundreds of times—at parties in north Texas, in clearings among tents of exhausted workers in California migrant camps, at hootenannies full of beer-soaked communist intellectuals in Los Angeles. And now here in New York City, where—but suddenly, a clatter of colliding limbs, and someone was splayed on the floor. This time, there was no laughter, just looks of concern and, he's afraid, some scowls in his direction. They were probably wondering how it could be so hard to play such a simple song at an even tempo. They might even be thinking he was a fraud. Why not just dance to records if it was going to be this much trouble, if people were going to get hurt? All the camaraderie and ease of minutes ago had dissolved, it seemed. Sophie might have already been considering other guitar players.

When he had arrived at the rehearsal, he had recognized one person in the room other than Maslow, and now she was approaching him. People here called her "Margie." She had introduced herself as Marjorie Mazia when she and Maslow had shown up unannounced a few nights earlier at the house he was sharing with a group of politically like-minded musicians called the Almanac Singers. Like Maslow, Mazia had been taken aback by Guthrie's *Dust Bowl Ballads*. In those 1940 recordings, both young women heard echoes of the Yiddish songs their parents sometimes sang to them as children, laments for a people that, just like the Dust Bowl victims, were made homeless by greed and exploitation. It made them feel a connection with a population they'd barely known existed.

Walking over to the singer, Margie held something in her hand: a stack of what looked like those cardboard cards that come in new shirt packages. Smiling, radiant, looking sharp-eyed but reassuring, she sat down on the floor in front of him and began to write numbers and cues on the cards. "Now Woody," she said, "if you can count, you can do this."[2]

That night in the dance studio, as Guthrie tried to do his part to assist Maslow's company in their endeavor, he required help achieving a more literal, microcosmic version of what his songs and writing encouraged others to do: get organized, become part of a planned movement, join in a united, collaborative process. And yet this personal intervention—in a scene of poor timing, disorder, bodies made vulnerable—helped set Woody Guthrie's life on a new course. It's a story that both Woody and Marjorie retold many times over the course of their lives, one that their daughter, Nora Guthrie, calls "a part of our family lore."[3] Fundamentally, it reflects the clash of two ways of keeping time, the loose and improvisational rhythms of folk music at odds with the intricate, precise timing of modern choreography—an unlikely alchemy with which not only Maslow but Martha Graham and other eminent modernists were experimenting. But as a family legend, it describes an inaugural act of intimacy, an unsolicited but much-needed offer of care in a moment of helplessness. Woody Guthrie's fascination with the revolutionary potential of intimacy, honed during a lifetime of contact with fragile bodies—including, just a few years after this dance rehearsal, his own—is the subject of this book.

It shouldn't come as a surprise that dance would be an arena of significant anxiety for Woody Guthrie. The slight man sitting on a folding chair with a guitar, struggling to hide his shame, knew very well that human bodies are precarious things, and that, consequently, they make us need the intimate care and attention of other people. That awareness filled his original songs, like the ones Maslow and Mazia had heard on his record, in which he described the human wreckage caused by dust storms, floods, and other "natural" catastrophes whose impact increased proportionally with the poverty of the people affected; it was in his persistent attention to the predations of capitalism, and the damage routinely done to workers laboring in substandard, even dangerous conditions. He knew the violent blowback they could expect from their bosses when they banded together as a group to seek a fair share of their labor's rewards, or a healthier working environment. He had sung about it in songs like "Dust Pneumonia Blues," "Dust Can't Kill Me," "Hard Travelin'," and many more.

Born in Oklahoma in 1912, Guthrie had grown up on soil with a deeply rooted history of vicious, unrepaired violence. Before being granted statehood in 1907, the region was initially designated as "Indian territory," a place for the federal government to stow several nations of indigenous people forcibly uprooted from their land in the South and Southeast in order to open up vast swaths of the continent for the use and profit of white settlers. On May 31, 1921, sixty miles north of Guthrie's hometown of Okemah, hundreds of white Tulsa residents launched a quasi-military assault on the Black neighborhood of Greenwood, dropping bombs from the air, setting buildings on fire, killing as many as three hundred people and razing the prosperous area once known as "Black Wall Street." More locally, in 1911, the year before Guthrie's birth, Okemah had been the site of a brutal lynching, in which a Black mother and son, Laura and L.D. Nelson, accused of killing a white police officer, were seized from a jail and hanged from a bridge over the Canadian River just south of town. Although no documentary evidence can confirm it, in the late 1970s, Guthrie's uncle Claude told biographer Joe Klein that Charley Guthrie, Woody's father, was a member of the lynching party. He was a Democratic Party operative in the South and, by virtue of having that role, almost certainly a white supremacist; some biographers suspect he was an active member of the Ku Klux Klan. He wrote reactionary articles for the *Okemah Ledger* with titles like "Socialism Urges Negro Equality."

An image of the Nelsons' bodies hanging over the water—rendered by the same Okemah photographer who had taken a family portrait in 1907 of the Guthries pre-Woody—circulated nationally as a postcard, and seared itself on Guthrie's memory, to the point that he occasionally claimed to have witnessed the event himself. In one of his last sustained acts of creative output, as illness and injury made it increasingly difficult for him to play the guitar, he produced a series of paintings of lynchings, expressionistic watercolor scrawls of naked bodies terrorized by Klansmen.

His acquaintance with traumatized, damaged, and vulnerable bodies had even more personal origins. His family life as a child was littered with them. All-out brawls were routine in the raucous world of local electoral politics, and some of little Woody's earliest memories were of his dad coming home bruised and bloodied, a sight that often sent his mother into fits of worry and despair. These scrapes eventually cost Charley one or two of his fingers.[4]

More searing, and more grim, were the fires.

Before Woody was born, the family's house burned down; according to Guthrie in his autobiographical book *Bound for Glory*, "nobody ever knew how or why," but no one was hurt.[5] Then, on the morning of May 18, 1919, when Woody was six, an argument between his mother, Nora Belle, and his fourteen-year-old older sister, Clara, turned into a full-on fracas, ending with Clara's clothing in flames, ravaging her entire body. She succumbed to the burns in her own bed that evening. The obituary in the local newspaper for "Little Clara Edna Guthrie" smoothed over the incident, reporting that she had died "from burns received while working about the stove."[6] And Guthrie himself never gave a definitive account of how it had happened.

The incident, while extreme, wasn't out of the ordinary for the family. For a couple of years Nora Belle's behavior had been confusing and erratic. Her moods jumped quickly between calm, anxiety, and intense anger. Sometimes she performed odd physical feats, like moving items of furniture around the family home. She would be found in town picking through heaps of garbage, even though the family was economically secure at that time. And one time, Clara had come home to find the family's then-youngest child, George, swaddled in newspaper and stowed in the oven.

Indeed, Nora's own body often seemed under siege by forces she couldn't control. One moment she would appear to be fine, and then the next, "her face would twitch and her lips would snarl and her teeth would show."[7] When Woody wasn't taking it personally, blaming himself for her plight, he blamed the family's economic insecurity and Charley's political battles for causing her such worry.

Then, on June 25, 1927, Charley awoke from a nap on the couch to find his shirt soaked with kerosene and his wife setting fire to his clothes.

He ran outside and rolled out the flames in the dirt, but not before sustaining severe burns across his torso. Two days later, Charley's Masonic lodge brothers arranged to have Nora committed to the Central State Hospital for the Insane in Norman, where she died three years later.

Guthrie's accounts of these dramatic events often changed over the years, a common phenomenon with deeply traumatized people. Sometimes, he went to extremes in an effort to protect his mother's reputation. For example, he told a fellow musician, singer Lee Hays, that his father had in fact been attempting to commit suicide. He also told Hays that he had seen Charley's ribs laid bare, the fire having consumed a swath of skin on his torso.[8] And fiery accidents, as we will see, continued to haunt both him and those closest to him.

Fifteen years later and half a continent away, the problems in the studio—young, agile dancers endangering their limbs and joints while struggling to keep up with Guthrie's muddled time-keeping—would seem to resemble slapstick comedy more than any of these disturbing, violent episodes. But Guthrie's long-lasting fixation on the rehearsal incident, his attention to what he would later call dancers "bomp[ing] and tromp[ing] on one another," illustrates his life-long preoccupation with the fragility of bodies, with their propensity for coming unorganized and undone, with their need for assistance, care, and repair.[9] That a trait of his own bodily comportment—his uneven sense of rhythm—triggered the dancers' mishaps resonated with his long-held suspicion that he was somehow at odds with, out of sync with, the world. It reprised something of his childhood belief that he had caused his mother's mysterious illness, a self-punishing fantasy he described in the autobiographical novel whose manuscript pages he was scribbling when he got home from *Folksay* rehearsals and performances. In fact, Nora Belle suffered from Huntington's disease—known before the 1970s as Huntington's chorea (the Greek word for dance, poignantly)—a hereditary neurological illness with brutal physiological and cognitive effects. But because so little was known about the illness, and because so few doctors had seen cases, she was treated as "insane" and sent to an early death in a state asylum. Sometime nearly two decades later, in the mid-to-late 1940s, after he had written and recorded many songs documenting the vulnerability of bodies to social, political, and economic forces, Guthrie himself began to experience symptoms of Huntington's, thus experiencing a new kind of intimacy with his mother's body.

The nervous, blustery man sitting on a folding chair in the downtown Manhattan dance studio, awkwardly participating in a performance conceived by a woman, and performed by a majority-female troupe, is not the Woody Guthrie we know. The familiar image is of a rough-and-ready folk singer who scrawled militant slogans on his guitar; a champion of the common man; a master composer of the protest song; a boxcar hopping "ramblin' man" in the romantic tradition of peripatetic figures like Mark Twain's Huckleberry Finn, James Fenimore Cooper's Natty Bumppo, and Herman Melville's voyagers on the *Pequod*; perhaps even a blueprint for the imminent emergence of Jack Kerouac and Neal Cassady in their roles as countercultural heroes. We know him as a fierce supporter of the labor movement, a passionate cheerleader for the public works projects of the New Deal, and perhaps some kind of communist. He is well established as Bob Dylan's idol and mentor. An anodyne version of his song "This Land Is Your Land," stripped of a verse indicting the concept of private property, circulates though elementary schools and various misbegotten political campaigns, making it easy for us to know him as a classic American mythical figure: the male wanderer unfettered by social conventions associated with home, work, family. It is a fantasy of rebellion so widely evoked for so long as to be, paradoxically, quintessentially conventional.

The magnetism of this Woody Guthrie has obscured another side of him, the side that is the focus of this book. "The lesson to learn, the only lesson to learn is just when to be and when not to be very personal," he scrawled during one of his frantic writing sessions in the mid-1940s, as he was trying to continue expanding his artistic profile while witnessing the labor-centered left, amid which he'd earned his reputation, struggle to resist the cold wave of postwar anti-communist hysteria. He was someone interested in thinking about how it feels to be in the world—with what makes us feel good (being close to others, sharing secrets with them, having sex with them) and what makes us feel bad (injustice and inequality, but also shame, insult, isolation from loved ones). This Guthrie was an artist in multiple modes—music, verse and prose, fiction, painting—who didn't set the personal against the political. The personal wasn't synonymous with the *private*, in the sense of that term suggesting a retreat from the public world of politics and power struggle. The political stakes of knowing "when to be very personal" reflected his deep concern with what our bodies tell us about life, with how they make us vulnerable to and dependent on others, with how they make the historical context in which we live not just an object of knowledge but something we *feel*. He conveyed this perspective in how he described his contact with the Communist Party in Oklahoma: "They gave me as good a feeling as I ever got from being around anybody in my life."[10]

He read Marx, but he was not a theorist or policy maker, at least not in the traditional sense. A just reorganization of the world, he believed, would occur not at the behest of some intellectual's insight, but because the people who made up the mass had been empowered to resist the feelings of demoralization and cynicism forced on them. Capitalism and fascism both secured hegemony by maintaining particular emotional environments, encouraging cruelty and shame, and persuading people that they were "born to lose." As with healing damaged bodies, overcoming this abject emotional atmosphere required interpersonal collaboration—acts of repair. Feeling shame was a kind of social wound that could be treated by love and reassurance. His role as an artist was, essentially, the role of a partner or other intimate—to salve these feelings and rejuvenate participation in the fight for justice.

Where has this history gone, and why is this not the Guthrie we know? Materially, most of it resides in Tulsa, Oklahoma's Woody Guthrie Center, just a few blocks from ground zero of the 1921 white supremacist massacre. The archive there hosts materials saved for years by Marjorie and sustained into the twenty-first century by Woody and Marjorie's daughter, Nora Lee. They present a far more multidimensional figure than the one with whom most of us are familiar. The vault holds several thousands of pages, both handwritten and typed, left by a man for whom writing didn't so much *describe* life as *constitute* it, or at least a vast part of it. Songs were only one form this expressive energy took. The frenetic activity of his brain, channeled through pens and typewriter keys, fills loose-leaf pages, onion-skin typing paper, notebooks, address books, calendars, DIY lyric books, and sketch pads. His scrawl fills cheap personal calendars and address books that he picked up at dime stores and adapted into journals—or more nearly, artist's books, with swirling figures, just on the verge of abstraction, painted in watercolor over handwritten musings, verses, essays, sermons, observations, overheard phrases, and sex fantasies. Here is a book filled with things his first daughter with Marjorie, Cathy Ann, said as a toddler. Here is a large ledger filled with pasted-in, typewritten lyrics, a do-it-yourself songbook. Here is a sketchpad of lyrics alternating with watercolor paintings of people being hanged. The materials cover his life, from early scribblings in Oklahoma to late, heart-wrenching, illegible letters written to his children from the hospital. There are manuscripts of novels, plays, and memoirs. There are many hundreds, perhaps thousands, of letters, some full of lucid ideological musings, many full of avowals of love and sexual desire. There are thousands of song lyrics, the majority of them never recorded. As has been evident over the past two decades in lyrics Nora Guthrie has bequeathed to contemporary artists (resulting, most famously, in the three collaborative *Mermaid Avenue* albums by the British folk-punk singer Billy Bragg and the American band Wilco), these songs often venture farther into personal and intimate matters than any of those he recorded during his lifetime. Except for the visual pieces included in the sumptuous 2005 volume *Woody Guthrie Artworks* and the writings included in a couple of now-out-print volumes, the majority of these materials have been seen only by scholars.

But this version of Guthrie has also gone missing in large part because of its incompatibility with the most dominant stories told about the history of the Left in the US, most notably its shifts between the 1930s and the 1960s.

"Old Left" and "New Left" are terms historians and political scientists have used to describe mid-twentieth-century shifts in what Michael Denning calls "the tradition of radical democratic movements for social transformation."[11] In this broad narrative, the Old Left arose in response to the economic crisis of the Great Depression; the New Left took shape in the midst of an existential crisis, a numbing of the creative spirit brought on by the Cold War culture of conformity. The Old Left, openly sympathetic to socialism and communism, championed workers, labor unions, and collective approaches to social problems. The New Left, more skeptical of political parties, advocated for individual freedom of expression, nonconformity, the rights to use one's body as one pleased. Commentators align each era's cultural figures with these frames: as the story goes, leftists in the 1930s and '40s looked to people like Guthrie to rally masses, fire them up, and teach them about specific cases of exploitation and repression, while 1960s leftists looked to the Beats, psychedelics, rock music, and so on to tell them who they were as individuals, to assist them in finding heretofore hidden, repressed parts of their selves. For the Old Left, the story goes, art was a tool, and usually direct and literal. For the New Left, art was a means toward personal exploration, and aesthetic challenges were meant to expand the realm of individual experience.

And yet, so much falls out of this broad narrative. For one thing, it is a white left. While the period usually associated with the fight for Black equality, for instance, is usually framed as falling into the New Left era, the Old Left—the Communist Party of the United States (CPUSA) in particular—devoted tremendous amounts of energy to fighting for voting rights, economic justice, fair housing policy, and an end to racist police violence. To identify civil rights activism with the New Left is to ignore decades of campaigns on these issues, organized by Black party members. Guthrie learned about civil rights in this context, from Black-led groups like the CPUSA's Civil Rights Congress, becoming quite militant in his views by the 1950s.

What also falls out is a more nuanced picture of the Left of the late 1930s and early '40s. As scholars like Denning, Paul Mishler, and Daniel Hurewitz have made clear, the Old Left, known at the time as the Popular Front, was far from narrowly focused. Its conscripts believed passionately in the political value of the expressive arts. A bevy of artists, working in a wide range of media, including Sophie Maslow and her mentor, Martha Graham, began to draw material from rural and regional American cultures, believing them less sullied by capitalism. Eventually, Popular Front leftism even seeped into the Hollywood filmmaking industry, in the class allegories driving movies made by eminent directors like Orson Welles and Preston Sturges. To US leftists in the '30s, activist work didn't just mean labor organizing; it included founding cultural institutions: "literary clubs, workers theaters, camera clubs, film and photo leagues, composers collectives, Red dance troupes, and revolutionary choruses."[12] Parents sent their children to leftist summer camps in the mountains north of New York City.[13] As a veteran of the Communist Party and '30s leftist theater in Los Angeles told Hurewitz some sixty years later, "There was a recognition that the cultural expressions in life were as essential as the political treatises."[14]

Artistic expression and progressive politics became intertwined in more involved, subtle ways. A rich culture of the Left emerged, ranging from explicitly Marxist night classes and summer camps to Hollywood films constructed as allegories of New Deal social and economic initiatives. But the point of music, literature, and the other arts was not simply the representation of political theory in another medium. Art's aim was not to dress up slogans. Politics and the arts bled into one another. Books, plays, films, concerts, records, and art created personal, spiritual, emotional attachments, and told stories through which people could understand their own lives and feelings within a leftist framework. A lively cultural arena served to bind people together—something particularly necessary in a movement made up of many different factions. The aim was to cultivate the "spiritual life" of the anti-fascist left. An outing to see *The Magnificent Ambersons* or Paul Robeson in *Ballad for Americans* might perform this function as well as or better than a reading group's discussion of Marx's *Capital*.[15] So might a show or performance featuring old folk songs. Leftist politics gave people something they needed *personally*—that is, to be fully a person. As Vivian Gornick boldly put it in her 1977 oral history of the Popular Front–era CPUSA, *The Romance of American Communism*, "Being a Communist defined [party members] in a way that is almost impossible to understand today. It was *the* overriding element of identity, the one which subsumed all others."[16]

And as the testimony of Popular Front veterans in Gornick's book shows, the Old Left's draw was by no means purely ideological; it drew people—especially middle-class people—who wanted to *feel* a certain way, believe themselves participants in the making of history. Guthrie and others—writers, visual artists, musicians—gave form to these people's feelings, and taught them that their feelings could help make a more politically and economically just world.

|||||||||

Around the time Woody Guthrie met Marjorie Mazia, he made a project of expanding his profile as an artist and intellectual. He had made waves in music and union circles as a musical documentarian of the Dust Bowl and labor history. Around the time of the dance rehearsal, however, he had begun writing fiction, memoirs, essays, verse, plays. He drew and painted. In this expanded range of his work, we see a pre-1960s US left with which we are not familiar. We see, in particular, a great deal of very direct material about life *as felt*—in particular about the dispiriting power of shame and being stigmatized, and about the need for intimacy as a salve for shame. We also see a lot of writing about sex—not a topic that tends to come to mind when thinking of cultural warhorses of the Old Left like John Steinbeck and Pete Seeger.

Guthrie became known as a protest singer, but that label fails to capture the extent to which a general practice of living, focused on concern for working and poor people's emotional well-being, drove him as an artist. To him, this view did not contradict commitments to the labor movement or even communism. Indeed, he saw capitalism as an economic system that worked the life out of people's bodies, and subsumed them in worry, shame, and guilt, all the while convincing them that they were, at base, faulty and inadequate. This poisonous process, in his understanding, infected both bodies and minds, making people physically, psychologically, existentially sick. His music addressed people feeling alienated, inferior, and out of sync with the way capitalist interests had choreographed the world in which they lived. There had been labor songs since the late nineteenth century; the Industrial Workers of the World (IWW), or "Wobblies," a radical labor movement Guthrie revered, in 1909 first published their *Little Red Songbook*, full of rousing tributes to workers and their fallen martyrs. But there was something distinctly different about Guthrie's songwriting. It sought a kind of connection via what Guthrie would have called "being personal." He did what the best writers of popular song do: establish an emotional connection with their audiences, making each listener believe the singer is singing about their life—their thoughts, feelings, and experiences—in particular. Guthrie was an artist of an era in which, as cultural theorist Lauren Berlant puts it, "the fundamental gift-message of popular culture is 'You are not alone.'"[17] To those dragged down into shame and self-loathing by structural inequality, he was friend, lover, therapist, even mother. For Guthrie, intimacy was the place where people made one another powerful.

In the world of IWW songs, righteous anger was always just below the surface, ready to be tapped by the sound of a rousing chorus. There was tragedy, martyrdom, but no existential doubt; no one got anxious or depressed. In the songs Guthrie sang and wrote, heavily influenced by African American blues and the Carter Family's adaptations of traditional balladry, the "hard"-ness riddling lives—"Hard Travelin'" and "Hard, Ain't It Hard"—sapped people's revolutionary spirit and muted their capacity to act. Guthrie knew moods were not simply inconveniences or frills; he knew they actually reflected political struggle. When Guthrie sang the song, it was a political problem that people went "down the road feelin' bad." His lyrics linked economic straits to emotional states, with "worry" a particular bugbear, conveying an airless blur of depression, anxiety, fear, and fatigue:

I mined in your mines and I gathered in your corn
I been working, mister, since the day I was born
Now I worry all the time like I never did before
'Cause I ain't got no home in this world anymore[18]

Guthrie believed that bad feelings, like the "worry" and sense of groundlessness in the singer's voice in "I Ain't Got No Home in This World Anymore," were not simply the result of political exploitation and social inequality; they were the lived form of them. Desperation and anxiety made people pliable, vulnerable to false promises. As he wrote to Marjorie Mazia in a sprawling letter nine months after *Folksay* closed a successful three-week run, "Fascism would like for you to weep and hang your head and cry and get so mixed up in your thinking that you'd walk into one of its own churches looking for some kind of a personal salvation."[19] His role in organized resistance to authoritarianism was to reanimate clear thought and feelings of self-regard.

Again and again, these patterns of his thought homed in on the physical body. In the winter of 1947, he wrote in a notebook: "Be you old, young, fat, slim, too young, too fat, too slim, too nervous, too rich, too poor, too drunk, too sober, too everything else, you are pretty in your private ways to the eyes and ears and to the fingers of others."[20] Bodies were vulnerable not only physically, but culturally; they laid people bare to ridicule, stigma. Guthrie knew that people were suffering from cruel economic exploitation; and what inhibited their capacity to resist, to come together and collectively refuse, had much to do with the deflating power of shame. Convinced that people are intensely vulnerable to such wounding, he tried to administer a dose of emotional repair amid the ongoing volleys. In this passage in his notebook and elsewhere, he reaches out to people told that their bodies are "too" this or that—that is, excessive, aberrant, deviating from the norm. Although he was eight years away from his Huntington's diagnosis when he wrote these words, they foreshadow the shift his own body would take in the direction of the so-called abnormal. Eventually, the slowly emerging, mysterious presence of Huntington's gave his work a special purchase on these matters, as he faced not only the undoing of his body, but also its stigmatization as abnormal, deviant, shameful.

Guthrie's conduct of his personal life was, at best, inconsistent; some of it blatantly contradicted the ethos of care to which he claimed fidelity. He repeatedly acted on his desire for women other than Marjorie, and while he was fairly open about his non-monogamy with her, most of the evidence suggests that this was behavior she chose to put up with rather than fully accept or encourage. In my research, reading the materials in Tulsa, at the Smithsonian, and in the home of a private collector, I would sometimes cringe or be disappointed, wanting him to be a better person, to put the empathy he theorized so well into more consistent practice. As much as I admired certain qualities of his erotic letters, like their idealism and openness, he used them as instruments of what we would now call harassment. Imagining them arriving in some unsuspecting young woman's mail, I could only wince. But by now, no one is really surprised to encounter flaws under the sheen of heroism.

But there is another aspect of Guthrie's life and work that has received insufficient sympathy and attention. Guthrie's postwar work, when it has received any notice, has often been described as limited and less significant because of encroaching symptoms of Huntington's, a condition whose major symptoms include loss of balance, loss of coordination, tremors, erratic behavior, loss of inhibition, and eventually, dementia. The slow

WOODY GUTHRIE: AN INTIMATE LIFE | 15

onset of a condition like Huntington's poses particular challenges to the interpreter of the life of someone who suffered from it—especially to the analysis of the period before becoming fully, obviously symptomatic. It is always there, lurking, tempting one to employ it as an explanation for a particular occurrence: an increasing focus on sex, a set of inappropriate letters, even particular turns in writing style. The truth is, we will never know precisely how, when, and to what extent Guthrie's illness affected his creative process. After all, it was *never* the Huntington's disease that was creating the work; it was still Woody Guthrie, responding in some complicated fashion to the presence of the illness inside him. Indeed, one might say that the illness was "inside" him from his birth—not only in the strict biological sense of his carrying what we now know to be the gene mutation that causes it, but also because he lived with it, intimately, in the presence of his mother.

I have tried to use this notion of Guthrie's looming, sick body, alongside the pleasures of the body that he celebrated, to argue for a kind of continuity across the "healthy" and "sick" years—a division that, because of the nature of Huntington's disease, will always prove impossibly blurry anyway. In a sense, this book is a biography of Woody Guthrie's body. It is, at the same time, part of a history of the Left, concerned with changes in how we think about what counts as political. The stakes of this shift are high. Looking back from the present, some radicals are likely to see any interest in sex, love, and the body as a turn away from the hardheaded materialism of the Marxist tradition, in the direction of a softer, more capitalist-friendly liberal individualism. And yet Guthrie claimed, enthusiastically, to be part of that tradition broadly inclusive of socialism and communism.

Left critique has often simply written off the influence feelings *do* have on how people imagine their place in the world—for everything from desire to melancholy to ecstasy. There are, of course, major exceptions: Emma Goldman's joyful anarchism, for instance, or Walter Benjamin's extended meditations on melancholia, or Raymond Williams's "structure of feeling" as a useful category of historical analysis. Guthrie's project is different from all of these, and to claim that he was an intellectual would be to violate something very fundamental about the way he saw himself. But he struggled with some of the same paradoxes and contradictions, ones that continue into the current moment: How do we make our private lives both reparative, rejuvenating spaces without turning them simply into realms of consumption, escape, and willed ignorance? With "random acts of kindness" reduced to that most clichéd mode of activism, the bumper sticker, is it possible to think in more complicated ways about how the worlds we make for ourselves, in our relationships with others, might serve a greater political purpose? This is a book about an extraordinary figure's realization that these things matter, of a traumatic life in a traumatic era teaching him new things about where politics lie, about how struggles for justice are lived, and how they might be won.

Chapter One

"I DON'T SING ANY SILLY OR JERKY SONGS"

I N THE 1970S AND '80S, young people may well have encountered Woody Guthrie most commonly in the form of an iconic poster, often frameless and tacked to the wall of a dorm room or activist organization's office. This poster had a little image of Guthrie in one corner, but mostly it was crammed with text, in a typeface designed less for clarity than to convey urgency and authenticity. Those who made the effort read a screed that began:

> I hate a song that makes you think you're not any good. I hate a song that makes you think that you are just born to lose. Bound to lose. No good to nobody. No good for nothing. Because you are either too old or too young or too fat or too slim or too ugly or too this or too that. . . . Songs that run you down or songs that poke fun at you on account of your bad luck or hard traveling.
>
> I am out to fight those kinds of songs to my very last breath of air and my last drop of blood.[1]

These words resonate with defiant, unadulterated anger, as he calls for artistic honesty to cut through the muck of American popular song— the ethnic and racial stereotyping, the glorification of consumption and wealth. But the poster omitted an earlier passage from the original text, a monologue Guthrie had presented during a New York radio broadcast in 1944, in which he stated: "I don't sing any songs that are not real. I don't sing any silly or jerky songs, nor any songs that make fun of your color, your race, the color of your eyes or the shape of your stomach or the shape of your nose."[2] In their editorial process, the poster makers suppressed the extent of Guthrie's focus on stigmatized physical features like skin color, eye color, stomach and nose shape, girth, attractiveness, perhaps thinking they added little of substance to our understanding of the singer's sweeping sympathy for the downtrodden. How important could it be, they may have asked themselves, to portray him as an early advocate against, say, fat shaming?

But Guthrie's attention to these bodily features, and to people's marginalization on the basis of them, drove his career as an artist with a guitar, a pen, or a paintbrush. He came to understand the shaming and stigmatization of certain bodies as working to isolate people, to prevent them from assembling as a collective—a proven way for those lacking financial resources to empower themselves—to demand a better life. The origins of this viewpoint lay in Guthrie's earlier life, in the tragedies that beset his family, all revolving around his mother's mysterious condition, her undiagnosed Huntington's disease.

Huntington's disease has three major symptoms: dyskinesia, or involuntary movements; dementia; and "disorders of mood and perception, particularly depression," though angry outbursts are also a noted symptom.[3] Its symptoms typically begin showing themselves in early middle age, usually between the ages of thirty and forty, but they often appear as minor shifts in mood and disposition, making their initial manifestations difficult to discern. Yet, there are many variations among cases. Nora Belle Guthrie may have been a bit younger than thirty when her family and neighbors began to notice behaviors they deemed strange.

Until the second half of the twentieth century, the condition was widely known as Huntington's chorea, the Greek word for dance or chorus, that is, a group of dancers. It is hereditary, a gene mutation passed down through generations, and as of the early twenty-first century, incurable. A child with one parent suffering from the disease has a 50–50 chance of developing it as an adult. Although the symptoms appear gradually, they eventually become dramatically visible—particularly as involuntary, jerky movements. This dyskinesia becomes far more drastic than the tremors associated with Parkinson's disease—hence, the association with dance, a spectacle of the body. Consequently, people suffering from the illness have long been told their bodies were aberrant, and faced ostracism and discrimination.

Before Dr. George Huntington named it as a pathology in 1872, those stricken with the disease were frequently assumed insane, their outlandish physical symptoms considered a manifestation of a deranged mind. In the early twentieth century, Alice Wexler's research shows, scientists and physicians saw the condition through the lens of eugenic theory, the racial pseudo-science built on the principle that certain categories of people should be encouraged to reproduce while others should be discouraged. Dr. Charles B. Davenport, a leading American eugenicist, "called for immigration restrictions, surveillance of families, and compulsory sterilisation of people with Huntington's."[4] In 1934, a British neurologist claimed that the mark of the illness spread beyond those carrying it, affecting their intimates as well; according to Wexler, "all members of families affected by Huntington's disease were [in the neurologist's words] 'liable to bear the marks of a grossly psychopathic taint, and the story of feeblemindedness, insanity, suicide, criminality, alcoholism, and drug addiction becomes enfolded over and over again.'"[5] In other words, the widely respected theory of eugenics subjected them to the same authority-imprinted stigmas, in many of the same terms, as it did people of African origin, immigrants from southern and eastern Europe, and even, as we will see, some poor white Americans.

In the early 1920s, as Nora Belle Guthrie's bizarre spells worsened, no one in the family or beyond knew to call what was happening anything other than insanity. The people of Okemah bandied about words like "batty" and "nutty." Both in the family and in town, there was some sense that madness had haunted the paternal side of her ancestry, the Shermans. But intimacy isn't always about sharing; it can also be about agreements to keep secrets. We don't know how much Nora Belle knew about this murky history, or whether she discussed it with her husband or children.

In any case, the town noticed Nora Belle's strange movements and sudden outbursts. They heard rumors of strange things happening at home, and suspected they weren't being told everything about the house fire or the incident in which Woody's older sister Clara sustained fatal burns. In the town's public spaces, they greeted Nora with stares and suspicious glances.

Clara's death was a turning point. After that, Guthrie wrote in an autobiographical sketch in 1946, "my mother's nerves gave way like an overloaded bridge." More tenderly and poetically, he wrote of her, "She sang in a voice that not everybody understood."[6]

Many afternoons, Woody's mother would grab him and retreat into the obscurity of the Crystal Theatre on Okemah's Broadway, doing her best to make her body disappear, at least as a spectacle for others. Mother and son would sit in the dark for hours watching matinees. If they were lucky, the program would include a film starring their favorite, Charlie Chaplin, a masterful physical performer who turned bodily struggles into comedy, making them a source of joy and release for his audience. So deep an impression did these movies make on little Woody that in later years, many people who knew him would call his bodily bearing Chaplin-esque.

The town's treatment of his mother, and these afternoons spent in hiding, introduced Woody Guthrie to shame as a force of social organization and disentitlement. At the theater, in the streets of Okemah, and at home, his primary relationship with an ill, disabled woman laid the foundation for his empathy and identification with the dispossessed, people robbed of their full personhood by stigma. In this sense, there is no pre- or post-Huntington's Woody Guthrie; he had lived with the disease since early childhood.

After Nora Belle was committed to the state asylum in 1927, Charley Guthrie moved to north Texas, where relatives helped him recover from the severe burns sustained, apparently, at the hands of his wife. In fact, his fortunes in Okemah had fallen dramatically from his earlier days as a real estate speculator, political powerbroker, and anti-socialist propagandist. Oil money now ran the town, and he was an insider turned outsider. But it was the aftereffects of the fiery calamity at home that sent him over the edge. He bolted across the southern state border, leaving his two oldest surviving children, Woody and older brother Roy, living in Okemah in poverty. It was Woody's first experience of rootlessness. Sometimes the two teens would stay with family friends, other times they would squat in one of the town's abandoned houses.

In the summer of 1929, just before the stock market crash undermined the global economy, Woody Guthrie moved to Pampa, Texas, where his father had resettled. It was here that Guthrie began to see a future as a musician. He'd learned harmonica from an African American man named George (presumably Guthrie never thought to ask his surname) in Okemah—though George's skin color dictated that he had to leave the town by dusk, given Okemah's "sundown policy." Then he learned guitar and got his first paying gigs, playing "hillbilly music," essentially the forerunner of country music, at barn dances in a duo with his uncle Jeff, a fiddler. In spare moments alone, he played the old, traditional songs his mother used to sing when he was a toddler. On stage, he had an uncommon gift for witty stage banter. He drew inspiration from his fellow Oklahoman Will Rogers, a humorist and political satirist of indigenous heritage. As more and more people lost jobs, homes, and savings, dry wit was an increasingly necessary form of sustenance.

Intellectually, Guthrie was a determined, ravenous autodidact. He dropped out of high school, finding the hours he spent reading in the Pampa public library more intellectually stimulating. According to biographer Ed Cray, he "systematically worked his way through the shelves, concentrating on psychology, Western religions, and Eastern philosophies."[7]

He started to build his own nuclear family in 1933, when he married Mary Jennings, the younger sister of his best friend in Pampa. She came from a stable, respected family; the town considered her a catch. He was twenty-one, she sixteen. Over the next seven years, they would have three children together: Gwen, Sue, and Will Rogers (Bill), born in 1935, 1937, and 1938, respectively. But over this time, as he was honing a political art of empathy, he would hypocritically neglect his loved ones, spending many days and nights away from them pursuing his own ambitions, or dragging them around the country as reluctant participants in his quest.

On Palm Sunday of 1935, Woody and Mary were together at home in Texas when they witnessed an environmental event that seemed to embody all the greed and depredation that had brought on the Great Depression. A massive dust storm engulfed Pampa, piercing the walls of their home and dimming the electrically lighted interior. Outside, people and animals suffocated, their lungs filling with the dry particles. The calamity inspired his first serious stab at songwriting: a composition called "Dusty Old Dust."

Witnessing vulnerability drew him in a political direction very different from his father's. Woody was no stranger to the Left; in Oklahoma, leftists were part of the ambient political environment. His father's fierce anti-socialist diatribes in the Okemah newspaper were in part a response to a very present, very vibrant radical left in Oklahoma. In 1912, the year of Woody Guthrie's birth, the state's electorate gave Eugene Debs, the Socialist Party candidate for president, a whopping 16 percent of its vote. Little Okemah even boasted its own socialist newspaper, the *Sledge Hammer*. As scholar Will Kaufman puts it, "The elder Guthrie could take little pleasure in the knowledge that it was *his* state—not New York—that was the epicenter of political radicalism in America."[8]

But his political consciousness blossomed in 1937 when he grew restless enough in Pampa to head west, among many thousands of other migrants, with little sense of what he would find. During the journey, he encountered desperate people, mainly poor and white, from the rural South and Midwest, individuals and families whose livelihoods in tenant farming and other forms of cheap labor had been decimated by the economic and environmental crisis, brought on by the carelessness of the owning class and the government that coddled it. His considerable gifts as a listener and interlocutor drew out the people's stories; his hungry mind devoured them. Even though he wasn't quite "of" these folks, he began to sense a kind of poetry, capturing something essential about modernity, in their transient, unsettled existences, akin to the dust particles being blown across thousands of miles of North America.

His wanderings terminated in Los Angeles. Hopping between the couches of relatives and friends, in a matter of months, he had his own radio show on station KFVD, playing hillbilly music with a partner named Maxine Crissman, who played under the handle "Lefty Lou from Old Mizzou." He was secure enough to send for Mary and the kids to join him, and they did. After a short period of living in their car, the family settled in Glendale, adjacent to the big city.

But rather than a new start for his family, Los Angeles offered Guthrie entry into a new social world, full of people—working-class union members but also, increasingly, middle-class leftists—channeling their outrage about the state of the world into organizing, activism, strikes, and creative production in the arts. There was even a single LA neighborhood where they tended to live and gather: Edendale (now Silver Lake and Echo Park), already known as a haven for LGBTQ people, far-left radicals, and artists. Here Guthrie would hang out with his friends Ed Robbin, a political commentator at KFVD, and Will Geer, an actor, both of whom regularly attended strikes and meetings sponsored by the CPUSA and other Communist organizations. Many nights, Guthrie would balk at making the trip back to his family's home, instead crashing on Robbin's couch after staying up late writing lyrics or political screeds. Before long, his connections and growing renown landed him a gig writing columns for the local Communist daily, the *People's World*.

He went to parties attended by European intellectual luminaries in exile, such as Bertolt Brecht and Thomas Mann.[9] But more significantly, he started to absorb a broader and deeper perspective on exploitation, capitalism, and fascism. The people around him talked in enthusiastic detail about the progress the Soviet Union had made against centuries of poverty and exploitation, and backed the revolutionary nation as "the organizer of all the forces of peace and progress everywhere in the world."[10] At the same time, the CPUSA cast its politics in nationalist terms, part of "American revolutionary traditions" like the revolutionary war and the defeat of slavery, "which are the heart of Americanism."[11]

Historian Daniel Hurewitz describes late 1930s Edendale as "a dynamic community in which leftist activists infused their politics with the deep feelings of intimate connection."[12] In an environment increasingly prizing emotional communication, both politics and art were considered expressive channels. It was a community that saw politics was a whole way of being, a model of the very self, not an abstract set of principles or commitments separate from one's private life: "The leftists' engagement with the public was the expression of their intimate emotions."[13] In addition to agitating with labor unions, they founded daycare centers and organized theater groups whose offerings often had no explicit connection to the revolutionary cause, other than to seal communal bonds. Those bonds were political in themselves. One veteran of this world told Hurewitz, "There existed 'no separation between explicitly political and implicitly nonpolitical' activities. . . . There was a recognition that the cultural expressions in life were as essential as the political treatises."[14] It was a "rich culture of participation" in which music played a particularly important role; from the late 1930s onward, CPUSA meetings often began with group singing, and participatory folk music became a staple of the party's gatherings.

The more glamorous of these get-togethers were, of course, as distant as could be from the rickety trucks and dingy trains Guthrie had ridden on his way out west, or the crowded migrant camps outside the city he visited with his new bosom buddy, Will Geer. But the Left was a motley collection of constituencies. In 1935, sensing the urgency of a moment when fascism was becoming ever-more powerful, the Seventh World Congress of the Comintern had directed that communists across the globe make peace with other left-of-center activists and parties; in the US, these ranged from socialists to New Deal Democrats. The resulting alliance became known as the Popular Front. In an effort to expand their membership, the CPUSA wrote glowingly of legendary figures in American history like Abraham Lincoln, whom they considered a revolutionary for ending slavery. General Secretary Earl Browder articulated the party's new creed: "Communism is twentieth-century Americanism." As Guthrie was expressing his political views in terms touted by the CPUSA with increasing explicitness, this turn permitted him (and others) to call on resources like the old folk traditions in which his mother had reared him.

Moving in these circles also helped a white man from the edges of Dixie begin to revise his views about people marginalized on the basis of their racial backgrounds. Especially since the 1930s, the CPUSA, which boasted a significant African American membership, had targeted anti-Black racism as a tool of capitalism and oppression. They considered Jim Crow and racial prejudice more generally a manifestation of home-grown fascism; this was a position Guthrie would hold for the rest of his life. The party's leadership on this issue likely reverberated for Guthrie when, a day after singing the song "Run, Nigger, Run" on his radio show, he read on-air a letter of protest from a young African American college student and swore never to use the word again.[15] In coming years, he would refine his anti-racist politics and, even as he grew ill, become more militant and focused.

In his song "Do Re Mi," Guthrie mocked the mythical idea that sunny California was a "paradise to live in or see," an oasis free of the troubles by which the rest of the US was beset; he and the masses of "Okies" had learned California was far from a social haven. And although he didn't broach the topic in the song, the state's residents of Euro-American origins already had a long, entrenched, all-too-familiar history of being racist. Upon obtaining territory from Mexico in the mid-nineteenth century, white settlers launched a concerted, genocidal campaign against indigenous people. That century's later decades saw a heightened bias against non-white migrants from Asia and Mexico.

In the 1930s self-proclaimed "native" Californians also extended their racial biases to the white migrants with whom Guthrie most empathized and, to an extent, identified with. The state's schools and cultural institutions were awash in eugenics, with some even proposing programmatic sterilization for certain categories of people. Browsing an LA newsstand, he might have picked up a copy of *Country Gentleman* and encountered an article lamenting the laziness of the migrants, comparing them to "Mexican" laborers (many of them American-born), and describing them in terms like "hordes" and "swarms." Or perhaps, while thumbing through *California, Magazine of the Pacific*, he'd come across a lavishly illustrated piece about the "Okies" despairing of their high rate of reproduction. Biology textbooks described these not-quite-white transplants as having mental deficiencies and physical oddities: they were "feeble-minded," small-headed, obese, women who looked like men, and so on. More than likely, Guthrie heard comparable terms and sentiments coming out of the mouths of police officers at a coffee shop counter, or bandied about by the customers chatting in his neighborhood grocery store.

In other words, though ostensibly white themselves, the migrants were victims of the long, ambiguous history of American whiteness, which had been used as a cudgel against Irish, Italian, and Jewish immigrants, among others. According to historian Peter La Chapelle, in 1930s southern California, "a group of ostensibly white citizens became fodder for the kind of race talk and eugenic baiting normally reserved for minorities and immigrants. . . . Eugenics and race talk allowed native white Californians to create myths that downgraded the status of white Dust Bowlers to such an extent that migrants were subjected to forms of harassment typically faced by racial minority groups." Eugenicists considered the migrants only "liminally white."[16]

Some on the Left addressed these claims by asserting that the migrant whites *did* descend from good, sturdy "stock." Devotees of this tack included author John Steinbeck, who had drawn national attention to the plight of Dust Bowl migrants with his best-selling novel *The Grapes of Wrath* (1939). A year before publishing *Grapes*, he titled a volume of his essays about the domestic refugees *Their Blood Is Strong*, hence reproducing eugenic logic in an attempt to redeem the desperate white migrants arriving from the South and Midwest. As disability studies scholar Lennard Davis notes of the era, "Socialists as well as others embraced eugenic claims, seeing in the perfectibility of the human body a Utopian hope for social improvement."[17]

As he moved more deeply into the world of the Popular Front left, Guthrie routinely pledged allegiance to socialism and communism as sciences of social and economic organization. However, throughout his life, his collectivist outlook consistently eschewed any faith in the "perfectibility of the human body"—perhaps, in part, because eugenics struck even closer to home. Eugenic theory represented the institutionalization and organized enforcement of attitudes like those that considered some people "too fat or too slim or too ugly or too this or too that," as he would put it in his 1944 radio monologue. And more specifically, it called for the sterilization of any family with a history of cognitive or physiological disability, such as the maternal line of Woody Guthrie's ancestry. Indeed, in 1931, Oklahoma gave the superintendents of state mental health facilities the discretion to sterilize their patients. Any evidence of hereditary insanity would make patients more likely to face involuntary sterilization. This directive's recipients included the Hospital for the Insane in Norman, the destination to which Charley Guthrie's friends delivered Nora Belle Guthrie in 1927.[18] Nora Belle died from Huntington's disease in 1929. But if her son had ended up in a particular place at a particular time, he might very well have faced the prospect of compulsory sterilization.

Eugenics valorized sameness, the conformity to strict ideals of health and beauty. From his time in California onward, Guthrie's outlook insisted on making room for, even prizing, variation, difference, and diversity. This view would become increasingly bound up with his politics as he began to suffer from an illness he either didn't know how to name or chose not to.

Meanwhile, he was living a huge contradiction: as he learned more about injustice and the emotional environment that kept it alive in the world, he neglected his commitments to his spouse and children. It was a pattern of lapse he would never fully solve. His most serious effort to do so came in the first five years of his relationship with Marjorie Mazia, during which he explored the role of sex, love, and domestic life in leftist politics.

In contrast, the close bond between Guthrie and the communist actor Will Geer continued to deepen; it would extend through the singer's life, becoming his most consistent and sustaining relationship aside from his partnership with Mazia. Geer persuaded his friend to make his first move to New York, in February of 1940, when the actor was tapped to play the lead role in the Broadway production of *Tobacco Road*, an adaptation of Erskine Caldwell's hugely popular novel about hapless poor Southern white people, essentially a comedy-exploitation version of *Grapes of Wrath* that, despite its author's Popular Front sympathies, relied on eugenics-derived stereotypes. Nonetheless, it was a huge boon to Geer's career, and allowed him to move into a spacious apartment with room for his friend to crash.

After a week of bunking with Geer and his wife, Herta, Guthrie moved into the Hanover House hotel, where he composed the song that, a few decades later, would make him a household name. He had grown tired of hearing Kate Smith's then popular version of Irving Berlin's "God Bless America," finding it a bloated, supercilious proclamation of nationalism during a time of grave crisis that was steadily increasing the ranks of the nation's vulnerable. He wrote a series of lines about traveling the continent, witnessing its beauty but also its despair and exploitation. Each verse ended "God blessed America for me." Later he would change this refrain to the now-canonical "This land was made for you and me," with the exception of one verse about poverty and starvation that ended with the more skeptical "Is this land made for you and me?"

In the first week of March 1940, Geer helped arrange a midnight benefit concert for the John Steinbeck Committee to Aid Agricultural Organization at the Broadway theater where *Tobacco Road* was running. The bill listed Guthrie as "'Woody,' a real Dust Bowl refugee," and his lively performance here gave him his breakthrough with the East Coast leftist folk music intelligentsia.[19] Earl Robinson, later to co-star in *Folksay*, was in attendance. So was Alan Lomax, folklorist and bearer of the unwieldy title Assistant in Charge of the Archive of American Folk Song at the Library of Congress. Also there that night was Lomax's intern, a gangly twenty-year-old named Peter Seeger, who had recently dropped out of Harvard to pursue a career as a folk musician and scholar.

Although only twenty-four, Lomax was well on his way to becoming the most institutionally and individually powerful figure in twentieth-century American folk music. Smitten by Guthrie's live performance, Lomax arranged for the singer to visit him at the Library of Congress. With an aluminum disc recorder running, Lomax and his sister Beth (later a member of the Almanac Singers) conducted a free-ranging conversation with Guthrie, in which the singer's stories of his experiences among the distressed rural, white populations of Oklahoma, Texas, and California flowed organically into performances of his songs, including such classics as "Do Re Mi," "I Ain't Got No Home in This World Anymore," and a handful of ballads about the Dust Bowl.

At one point early on, Lomax asked Guthrie to define the blues. The singer responded:

> I always just called it plain old being lonesome. You can get lonesome for a lot of things. People down around where I come from, they're lonesome for a job. Lonesome for some spending money. Lonesome for some drinking whiskey. Lonesome for good times, pretty gals, wine, woman, and song that they see stuck up in their face by other people. Thinking maybe that you were down and out, disgusted, busted, and can't be trusted gives you a lonesome feeling. That somehow the world sort of turned against you or there's something about it you don't understand.[20]

Guthrie's thinking about racial politics wasn't yet evolved enough for him to realize he was erasing the specificity of the blues as an African American cultural form, shaped by a particular set of struggles faced by Black people in the US. But he had struck a note that would, in the coming years, resound through his work: for people whose lives are economically and otherwise subject to the whims of the wealthy, dispossession and oppression manifest as feelings of emotional and intellectual isolation.

After Guthrie's performance at the Library of Congress, Lomax recognized that his art was not just his singing but his very person, the particular way he embodied the emotional capacities of humanity. He could do so much more than just record songs, the archivist thought. He should write a book.

In the spring of 1940, Lomax arranged for Guthrie to record songs at RCA Victor's studio in Walt Whitman's old hometown of Camden, New Jersey. In a single day, April 26, he made the lion's share of the album that would soon catch the ears of Sophie Maslow and Marjorie Mazia:

Dust Bowl Ballads. The pathos-laden songs give voice to poor people in dire circumstances; they remain some of his deservedly best-known work as both a performer and a songwriter. The album followed closely on the release of director John Ford's adaptation of Steinbeck's *Grapes of Wrath*, and the novel, film, and record became tightly associated, Guthrie often standing as a real-life version of the scrappy hero of the novel and film, Tom Joad.

In New York, Guthrie's reputation grew and excitement around him mounted. He played at fund-raisers, labor events, and on the radio. He made more friends in the music and political worlds, among them Huddie Ledbetter (known in the music world as Lead Belly) and his wife, Martha, with whom he remained close for years. Politically, he became more and more aligned with the CPUSA's official positions. He followed the party line on the Soviet Union after its pact with the Nazis, criticizing calls for US intervention in the first rumblings that another world war was erupting in Europe.

As lively as the past few years had been, Guthrie still had little sense of where his life was headed, and where his work as a musician would lead. Although he was still married, and ostensibly trying to keep the family together, it was clear that his ambitions were at odds with what Mary wanted and expected from their relationship. He brought the family to New York, then back across the country to Los Angeles, then up north to Sonora. When he received a commission from the Bonneville Power Administration to write and record a suite of songs about the Columbia River and the building of the Grand Coulee Dam, he dragged her and the kids to Portland, Oregon. He wrote another set of powerful songs, but Mary was miserable. After a month, they returned to Texas, but Guthrie started making plans to return to New York. That sealed the end of the relationship. With no lack of justification, Mary was tired of his callous disregard for her feelings and the kids'—the long periods of absence, the sudden moves, the financial uncertainty. She said she wasn't going, and in everyone's eyes but the law's, the marriage was over.

He returned to New York, where *Dust Bowl Ballads* had captured the ears of a small but growing world of folk musicians and fans. They were eager to hear more from this odd little figure from Oklahoma, this Tom Joad come to life. In downtown Manhattan, artists adjacent to the folk music world were catching the bug too. Striking out from the Martha

Graham Company, which tended to submerge politics in formal experimentation, Sophie Maslow had already used a few of the songs in a dance piece that borrowed the record's title. More immediately, Lomax's young intern Pete Seeger—who now had dropped the *r* from his first name in a populist gesture—was in New York starting up a group dedicated to traditional music as well as topical songs written from a radical left perspective. They called themselves the Almanac Singers, and they invited Guthrie to join. He did.

The Almanac Singers weren't only a musical group; they were an experiment in living Popular Front values, a kind of commune. Their members, who also included Lee Hays, Millard Lampell, and a rotating cast of others, lived together in a loft on West Twelfth Street in Greenwich Village. In 1941, they moved to a townhouse at 130 West Tenth Street, a building that soon became a performance space, crash pad, and general social center for the politically invested folk music scene. The denizens of Almanac House were uncompromising in their anti-fascism, and their ideology leaned in the direction of communism; they attracted like-minded people from the Village and beyond. Here, Guthrie would first encounter Marjorie Mazia and Sophie Maslow.

According to Richard Reuss, the Almanacs, as they were often called, were a landmark in the history of American popular music. In addition to their strident politics, they were the first group to fully wed folkways and folk traditions to their political ideology. They were a group "for whom the people's folk songs and folkways were central to their political ideology, attempts at agit-prop communication, and lifestyle. More than any other segment of the communist movement, they attempted to implement a proletarian culture based on American traditions, one that they and others might live as well as speculate about in the abstract." They "laid down the practical foundations for the socially conscious use of traditional materials in an activist context."[21]

But living there also helped cultivate a new Woody Guthrie. As music scholar Robert Cantwell phrases it, "It was the Almanac House that put the finial on his bohemianization."[22] As in Edendale, Guthrie looked around and saw himself in a world of avant-gardists, literati, and lifestyle experimenters. But now he was beginning to see himself as their artistic comrade and, in at least one case, collaborator.

Chapter Two

CHOREOGRAPHING THE REVOLUTION

ACCORDING TO VARIOUS ACCOUNTS from years and decades later, the events that led to the rescue at the *Folksay* rehearsal went something like this:

Marjorie Mazia bounded up the stairs of a Greenwich Village townhouse alongside her friend and colleague, Sophie. Marjorie was happy to be an accessory to her friend's plan, though she worried that she ought to have been back in Philadelphia with her husband, Joe. But the things the other girls who danced for Martha did in New York, beyond the little studio, were so much more exciting. The quest today: mounting a charge on the place where the Almanac Singers live and rehearse, which everyone called "Almanac House," to recruit this Woody Guthrie fellow for Sophie's new production. It was New York in late February—hence likely cold and gray, a time normally full of tired faces reaching their limit of winter. But in the early months of 1942, everyone had wide-open eyes and a tingle in their stomach, symptoms at that time of the global atmosphere of terror and determination. In the face of impending war with the Axis powers, even everyday tasks took on enhanced meaning; working with a dance group that explicitly conceived of itself as anti-fascist felt like opening up a skirmish on the domestic front.

Marjorie felt sorry about how she was treating Joe, leaving him alone so much in the "band box" house they shared in Philadelphia, but she had to make space for this adventure. They were going to see, in the flesh, the man whose voice she had heard on her sister's phonograph in Missouri. She recalled the voice floating out of the phonograph, full of weary strength—not the he-man might that some wanted in their male vocalists, but a vulnerable fortitude, still carrying traces of woe, and tinged with a wryness that had no doubt served the singer well as a survival strategy in the trying times he'd lived through. The lines she would never forget were direct, plaintive, and genuine:

Wherever little children are hungry and cry
Wherever people ain't free,
Wherever men are fightin' for their rights,
That's where I'm a-gonna be, Ma.
That's where I'm a-gonna be.[1]

At the moment Sophie rapped on the door, Marjorie heard these lines in her head, and the usual image of the man singing them took shape in her mind's eye: tall, gaunt yet imposing, Lincoln-esque. Sculptural. Or, she might have to admit, maybe a little like Henry Fonda, star of the film version of *The Grapes of Wrath*. Sophie, too, loved "Tom Joad" and the other songs on *Dust Bowl Ballads*. She'd agreed when Marjorie said there was something in them that evoked the plaintive Yiddish songs their parents used to sing, doleful tales of exile and exodus. Months earlier, she'd even tried to get Guthrie's assistance with a dance piece based on the songs, but to no avail.

The first signs this time around did not look promising. An unsmiling man opened the door, his face showing no sign of recognition, much less of being impressed, when the visitors told them their names, that they danced with the Martha Graham Company, and that they were here to talk to Woody Guthrie. He introduced himself as Arthur Stern, but said he and the other musicians weren't interested. There was even a hint of a sniff at their boss and her reputation for haughtiness.

Behind Stern, down the hall, Marjorie saw a small man standing at a window. Once they'd worn the de facto doorman's resistance down, she and Sophie were led to the room where the man stood next to a long table flanked by picnic benches. It was a kind of combined dining room and kitchen. The oven door was open to contest the late-winter chill in the air. On one end of the table was a typewriter, an inch-high stack of yellow-pad paper, apparently all covered with words, and a coffee pot. He looked disheveled, unshaven—sort of like a rabbinical student, Marjorie thought to herself. Just then, the small, huddled figure turned around toward them, his faraway expression turning bright and inquisitive. An instant later, Sophie, without a trace of hesitation, said, "Hello again, Woody." Could this be him? The little thing before them, barely bigger than she, looked more likely to be blown away by a dust storm than to stride resolutely through one.[2]

Two hale and hearty daughters of Russian Jewish immigrants, performers at the epicenter of modern dance, standing before a bedraggled troubadour from poverty-stricken Oklahoma: a couple of decades earlier, virtually no one could have been bothered to imagine such a scene possible. But here in Greenwich Village in February 1942, historical forces, political passion, and artistic energy had all aligned to bring them together.

The encounter that night had a deep history; it was an instance of the Popular Front enabling the crossing and merging of two different histories of radicalism. The importance that the Popular Front gave to artistic expression provided a reason and means for Maslow and Mazia to reach out to Guthrie. Its political mission made new intimacies possible.

Guthrie's political inspiration came out of a socialist genealogy rooted in the American heartland. He spent his young childhood years in a middle-class environment where books were purchased and valued. But after illness and tragedy all but destroyed his family of origin, he gravitated toward a populism whose heritage was as spiritual as it was scholarly, a tradition drawing its conceptual weaponry from the words and deeds of charismatic leaders like Joe Hill and Eugene Debs. In contrast, for Sophie Maslow (born 1911, a year before Guthrie) and Marjorie Mazia née Greenblatt (born in 1917), revolutionary fervor drew from a place far more remote, with roots in a tradition of learnedness—and a history of sometimes violent ethnic marginalization—extending back through generations of ancestors in eastern Europe. Maslow was born in New York City to working-class parents whom she described as part of a "Russian Jewish intelligentsia." Her father had spent time in a Russian prison during the "bloody Sunday" revolution of 1905.[3] The Greenblatts had met at a socialist bookstore in Philadelphia shortly after both had come to the US. Marjorie's father was a successful merchant, her mother a poet who, by the end of the 1930s, had published two books and established a strong reputation among people who read Yiddish literature. Despite their class differences, both women had grown up amid conversations about how to build a more just, equitable world. Over meals, they discussed books about socialism, anarchism, and Zionism.

In the urban Northeast, Mazia and Maslow had access to cultural institutions—museums, galleries, theaters—whose existence Woody Guthrie would have known of dimly, if at all. The modernist movement was bringing new theories and methods to virtually every expressive medium, but it was the female-dominated art of dance that captured the imagination and desire of these Jewish American teens. Maslow's mother took her young progeny to see Isadora Duncan dance in New York; Marjorie somehow ended up at a Philadelphia performance by important choreographer and theorist Mary Wigman. Each was enraptured by what she had seen, and each signed up for dance classes at the Lower East Side's Neighborhood Playhouse—Marjorie a few years later than Sophie. The Playhouse was an offshoot of Henry Street Settlement House, founded by the Lewisohn sisters, a pair of older German-Jewish Americans intent on helping more recent immigrants adjust to their new surroundings, which largely remained the rough world of tenements. Financially and culturally well established, the Lewisohns believed the new arrivals needed to shed their old-world ways and assimilate to American cultural modernity. The sisters brought in eminent choreographers like Martha Graham to educate the offspring of these "greenhorns" in the vanguard of aesthetic experimentalism.[4]

In 1935, Greenblatt joined the Graham Company, where she met Maslow, who had joined four years earlier. Training in the Graham technique of contraction and release, a disciplined method that expanded and celebrated the expressive capacities of their bodies, must have offered these young women a thrilling sense of freedom and empowerment. The radical movements of their bodies mirrored the political spirit of the time. Greenblatt and Maslow found themselves among people of the conviction that, as dance theorist Oliver Sayler put it at the time, "esthetic revolt is the concomitant of social revolt."[5] Over the course of the 1930s, the formally groundbreaking modern dance world came to embrace the anti-fascist politics of the Popular Front. Choreographers and critics quarreled over whether an art of democracy, striving to support (and, in some cases, speak for) the working class, ought to focus on formal innovation or on introducing new, more explicitly revolutionary subject matter; they disputed whether formal innovation or cultural heritage ought to be prioritized in the process of transforming dance into an art of the masses.[6] Graham was turning to folk sources and interpreting indigenous and African American forms. Some leftists occasionally criticized her for not bringing politics into her work more explicitly. But in 1938, her *American Document* debuted, featuring sections addressing leftist rallying points, such as the execution of anarchist immigrants Sacco and Vanzetti and the racist prosecution of the Scottsboro Nine. Both Maslow and Mazia were among the lead dancers.

More so than Mazia, who never worked professionally as a choreographer, Maslow's career reflects the radical dance world's preoccupations of the time. She shared Martha Graham's interest in folk culture. But even before joining her mentor's troupe, thanks to her father's persecution in Russia, she had become intensely committed to the political ideas of the radical left, centered on the work of the CPUSA. This revolutionary fervor inspired her to begin working independently as a choreographer, developing pieces rooted in CPUSA members' reverence for the Bolsheviks and the Soviet Union. She collaborated with two new, self-identified radical dance groups, the Workers Dance League (slogan: "Dance is a weapon in the revolutionary class struggle") and the New Dance Group, ensembles which, as scholar Julia Foulkes has written, "merged art and politics, finding ways to respond to social conditions and make political statements through dance."[7] The latter group provided the bulk of the dancers for *Folksay*.

Marjorie Greenblatt shared many of these interests and views. But her personal situation was more complicated. Despite dancing with the Graham Company, she still called Philadelphia her home. Indeed, the same year that she began lessons with Graham at the Neighborhood Playhouse, she married a serious young man with strong, straightforward ambitions, a senior chemistry major at the illustrious University of Pennsylvania named Joseph Mazia.

For seven years, she commuted the two hours between Manhattan and North Philadelphia. It was draining. But how could she imagine abandoning the Graham Company, especially as her star rose there, and Martha took her on as her personal assistant? In the years before *Folksay*, Mazia performed in such well-received pieces as *Primitive Mysteries*,

Every Soul Is a Circus, *American Document*, and *Appalachian Spring*. She was renowned in the troupe as an especially good teacher of the newest dancers; her mentees included future avant-garde legend Merce Cunningham. She was blessed with a skill set that spanned multiple senses of the term *choreography*: she excelled at planning, at organizing people so they could realize their full potential. Known well for her administrative adroitness, she had a reputation for keeping things from falling apart.

These skills also served her in initiating intimacy with the wiry folk singer who had arrived in the dance world after following a very different path. As their relationship intensified after the awkward dance rehearsal, she would inevitably take on a maternal role—hardly a radical position for a woman in a heterosexual couple to stake out. Yet she also modeled many of the traits he hoped to bring into the world via his writing, both musical and literary: an attentive and empathic approach to people's neediness, and an ethos of repair, of helping to heal the physical and emotional wounds the world inflicted on them.[8] His notebooks, journals, letters, and artwork make it crystal clear: Woody Guthrie considered these qualities revolutionary.

Folksay proved a vital turning point in Guthrie's public and private life.

Although the piece was less abstract than the experiments in which Mazia and Maslow participated in the Graham studio, the ideas behind it were still acutely modern. Maslow's concept for it derived from a form of performance championed by the Lewisohns at Neighborhood Playhouse, the "lyric genre": pieces based on long poems, featuring a mix of dance, song, and verse.[9] The poem at the core of *Folksay* was Carl Sandburg's 1936 *The People, Yes*, his epic paean to the resilience of the American citizenry. The dancers—Marjorie Greenblatt Mazia among them—dressed in plaid shirts, blue jeans, long skirts, and cowboy hats. In solos, duets, and small group and company numbers, they performed steps that drew from square dancing and other folk forms associated with rural white America. Guthrie and Tony Kraber handled the music and the recitation of the poetry, with some comic dialogues thrown in. Maslow designed the set and players to look like what she imagined to be a typical Saturday night in a typical American small town, maybe one in Oklahoma.

In March 1942, *Folksay* opened at the Humphrey-Weidman Studio Theater at 108 West Sixteenth Street, with Guthrie and Kraber intoning these lines from Sandburg:

> *The people is Everyman, everybody.*
> *Everybody is you and me and all the others.*
> *What everybody says is what we all say.*
> *And what is it we all say?*[10]

As the duo recited the lines, the dancers roamed freely over the stage, embodying the "many becoming one." It was a spectacle that, like so much of the art associated with the Popular Front, could be cast as either deeply American or radical and socialist—the idea, just edging into broad plausibility, was that these could be the same.

The dances, songs, and skits that followed conjured the well-tested social rituals of rural and small-town white America, a demographic considered marginal to modernity's onrushing flow. It was a small production, performed in this initial incarnation just a few times for likely a few hundred people, at most. But its critical reception made it a quiet triumph across a wide span of reviewers. The production left critics from a range of ideological poles deeply impressed. Reflecting a growing ambivalence toward more direct agitprop on the radical left, the CPUSA's East Coast organ, the *Daily Worker*, wrote that "the day of gloomy grotesquery, when modern dancers drove their points home with hammer and blows . . . is gone."[11] Curiously, neither they nor any other outlet mentioned the phrase scrawled across Guthrie's guitar: "THIS MACHINE KILLS FASCISTS." In the *New York Times*, John Martin wrote: "The wide range and incident of their talk about 'the people' is illustrated by Miss Maslow and her group in some pungent miming or . . . carried off into realms of poetry by dances of tenderness and charm. Unless you are pretty insensitive to the people that are America, it is guaranteed to leave you with a lump in your throat." He singled out Guthrie for praise, as would legendary dance critic Edwin Denby when he reviewed a revival of the show for the *Herald Tribune* in December. The initial review of the production in the *Herald Tribune*, by Walter Terry, called it "just about the most successful American ballet I have ever seen."[12] The radical visionaries of Russia, Oklahoma, north Texas, southern California, North

Philadelphia, the Lower East Side, and Greenwich Village had found their common medium and triumphed in a range of daily papers.

Decades on, only serious fans and students of Guthrie know about his work on this dance project, and Maslow and the New Dance Group never attained the eminence of Martha Graham and her company. But revivals of *Folksay* remained a reliable and steady gig for him for the following eight years. Even in the summer of 1950, when his career, health, and personal life had taken a turn for the worse, he performed in the piece at the American Dance Festival at Connecticut College. *Folksay* also resulted in his only television appearance, when CBS staged a performance of the piece in their studios for broadcast in November 1944. The reviewer from *Billboard* magazine called it the best-produced program they had ever seen on the new medium (sadly, no video footage appears to exist).[13]

Folksay brought new attention to Guthrie's career, signaling the possibility that he could reach beyond the audiences he'd captivated on the radio, at union rallies, and with *Dust Bowl Ballads*, that he could contribute to a broader range of art-making. It also brought Marjorie Mazia into his intimate life. The piece and his new love—which, he soon began to intuit, offered a chance at the stable private life he had never yet enjoyed—were forever fused.

Some of Guthrie's associates—testy Arthur Stern, for example—might have seen *Folksay* as an easy one-off, or a fairly undemanding opportunity to spend a couple of weeks in the company of some attractive young women (and men). But in the year following the premiere, the production for Guthrie inspired a burst of speculative writing about work, art, politics, and human relationships that would fill out his notebooks and letters for the next few years. In notes and little essays, he articulated new priorities and described old ones in original ways.

In approaching dance, Guthrie immediately fixed on one thing in particular, and that was the way the art form reverberated with collectivist principles. It required coordination, organization, and planning—practices that resonated with socialist strategies like the Soviets' Five-Year Plans, sweeping programs meant to modernize industry and collectivize agriculture, all in the name of eradicating poverty and the exploitation of labor. To leftists supporting the Popular Front, Roosevelt's New Deal represented the United States beginning to move in a similar direction. The dancers in Sophie Maslow's troupe offered an embodiment of these principles, and Marjorie Mazia offered a way to make them palpable in his life via the mediums of love, sex, and intimacy.

And so, months after the first, brief run of *Folksay* in the spring of 1942, the experience was still with him. He was in love with Marjorie. But he'd also extracted from the experience a *feeling* of the ideal of "organization." Dancers, after all, literally embodied that principle, which not only drove the labor movement but also lay behind the veneration of social planning in the Soviet Union and, with the New Deal, in FDR's America. On a frigid night, likely the following winter, after he'd ditched Almanac House for his own tiny place farther downtown in the Village, he opened up a new composition book, blew warm breath on his stiff hands, and started writing about his work on Maslow's piece.

Indeed, he started out by musing about performance more generally (the notebook's title was, or later became, "Acting and Dancing"). He recalled Earl Robinson mocking him for having enjoyed wearing makeup for the production. "I'd like to learn all sorts of ways to make up. I'll buy me a kit and practice." He was showing an openness not just to another medium, but to women in particular, earning him the ridicule of a male colleague. He indulged this interest in what being female felt like sporadically, but it was a marked characteristic of his at this particular point in life—as his autobiographical writing would soon show.

That feminine practice of "mak[ing] up" was part of a broader theory of performance—of the self *as* performance. "I take a different slant on acting than most everyone else," he wrote. "To me acting is being your self. There ain't no one little 'self' that is you. I'm no one certain 'self.' I'm a lot of different 'selfs.'"[14] This kind of vernacular version of academic social theories—here, for instance, he anticipates everything from sociologist Erving Goffman's influential *The Presentation of Self in Everyday Life* to multiple branches of postmodern thought—pops up regularly in Guthrie's writing. What's striking in this notebook, though, is that he moves away from what initially seems to be a focus on individual freedom to be who he wants to be and toward the more concrete and collective aspects of dance. Ultimately, the idea that he can be different "selfs" seems more about the very fact that he can go from being the rugged folk singer people like Robinson see him as to a performer in a dance ensemble wearing makeup.

In the pursuit of his expanded artistic profile, he reaped the benefits of the diverse but close networks of Manhattan's Popular Front cultural producers. His commitment to *Folksay* was clear enough to prompt Louis Horst, the editor of the magazine *Dance Observer* and Sophie Maslow's former teacher, to invite him to pen an article about his encounter with the dance world. Ordinarily, the magazine published reviews by well-known critics and theoretical essays by choreographers; Guthrie's voice broke new ground.

Most of the writing came from the "Acting and Dancing" notebook, though it left out the original text's repeated references to the cold making his writing hand shake. Typically hyper-productive, he wrote enough for two articles, and though the pieces have the feel of being written around the time of the initial performance, they appeared in consecutive issues in November and December 1943, possibly scheduled to coincide with a revival of the production. In the first essay, "Singing, Dancing, and Team-Work," Guthrie retold the story of his difficulties at the rehearsal, the discord between idioms, during which his "old philosophy of 'inspiration' and 'feeling'" clashed with the dancers' practiced order, and the dancers risked injury as they tried to compensate. "I watched their pretty bodies and wished I was a dancer," he wrote. That sense of longing for a powerful, expressive physicality ran deeper than simple sexual attraction. The essay expressed a gentle sense of envy, a desire for stability within his own person, his own body and actions. He focused this longing not on his sweetheart, Marjorie Mazia, but on the leader of the troupe, choreographer Sophie Maslow, writing admiringly: "Sophie's body looked so healthy and so active it looked like it would do almost anything she told it to do. All she had to do was notify it." For Maslow, it seemed, there was no space between thought and action; she was efficient and effective like a smoothly running machine. He venerated dancers for pushing through their copious injuries in the service of their art: "Dancers all have got a busted foot or ankle or back or shoulder or some certain mixture of it all. . . . You can shake one's hand and always some other part of their body will fall off, a leg, an ear, their hair. I shook hands with one lady and her left hip dropped four inches." Despite this tragi-comedy of anatomical dissolution, he reported to *Dance Observer* readers, their commitment to their art persists.

Both this essay and the other one for *Dance Observer*, titled "People Dancing," make clear that for Guthrie, watching these women move their bodies was a deeply restorative, deeply *political* experience. The dancers' gritty resilience obviously recalled the time he'd spent among people fighting seemingly insurmountable economic and environmental adversity. But dance also stood out to him because it seemed so essentially a collective art, individuality subsumed to a greater whole. At some level, the same was true of folk music, with its group sings and freewheeling hootenannies, raucous musical parties where anyone might contribute a song. But in truth, he was growing dissatisfied with the Almanac Singers. They were insufficiently committed to musical quality, he thought, and they bickered for hours on end about political minutiae. Maslow's dancers, in contrast, seemed literally to embody a more cooperative and collectively oriented world—much as labor unions did:

> I learned a good lesson here in team work, cooperation, and also in union organization. I saw why socialism is the only hope for any of us, because I was singing under the old rules of "every man for his self" and the dancers was working according to a plan and a hope. (I learned that a planned world is what you need.)
>
> [. . .]
>
> I fell in love with two of the dancing girls just by the horse sense they used in explaining to me the business of organization. One girl told me the theatre was like a factory. The people are like the wheels. If they don't all turn the same way at the same time they'll tear each other up.[15]

Planning, organizing, hoping: what he'd seen in Maslow's company was what everyone needed to become versed in to bring about social change—indeed, to bring about socialism. That he "fell in love" with two of the dancers as they explained "the business of organization" might at first seem a rather conventional heterosexual paean to their "pretty bodies." But more nearly, it illustrates the powerful emotional bonds he saw taking shape in concert with this collective acumen, a clarity of purpose transcending individual ambitions and afflictions. Socialism, for

Guthrie, meant not only a set of political positions but an underlying injunction to be radically available and open to others—in other words, radically *social*. The tone of the piece was homespun and affable even as it subtly urged its readers toward collectivist principles—a voice he had honed writing his "Woody Sez" column for the *People's World* and *Daily Worker*, though those tended to be still more slangy.

The second piece for *Dance Observer*, "People Dancing," made clear why the dancers' example was not only important but timely: acting collectively, embracing the fundamental principles of socialism and communism, was a powerful weapon necessary to defeat the growing global menace of fascism. All workers needed to increase production, from factory workers to dancers. But the point here wasn't simply to amass goods and commodities, or even to strengthen the wartime economy. Work—especially the work that went into an art like dance, if aligned with the "new kind of dance budding on our tree"—cultivated relations, intimacies: "people know[ing] people." And intimacies revealed and healed otherwise disempowering truths, which festered miserably in an individualist culture: "Trouble and worry grow best when you hide them." Ultimately, freedom—the opposite of fascism—meant the ability to realize and express one's need for other people—this is what the *Folksay* experience had brought home to him. With this driving principle, all workers, from railroad workers to sharecroppers to the practitioners of this new, visionary dance, who "liv[e] just to keep working for everybody else," could be members of the same labor union.[16]

Dance offered Guthrie a theory of artistic practice at a time when he was working hard to prove himself more than a hayseed, more than a Tom Joad–like figure straight from the pages of a book or a movie screen. Unfolding in real time, in immediate physical actions, dance challenged the boundary separating representation and reality, expression and action. It must have drawn him in powerfully. As dance scholar Mark Franko writes, "Consider that modern dancers were engaged in deeds, not words. The energy, alacrity, and stamina they evinced as well as the live contact they sustained with a sympathetic audience narrowed the gap between performance and political action."[17] Guthrie meant to perform a similar feat with his music and words, even his prose; in a piece from a few years later, "People as Words," he wrote that he saw words as forces in themselves rather than mere vehicles for the delivery of messages. They could be wielded to hurt, and called upon to repair hurt. This perspective was fundamental to how he viewed himself as an artist: he was not just an expert at creative expression, but, as a practitioner of the arts, a caretaker, a healer, and an organizer.

Nonetheless, when he recalled the night of the rehearsal in a letter to Marjorie months later, after they'd become a couple, he described being surprised and confused by her sudden appearance to repair the awkward situation. He recalled how they'd sat on the studio floor together, going over the counts, until he could put together passably steady versions of songs like "I Ride an Old Paint" and "Dodgers." When the rehearsal ended, he was still ashamed of his clumsiness. So, when she caught up with him as he was walking out, he initially tried to forestall any conversation. But her bright radiance calmed him. She betrayed no pity or condescension.

As they walked and talked their way down West Twelfth Street he began to feel a measure of freedom and ease that still didn't always come easily in this strange, vast city. He felt his muscles relax out of the taut battle-pose they usually assumed here. If a young girl like this could be so carefree, clear-headed, and independent amid the bedlam of Manhattan, surely so could he. They parted at Sixth Avenue, where she headed uptown to Fourteenth Street and he downtown to Almanac House on Tenth.

Then, as he walked home, an unfamiliar vision took shape in his head: an image of tranquil, nourishing domesticity—something he'd barely experienced in his trauma-scarred childhood. As an adult domicile, Almanac House was the veritable headquarters of the folk music world, but it was bare, functional, and chaotic, people going in and out day and night. It was a place to sleep, write, and occasionally strum the guitar. Something in Mazia's face conjured a vision of a very different home environment. As he mounted the steps of the big, shambling, impersonal place with a rotating cast of housemates, he imagined her arriving home to a warm, snug apartment, her parents asleep in one bedroom, a sister snoring softly in another. If she lived on Fourteenth Street, the place couldn't be huge or luxurious. But the confidence and calm she exuded made him picture a quiet space of peaceful intimacy—an atmosphere that was taken from him early in childhood and he had willingly rejected as an adult. That fantasized scene would dissolve soon enough; in the next few days, he learned that she was twenty-five years old, not seventeen as he'd imagined; what's more, she had been married for seven years.[18] Indeed, he wrote out his memories of this evening in a letter addressed to her at the house in Philadelphia that she shared with her husband, Joseph Mazia.

The fantasy of Marjorie as a nearly grown daughter nestled in a happy, comfortable family setting conjures poignant images of his lost sister Clara, and of how she might have thrived in a different domestic environment. Indeed, the whole imagined scene of the sleepy apartment dwellers contrasts poignantly with the chaos that descended on the Guthrie family of Okemah, Oklahoma, as Woody was growing up. As it happened, his other major creative undertaking at the time demanded that he revisit that chaos—a project demanding far more of him, in a personal vein, than any he had yet taken on. It was painful, but it seemed that the recent experiences with dance, and with Marjorie Mazia, offered some new ideas, some new ways to understand what had happened.

Chapter Three

"I HATE TO DESCRIBE MY MOTHER IN TERMS SUCH AS THESE"

PHYSICALLY, WOODY GUTHRIE WAS A SLIGHT MAN. The most common word his friends and associates used to describe him was "wiry." He was usually moving, slightly frenetic, even before that motion started to look "abnormal," excessive, a pathological symptom. Associated in most people's minds with freight-train jumping and walking "that ribbon of highway," he is, of course, among the legendary emblems of unrestricted mobility. A quintessentially American ideal, it is part of a myth that covers over the ruthless violence perpetrated by white settlers against indigenous people across the continent, and is repeated in the mythos of the "frontier." The romance of the American wanderer itself depends on unspoken privileges of whiteness and maleness. A considerably different picture of freight-hopping during the Depression appears in *America Is in the Heart*, a 1946 memoir by Filipino American writer Carlos Bulosan. A contemporary of Guthrie's and organizer of California migrant farmworkers, Bulosan describes being victimized by racist violence while riding freights up and down the West Coast. He also witnesses the gang rape of a woman in a moving box car.

Nevertheless, mobility remains a vexed issue in Guthrie's songs. Their narrators get tired, physically, emotionally, existentially. They go "down the road feelin' bad," as one of the old songs he often sang went. More significantly, the songs illustrate how social inequality—particularly as caused by economic disenfranchisement—constrains freedom of movement. The narrator of a relatively little-known verse of "This Land Is Your Land" finds his roaming and rambling footsteps tripped up by the appearance of a sign that says "Private Property." And although he responds defiantly ("On the other side, it didn't say nothing / That side was made for you and me"), it is hard not to worry that by disregarding the sign, he places himself at compounded risk, akin to the "wandering worker" in "I Ain't Got No Home" who bemoans how "the police make it hard / wherever I may go." The narrators of these songs, made vulnerable to power by their class status, face very real limits on their bodily freedom. Still, like the vast majority of their peers in American literary history, their bodies are, by conventional standards, intact and, in more recent parlance, fully "abled." They can fight the power with brio, and from this resilience comes the mythic quality of much of Guthrie's best-known music.

In early 1942, he had seen another sort of resilience embodied in the largely female modern dance world of bohemian Manhattan: that of women like Marjorie Mazia and Sophie Maslow, whose bodies, vulnerable yet strong, always seemed to be both hurt and healing. His major project, ongoing at the time when he met Marjorie, was an "autobiographical novel," initially called *Boomchasers*, but eventually titled *Bound for Glory*. He was working to craft a narrative that presented him as a representative "hard traveler," a knocked-around but sturdy survivor of the Depression and the Dust Bowl, while also giving a sense of his unique experience. Yet revisiting his early years meant that he also had to decide how to treat the fate of his mother, a woman whose body had met an insidious foe of massive proportions—one he may or may not have known to call Huntington's chorea. He had to decide how to represent her decline—and the mark it had left on him—as part of his story. His experience left a deep but often overlooked mark on the book, which continues to be widely read into the twenty-first century.

The literary project's existence came about because of the patronage and connections of Alan Lomax, the influential archivist he'd met at his first New York concert in 1940. Guthrie's performance in their hours-long recording session at the Library of Congress, in which he discussed living in unemployed economic strife as being "lonesome for a job," had beguiled Lomax. Reflecting on the session in later years, Lomax described a performer who "bit at the heart. A low, harsh voice with velvet at the edges, the syllables beautifully enunciated, the prose flowing with a professional writer's balance of sentence and the salt of folk wit."[1] He chatted up friends and associates in Washington, DC, and New York, looking to create writing opportunities for Guthrie (beyond his regular column for the *Daily Worker*), and predicting that his literary impact could rival that of authors like Mark Twain and James Joyce.

Eventually, Lomax arranged a book contract with E. P. Dutton & Company, a small publishing house with a strong reputation in the serious literary world. The contract brought another powerful woman into Guthrie's life: his editor, Joy Doerflinger. In the summer of 1942, every week or so, Doerflinger would show up at Almanac House, treating residents and hangers-on to a spectacle that seemed at once absurd and, in Manhattan, wholly predictable: a tall, slender, expensively dressed young woman of elegant bearing blithely entering the residence's shabby interior, trailed by her two tiny, leashed dogs—a procession that soon reversed course and exited in the same formation, its leader carrying a packet of Woody Guthrie's typed pages tucked in her purse.[2]

Guthrie was well into the writing process when he met Marjorie Mazia that spring. Their relationship quickly grew intense. They first spent the night together after the cast party following the first *Folksay* performance—just talking, Marjorie assured Joe Klein, the singer's first major biographer, four decades later. But soon, despite their both being married to other people, he was a fixture at her Fourteenth Street room—talking, having sex, writing, and one day answering the door to a startled Sophie Maslow, who'd stopped by to ask Marjorie something. Mazia offered him free use of the space when she was away on tour with the Graham Company, which in 1942 was quite frequently, or when she was down in Philadelphia with her husband, Joe. While the small room, containing just a bed, sink, and desk, was far from the domestic paradise he'd imagined her in on the night of the first rehearsal, its quiet and orderliness provided welcome respite from the chaos and bustle at Almanac House.

The manuscript became a kind of collaboration. She would read pages, copyedit, ask questions, comment. He began to refer to it as "our book." He wrote of her work on the project: "She jumped in and took about three or four flying leaps, and sailed handfuls of loose papers all over Fourteenth Street—and when the air got clear again, I was surprised to see all the notes, and papers, and papers stacked in their proper order and labelled and naturalized—all meaning something."[3] More personally, she encouraged him in his growing sense that he could expand his profile as an artist. She told him he was a writer, not an entertainer.

One night she read over one of the passages describing his mother's illness. She stopped and asked him, "Woody, could you get sick like that?" He replied: "No. Only women."[4]

The charged global environment also helped Guthrie focus on his writing. After the Nazis invaded the Soviet Union in June 1941, he had followed the CPUSA in reversing his anti-interventionist stance and endorsing US military involvement in the conflagration unfolding across the Atlantic. His enthusiasm for the cause intensified following the bombing of Pearl Harbor in December of that year. He and Marjorie worked on the manuscript in an atmosphere of heightened fear and excitement, as German bombs tumbled down onto the streets and buildings of London and other British cities, with an invasion from occupied France presumed imminent.

When summer came, she and her colleagues from the Martha Graham Company left New York City for Vermont to spend several weeks performing and leading master classes at the Bennington College Summer School of Dance. He was still awestruck at what he'd seen working with Sophie Maslow's troupe, and as the war in the Pacific intensified, he began to see female modern dancers as models for the anti-fascist military fight. With a playfulness typical of this period, he made up a mock newspaper with news from the Greenwich Village homestead. The lead story ran:

> "Famed Dance Troupe Skipping Through Dew"
> Bennington, VT: MARTHA GRAHAM and her dance groupe [sic] arrived in town a few days ago . . . Local citizens at first, noticing the tired looks, the crippled feet, busted limbs of all kinds and newcomers, mistook them for war casualties . . . Dancing is just as rough and tough, just as risky and dangerous as soldiering, in view of the condition of many of our stages they are called upon to perform their art for the building of national health, unity, and morale.[5]

The humor masked the growing trepidation about the grand military conflict subsuming an increasing portion of the globe's civilians in violence. But the passage also showed that his infatuation with Mazia and the other dancers' physical feats wasn't separate from his enthusiasm for what he and others on the pro-war Left called the "War Against Fascism."

She remained on the road into the fall. When he moved to a fourth-floor walk-up at 74 Charles Street in the West Village, he worked with as much purpose and focus as he'd ever done. The book he finished has multiple dimensions, and some run at cross-purposes. It begins in what's come to be thought of as classic Woody Guthrie territory—a boxcar full of hobos riding the rails to who-knows-where, but "bound for glory" regardless. The poster for the 1976 film of the book shows lead actor David Carra-dine perched atop a train car with his guitar, and the film, described on the Internet Movie Database as a portrayal of "the early life of Woody Guthrie as a vagabond folk singer," no doubt did much to promote Guth-rie's widespread association with hopping freights and freely roaming the distances described in "This Land Is Your Land." For Bob Dylan, who was initially offered the lead role in director Hal Ashby's film, it was this "whirlwind" aspect of the book that "sang out to him . . . like a radio" when he read it in Minnesota at age nineteen.[6]

According to Alice Kessler-Harris and Paul Lauter, "the cultural apparatus of the Left in the thirties was, if anything, more masculinist than its political institutions"; similarly, Paula Rabinowitz describes the period's "equation of literary and political vitality with masculinity."[7] Leftists, particularly male ones, tended to associate femininity with bour-geois weakness. Indeed, most scholars of the era place Guthrie within this macho hardscrabble tradition. At first glance, Guthrie's *Bound for Glory* seems a slightly belated example of that radical masculine aes-thetic, a book about the thrill of freewheeling wanderlust, where "glory" means, essentially, a man's escape from the burdens of work and fami-ly—a well-established American genre that feminist literary critic Nina Baym once dubbed "melodramas of beset manhood."[8] In this frame, the book looks back both to nineteenth-century works like *The Adventures of Huckleberry Finn* and forward to texts that would help form the bed-rock of the New Left counterculture, like *On the Road*.

But upon a closer read, a far more complex and sensitive work emerges, with a far more nuanced understanding of the meanings of re-sistance, revolution, and gender. To a significant extent, Guthrie used the book as a thought experiment on the politics of intimacy, of how conducting oneself in the face of others' vulnerability helped mitigate the effects of the cruel exercise of power that fascism and capitalism performed on a state level.

These aspects of *Bound for Glory* bear the imprint of Guthrie's recent experience of collaborating with Maslow on the piece *Folksay*. In particular, the book focuses on weakness and exploitability across gender—an emphasis that resonates with the priorities of modern dance. For choreographers like Maslow and Graham, writes dance scholar Mark Franko, "the radical body in motion was feminine and always political . . . the female body's emotional expression enacted a positive valorization of a position of weakness, whereas the male body represented a negative embodiment of what, in other circumstances, would be a position of strength."[9] Looking for an option that provided the necessary scope, Guthrie would use the literary form of the book to tell the story of his interest in troubled people and damaged bodies that needed intimate attention.

The book does, indeed, begin in what many take to be the most Guthrie-an of environments: a moving box car. But the message of the first chapter is far from a celebration of individual (masculine) freedom; it is, if anything, radically *anti*-individualist. The chapter portrays men improvising relations of care, of quasi-domesticity, in disorderly, physically chaotic conditions. It depicts men mothering other men in the absence of women.

The opening lines of the book read:

> I could see men of all colors bouncing along in the boxcar. We stood up. We laid down. We piled around on each other. We used each other for pillows. I could smell the sour and bitter sweat soaking through my own khaki shirt and britches, and the work clothes, overhauls and saggy, dirty suits of the other guys. . . . Part of us waved our hands in the cloud of dust and hollered out to the whole crowd. Others was too weak, too sick, too hungry, and too drunk even to stand up.[10]

With the reference to "men of all colors," Guthrie immediately makes the scene an allegory for the possibility of social unity, across difference, in adverse conditions. His protagonist, Woody, quickly sets to work at this goal, befriending an unnamed "Negro boy." Together, the pair set about contesting not only the chaos, squalor, and disorderly movement—they choreograph a system in which men take shifts sitting by the open door—

but the casual cruelty the environment inspires toward the weaker, the vulnerable, the different. Woody and friend make sure that the first passenger to get a spell of fresh air is an elderly man suffering from "rupture" whose foot has just been burned by young, mean-spirited pranksters. Guthrie then describes a scene of poignant emotional vulnerability, particular for a man: a sleeping young male passenger "hugging his bed roll and moving his lips against the wool blanket," presumably dreaming about a distant lover. Woody shoos away a group of men mocking him (24).

The most tender scene of intimacy among men in the chapter comes a bit later. Woody, the "Negro boy," and two adolescent boys are exiled to the top of the car, in a driving rain; the boys quickly act to *clothe* Woody's guitar, removing their own shirts to shield the instrument, thus figuring it as a kind of vulnerable child whose body requires care and protection. In turn, when the boys settle down to sleep, Woody offers the younger one a restorative gesture of bodily intimacy: "He scooted his body closer to me, and I laid an arm down so he could rest his head. I asked him, 'How's that fer a pillow?'" (34)—a scene that nearly replicates the staging of a publicity photograph of Guthrie with his fellow singer Burl Ives in 1940. Few passages in his writing so plainly illustrate scholar Bryan Garman's insight that for Guthrie, as for Walt Whitman, "physical contact between men constitutes an important part of [his] idealized politics."[11] But the form this physical intimacy takes is also profoundly maternal, a sentiment echoed in one of Guthrie's favorite songs, Goebel Reeves's "Hobo's Lullaby."

> Go to sleep you weary hobo
> Let the towns drift slowly by
> Can't you hear the steel rails hummin'
> That's the hobo's lullaby
> I know your clothes are torn and ragged
> And your hair is turning gray
> Lift your head and smile at trouble
> You'll find peace and rest someday
> Now don't you worry 'bout tomorrow
> Let tomorrow come and go
> Tonight you're in a nice warm boxcar
> Safe from all that wind and snow[12]

Indeed, a habitual desire to see a classic American model of masculinity in *Bound for Glory* has obscured the fact that it is, in a fundamental sense and from its very beginning, an exploration of the vital importance Guthrie's mother played in his self-identity. Ultimately, the well-ordered, reparative mothering of the first chapter essentially represents the book's purpose as a whole. We learn this to be the case, most poignantly, through his deeply traumatized depiction of his own mother's decline. His relationship with his mother haunts the book and, the book suggests, haunted him as well.

Maternal figures did loom fairly large in leftist political and literary culture—witness, for instance, the female labor leaders dubbed with nicknames like Mother Bloor and Mother Jones. Mothers played central roles in many novels by leftists, but they tended to be heavily romanticized, earthy figures like Steinbeck's Ma Joad from *The Grapes of Wrath* or Mike Gold's mother as depicted in his autobiography *Jews Without Money*—a strain in leftist literary culture so prominent in the 1930s that scholar Michael Denning calls it a subgenre: "sentimental maternalism."[13] In the summer of 1942, as he worked on *Bound for Glory*, Guthrie read Gold's book, along with Langston Hughes's *Shakespeare in Harlem* and George Bernard Shaw's *An Intelligent Woman's Guide to Socialism and Capitalism*. He enjoyed them all, but Soviet novelist Maxim Gorky's *Mother* (originally published in 1906) enthralled him the most. It tells the story of Nilovna, an apolitical, bullied, physically abused middle-aged wife and mother who is transformed into a supporter of the failed 1905 Russian revolution. Toward the middle of the novel, she tells younger revolutionaries what she admires about their approach, in words that must have drawn vigorous head nods from Woody Guthrie: "It makes me happy to see you've found the way to the human heart. A person tells you all that is going on inside him without fear; opens up his soul to you of his own accord. And when I think about all you people, I'm certain you'll overcome the evil in life—I'm certain of it."[14]

The depiction of Nora Belle in *Bound for Glory* is not sentimental in this manner; on the contrary, Guthrie seems highly aware that he is doing something groundbreaking and possibly shocking by *not* presenting her in the typical fashion, as a relentlessly sacrificing, unassailably virtuous workhorse. He does not seek to make her or her illness disappear, as they had conspired to do on those childhood afternoons by disappearing into the dark auditorium of Okemah's Crystal Theatre. He does erase, or blur, some details about the family's most brutal tragedies, seeking to absolve or muddy her responsibility for the fiery incidents that killed daughter Clara and severely injured husband Charley. But overall, her illness is not an outside invading force but a central part of her identity, as driven by culture and politics as it is by physiology. And, in a very atypical fashion for the period's sentimental maternalism, he presents himself, a young boy, as so deeply connected to her that their identities mesh across lines of age and gender.

Indeed, the Woody Guthrie of 1942 was intent on depicting not just the sacrifices his mother made for him, but his mother's centrality to his own identity. They share, in particular, a penchant for low-simmering psychic turmoil, worry. She worries about the family's economic stability, and about her husband's physical safety as he is repeatedly involved in altercations linked to local party politics. "Almost every day when Papa rode home," Guthrie remembers, "he showed the signs and bruises of a new fist fight."[15] At the same time, even when barely more than a toddler, he earns a reputation as a "worried little man." Although both parents are musical, because they share this affliction, she teaches Woody how music, particularly "old songs and ballads," can help with the "deep-running thoughts" that trouble them.[16] Guthrie is very clear: in his formative environment, singing traditional songs was not about the preservation of old ways; it was a response to very urgent needs in the present. Hence his approach to folk-singing as repairing hurt in the vulnerable people around him.

However, he bears witness to the fact that this quasi-therapeutic method doesn't always work, that sometimes signs of the condition the town just calls "crazy" emerge, like "the look on her face [that] twisted and trembled and it scared everybody."[17] Eventually, "she concentrated on her worries until it got the best of her," and the symptoms worsen:

> The whole town knew about her. She got careless with her appearance. She let herself run down. She walked around over the town, looking and thinking and crying. The doctor called it insanity and let it go at that. She lost control of the muscles of her face. Us kids would stand around in the house lost in silence, not saying a word for hours, and ashamed, somehow, to go out down the street and play with the kids, and wanting

to stay there and see how long her spell would last, and if we could help her. She couldn't control her arms, nor her legs, nor the muscles in her body, and she would go into spasms and fall on the floor, and wallow around through the house, and ruin her clothes, and yell till people blocks up the street would hear her.[18]

The most heartbreaking thing about this atmosphere of shame and helplessness is that young Woody, as the adult Guthrie portrays him, blames himself for his mother's illness. Or, more nearly, a rumor circulates around town that she "got awful bad sick when I was borned under th'covers," as he puts it to a young friend.[19] Of course, it is not uncommon, though no less heartbreaking, that children in broken domestic situations will blame themselves as an assertion of control amid turbulence. But here we have an adult man writing his memoirs and indicating that his very formation as a person is inseparable from his mother's illness and decline. In other words, whether voluntarily, involuntarily, or a combination of the two, Guthrie gives readers a sense of himself as still deeply connected, both physically and through the medium of shame, to his mother.

Marjorie Mazia is here, too, between the lines. The intensification of their love, as he wrote the book, drew on an apparently mutual desire for her to offer him a kind of maternal care that he had lost early in life. Marjorie, though five years his junior, assumed the role with ease. In letters from the road, she repeatedly urged him to shower, brush his teeth, eat well, sleep enough, drink in moderation, and engage in other typical practices of self-care. She signed off her New Year's Eve letter, "Be my goodest baby and I'll always be your Mama!"[20] Guthrie, in turn, repeatedly addresses her as "Mama" and even "Mommy." The former, of course, is familiar as an expression of sexual intimacy—even desire—and Guthrie's use of it embodies the way two forms of intimacy often considered distinct became hard to distinguish in his nascent partnership with Marjorie. And, in passages like the opening box-car scene, the book suggests, against the conventional understanding of gender, that he at times wanted to *become* his mother, or become a mother of a type she was ultimately not able to be for her family.

Young Woody's confession of shame about his mother's illness precedes a truly horrific scene of violence. One day Woody sits with a young uncle (a son of his grandmother's who is the same young age as he), sharing observations while playing with a new litter of kittens. Another, slightly older young uncle interrupts the fun, sadistically killing the kittens and torturing their mother, who is described in the aftermath in terms that evoke the symptoms of Huntington's, "moan[ing]" and "chok[ing]" and "throwing her head first to one side and then to the other." The cat's body works like a surrogate for Nora Belle's, allowing Guthrie to describe a degree of violence, pain, and disorientation that, presumably, would be too devastating (or shameful) to represent as directly ravaging his mother.

These vivid descriptions of damaged bodies cause the author to break down and address the reader directly, drawing attention to the challenge of writing this story: "I hate a hundred times more to describe my mother in any such words as these. You hate to read about a mother described in any such words as these. I know. I understand you. I hope you can understand me, for it must be broke down and said."[21] As a writer, Guthrie takes a nuanced approach here (one that he would employ repeatedly in coming years), for as he announces his shame about exposing the details of his mother's decline, he makes that same shame the means through which he forms an intimate bond with the reader.

Like all autobiographical books, *Bound for Glory* was an attempt to bridge the gap between the author's present and the raw material of their past. Juxtaposed with his collaboration with Maslow and her dancers, his work on this poignant aspect of the book is akin to his fascination with the vulnerability and strength of female bodies. Indeed, the timing suggests the possibility that one of the reasons he was so drawn to dance was that it served as a salve for the pain of recreating the traumatic scene of his mother's breakdown.

As soon as *Bound for Glory* was published in March 1943, reviews came in, the positive ones well outnumbering the negative. Critics made it clear that the book had done much of what Lomax had hoped it would do—bring out Guthrie's voice, his way with words. One reviewer noted that the book's appeal was more emotional and less directly political than might have been expected: "Guthrie writes (at times with touches of sheer poetry) from the heart and not from the economic perspective."[22]

At the same time, the reviews initiated the tradition of suppressing other aspects of the book in favor of the portrayal of Guthrie as romantic wanderer. In a review titled "A Guitar Busker's Singing Road," Horace Reynolds of the *New York Times* wrote: "Its action is the picaresque loafing, singing, starving, freezing, carousing life of the American road. Smoke boils out of the stacks of overworked locomotives, and Woody sweeps across the country from the green orchards of California to the sodden stones of New York's Ninth Avenue."[23] The *Tulsa World* referred to him as an "Okie troubadour" and "Skid Row, U. S. A. in person."[24] Some friends and associates groused that the book's editor had sanitized the rawer, more imaginative artist they knew—an opinion Guthrie himself would endorse not long after. Very few of the reviews mentioned his mother—and those that did, did sparingly.

With its tender and painful depiction of his mother's failing health, Guthrie's first major foray into literary writing also provided another, slightly submerged narrative about his formative environment of trauma and shame—one that morphed, implicitly, into the ethic of care for the vulnerable that underpinned episodes like the maternal box-car scene. It's as if Guthrie's readers—the professional ones, at least—either didn't care much about the book's other line of narrative or, though they were unlikely to admit it, found it too traumatic.

With hindsight, it's also possible to see something larger than Guthrie at work here, responsive to the economic and social trauma that had enveloped the globe in the 1930s. Where nations like Germany and Italy sought a strong father figure to protect them, countries drifting leftward, like the US, began to envision governance as something more akin to maternal care. While by no means a systematic challenge to capitalism, the modern welfare state modeled by the New Deal provided for its people, understanding its role as that of a caretaker for the vulnerable and distressed. The spectrum of views in the Popular Front varied mainly on whether, within the maternal state, capitalism should ultimately be maintained (New Deal Democrats) or jettisoned completely (the CPUSA).

The strength of female bodies continued to occupy Guthrie's thoughts as the years went by. Much of his artwork, particularly as it became more abstract over the course of the 1930s, depicted bulky figures with identifiably female features. Many of these images look like dancers, some have a melancholic cast; the figures often seem a mix of feelings of loss, awe, and desire. One stands out as brighter, though. A large figure performs a dance move or stretch in front of a smaller figure, presumably Guthrie's surrogate in the drawing. The handwritten caption reads: "Not ever to be afraid of my sexy odd position nor ever get afraid of creations ways with me."[25] It is a pledge to what he had learned from Marjorie Mazia and, in a more tragic way, from Nora Belle Guthrie.

Meanwhile, the good people of E. P. Dutton & Co. saw *Bound for Glory* as the first salvo in a promising literary career. They offered Guthrie a contract to write three more books. They were confident that he would continue to grow and achieve eminence in the world of letters. At this point, there was no reason to doubt it. Everyone just had to figure out how to defeat fascism while living through a war.

Chapter Four

THE WAR AGAINST LONELINESS

S INCE THE 1960S, many people associate the Left with permissive views
about personal behavior and self-expression, the letting-it-all-hang-out
ethos of the hippie generation. For the radical left of Woody Guthrie's
time, at least publicly, such matters held less importance. Particularly in
a time of stricter gender roles, such "personal" concerns didn't signify as
politically significant. The public sphere, the male-dominated worlds of
politics, law, and finance, was the real realm of focus, the arenas in which
oppressive class relations and racial injustice were maintained. Most leftists in the socialist or communist tradition believed that love and domesticity were false idols; the capitalist bourgeoisie idealized them in order
to sap the time and energy of people who might otherwise devote themselves to challenging the dominant economic structure and overturning
the ruling class. The significance of individual emotional experiences
needed to be sacrificed to the commitment to a larger cause. Moreover,
they were considered feminine concerns that ran counter to the masculine
struggle for revolution.

Guthrie's letters to Marjorie Mazia during the war years, however,
show a committed leftist thinking along very different lines. They are the
record of two people—one in particular—striving to make an intimate
relationship between lovers historically and politically consequential. To
an extent, these efforts reflected the Popular Front era, when a shift in
focus from revolution to anti-fascism brought FDR-supporting liberal
Democrats into the fold with socialists and communists, making the Left
as a whole more middle class and female, and the more radical left less

bound by ideological orthodoxy.[1] But the first years of his correspondence with Marjorie make it clear: Guthrie didn't consider this shift a
watering down of the Left's work.

As the summer of 1942 turned into autumn, Woody Guthrie came
to believe that his bond with Marjorie Mazia reflected not only their
attraction to one another but also the possibility of fusing one's personal
and political commitments. Unlike his estranged wife Mary, Marjorie
was well-read and came from a leftist background. She had an independent and unconventional personality. The fact that she was an artist enraptured him, as did their shared commitment to expressive forms that
would "attratct [sic] every honest ear and eye and human mind on this
planet" in order to expose the destructive nature of fascism.[2] Marjorie
was less declarative, but did nothing to discourage her lover's sentiments.
Their closeness seemed a medium for discovering ways to make sense of
the world, to change it, to make their lives consequential. The magnetic
pull between them felt mighty; surely it was meaningful not only to them,
but to history writ large.

Mary Guthrie, back in north Texas, and Joe Mazia, just a couple
of hours away in Philadelphia, became the unwitting victims of these
grandiose ideas. To be fair, Mary had given up on Woody when he de-
parted for New York for the second time. She didn't actually expect him
to return to her and the kids. Marjorie, however, kept Joe in a kind of
marital and geographical limbo. Working with Martha Graham always
gave her an excuse to stay in New York, and the company's heavy touring schedule demanded regular travel around the country. She seems to
have tried to hide the affair with Guthrie in the open, actually bringing
Joe to at least one folk music jam, or "hootenanny," in the basement of
Almanac House. Later, she would tell friends that her marriage to Joe left
her sexually cold.

In a head-on collision between intimate life and the state, the FBI
pierced through her charade. During a rehearsal in late May or early June
1942, one of Marjorie's Graham Company colleagues abruptly called
her to the studio's telephone. She ran to the phone worrying that something had happened to one of her parents, but discovered an agitated Joe
on the other line. He told her that he had just opened the door of their
North Philadelphia row house to two men identifying themselves as FBI
agents. "Do you know your wife is having an affair with a communist?"

one asked, flat out. To the US Department of Justice, there was no need for deliberation: Woody and Marjorie's relationship represented a potentially revolutionary act. Once the Nazis attacked the Soviet Union in June 1941, the people the FBI watched going in and out of Almanac House mostly shifted their anti-interventionist stance and supported the war effort, following the lead of the CPUSA. But the terms through which radical left groups expressed that support—the links they drew between American racism and Nazism, the talk of a "soviet" world in the offing—meant they were still threats to the stability of the nation, at least in the minds of a Bureau led by the notoriously anti-communist J. Edgar Hoover. Joe Mazia wasn't politically outspoken. Indeed, as a metallurgist for the Frankford Arsenal, where secret weapons projects were underway, he likely found the FBI's scrutiny of his private life especially alarming.

Confronted on the phone, Marjorie immediately owned up to the affair with Woody. She also seized the opportunity to share another piece of news with her husband: she was pregnant, and Guthrie was the father, not him. Joe demanded that once the summer dance season had ended, she return to Philly and stay. Reluctantly, she complied, telling Woody that after she had the baby she would come back to him and New York, but that she could receive better prenatal care in her ostensible hometown.

The situation was complicated, but the complications helped to engender some of Woody Guthrie's most far-reaching thoughts about the politics of intimacy, culminating in a fantastic literary and political experiment with the many senses of a single term that spanned the public and the private, the personal and the political: *union*.

Guthrie was game to see this tangled situation as a test of his political principles. He initially urged that the trio assume a "scientific" or objective mind-set, suggesting that their individual feelings might be less than helpful. His point of reference was less laboratory science than the "scientific" tradition in socialism, which dated back to Pierre-Joseph Proudhon, who coined *scientific socialism* in 1840 to describe a state ruled by careful, reasoned study and planning rather than by the will of its leaders.[3] It's unlikely that Guthrie had read Proudhon; more likely, he encountered the term, as filtered through Marx and Engels, while reading leftist journals connected to the CPUSA, like the *Daily Worker* and *New Masses*. However it entered his vocabulary, it embodied his faith that not just the social structure, but individual relationships, too, could be brought to their full potential by means of careful study.

In regard to this love triangle, that faith was genuine, although at times his expression of it veered into a display of plumage in the direction of his rival for Marjorie Mazia's affections. He filled a composition book with writing addressed to both Marjorie and Joe Mazia, as well as to Woody and Marjorie's yet-to-be-born child, whom Guthrie had taken to calling "Pete," presuming it would turn out male. For the greater part of this document, Guthrie maintains a generous and fair tone, depicting the three adults as stuck in a situation none of them wants, but that is nonetheless not only unavoidable but a symptom of humanity: "All of our tangles and mix-ups are THE ONLY REASON FOR LIVING—WORKING—GOING ON. And our loves and kisses and passions and flights of mind—they give us the gas and the juice to keep going on and on." He assures them that he has no special purchase on what is right, that he "need[s] fixing" just like landlords, the mayor, Eleanor Roosevelt, fascism, Jim Crow, and other public people and issues do. He claims he will be fine if they decide to stay together, because "hurt" and loss are a shared currency of humanity: "Everybody seems to of lost something. Something they haven't ever advertised in the papers but something that everybody is looking for. You. Me. All of me."[4] But there are times in the notebook when an underlying anxiety surfaces, as when Guthrie offers Joe advice on how to deal with premature ejaculation, thus passive-aggressively signaling to his rival that Marjorie has shared this deeply personal information with him. Clearly, Guthrie's attunement to the sustaining powers of intimate knowledge meant that he also understood its powerful capacity for shaming people.

There is no sign that Joe Mazia ever responded to this long missive. And the remainder of the documents of the first few years of Guthrie's relationship with Marjorie Mazia are in the more conventional format of one-to-one correspondence. The pair exchanged letters frequently, bridging the distance brought about first by Marjorie's exile to Philadelphia, and later by Guthrie's entry into the war as a member of the Merchant Marine in April 1943, just after Mazia had returned to New York with the couple's infant progeny, now named not Pete but Cathy Ann. As the weeks, months, and eventually years passed, this correspondence blossomed into a fascinating document of love in a time of massive upheaval as lived by people open to radical transformations in their personal and political lives. They also reveal Woody Guthrie allowing himself to write in a more theoretical and exploratory mode than perhaps any other place in his archive. The writing is more expansive and abstract than what was contemporaneously appearing in public outlets, like his articles for the *Daily Worker* and *Dance Observer*, where he tended to play up his hillbilly voice.

The wartime letters leave no ambiguity: Woody and Marjorie understood the historical moment to demand a relationship in which intimacy aligned with anti-fascist principles, in which love and sex buttressed the ideals to which they had committed their lives. Everything they did, everything that happened in their home(s) or in their bodies, bore potentially world-historical implications. Thus, in the months leading up to Cathy's birth, Marjorie described feeling the little fetus "Pete" kick in her uterus: "Maybe he's saying that I've passed over the fire and he's leading me on to a very beautiful soviet world—where love and courage and good work are there a plenty for all good people!"[5]

The political climate of the time provided Woody Guthrie and Marjorie Mazia with certain terms and concepts for understanding their feelings toward each other. Inversely, the feelings their intimacy generated fed their political commitments. They weren't theorists; they didn't make sense of their lives or relationship through specific writings; they didn't quote Marx, Lenin, or Goldman to one another, or argue over fine points of political strategy. Their engagement with left politics was, broadly speaking, more atmospheric. Left anti-fascism provided a language of mutuality, of shared purpose. It was there for the broad purpose of making a better world, but it was also there *for them*, to bring them closer, and to help them negotiate the unsteady ground of their increasing intimacy.

Marjorie took up this tack in response to Guthrie's anxiety about her move to Philadelphia while she was pregnant. She affirmed her commitment to him but claimed that she couldn't leave Joe when his job was so important to the war effort. More pertinently, she said, she had better prenatal care in Philadelphia, and they needed to make sure "Pete" would be the healthiest, strongest anti-fascist baby possible:

> I shall stay here in Phila. and give Joseph the courage he needs to fight a battle that is not only his but all of us who suffer the tortures of fascism. . . . My baby must live in a healthy world where the sick are helped but don't rule because they are so sick and unbalanced that nobody knows how to cure or hold them down. . . . I imagine Hitler must have been delighted these past few weeks to see such enemies as we three fighting so much between ourselves that we almost forgot that he's the real enemy! . . . Thank goodness it's over and three more healthy strong people have rejoined to battle fascism and greed. . . . Lets all help each other—you to write the songs that give our people courage—Joseph to give our boys the physical weapons with which to do the job and me to add Pete to this world to do his part and give all of us the strength and courage it takes to win such battles.[6]

Along with being an anti-fascist screed, this passage inadvertently shows how such momentous language can also hint at justification for potentially hurtful choices. The converse, however, is that the ideologically inflected discourse provided a useful floating device in rocky relationship waters. They took politics seriously. But the politics were also a prop within the everyday push and pull of an intimate dyad, not unlike the way some couples use children or in-laws. It was easier to shut down an argument when Hitler wanted it to continue.

It was clearly an odd ménage for Marjorie Mazia. On one side was Joe, a trained scientist working with the laws of chemistry to bolster the war effort. On the other was Woody, working against fascism with words, verses, choruses, melodies, emotions—all of which he nevertheless described in starkly physical terms, as parts of a *machine*, as attested by the famous slogan scrawled on his guitar, THIS MACHINE KILLS FASCISTS. At times, the lovers fought, each accusing the other of straying in the direction of other people (that is, besides their respective spouses), and Guthrie expressing off-and-on bitterness about Marjorie's decision to retreat to Philadelphia.

But Guthrie, in particular, also used the correspondence to hone ideas about how to fuse one's political principles with the events and emotions of everyday life. The letters both declare and embody what, for him, was a foundational axiom of anti-fascism: the emotional and the rational are not opposed but fundamentally entwined with one another—what a Marxist, using language that Guthrie occasionally employed in other contexts, would call dialectical.[7] Attempting to be "scientific" about intimate matters didn't preclude avowals of political commitment. Hence, his declarations of devotion tended to be constructed, in part, out of references to the historical events engulfing most of the globe:

> BUT YOUR PHONE CALL JUST CAME, and that changes not only all of this, but me, and the world, and everything, even my part in the war.[8]

> I know from very very personal experience that by my lonesome self I ain't worth a dip of snuff. But with you helping me I don't think a thousand fascists and ten years of bad weather could stop me.[9]

In early December of 1942, nine months after their first meeting, and after several months of angry back-and-forth about Joe, liberally interspersed with sojourns in the blissful space of their new relationship, Marjorie wrote Woody describing herself as "at the low point right now" and complaining that "I really feel like a tortured person."[10] His response illuminates how their correspondence afforded him an opportunity to think through the relationship between their closeness and politics on a global scale. He opens by assuring her, "I'm sorry you're crying, mama, and I wish I could hold you until the tears all run out."[11] He describes the snowflakes falling outside the window of his Charles Street apartment, comparing them to parachutists sacrificing their lives (in this case, to make the sidewalk cleaner, and to fill the rivers to hold up Allied warships), and to her falling tears, which, he writes, "will be like oil, mama, to grease our machinery to get us where we want to go."

He then described his view of the war's purpose:

> We're fighting this war to end slavery, thievery, and loneliness, and it is kind of like a big school, where you go to learn, sometimes, about these three things, and to feel them inside you, taste them in your mouth, and see how useless and bad they are, whip them personally, and then when you get to where you can lick them every time you meet up with them, you soon get to be a soldier, showing other people how to see them, know them, and destroy them, too.[12]

The message to his beloved: your sadness allows you to feel what life under fascism—with its embrace of slavery and thievery—is like, at the most visceral, sensual level ("feel them inside you, taste them in your mouth"). Think of your "loneliness" as a kind of knowledge, taught through mood and the senses. Knowing it will help you fight it. Her personal fight against it—indeed, everyone's struggle with bad feelings—qualified as its own front in the war.

If there is a single argument of sorts running through the letter (and others from this early period in their relationship) it is this: the vulnerability to hurt and shame that intimacy both produces and salves is not simply analogous to vulnerability to political power; it *is* the same vulnerability. Thus, Guthrie, now addressing both his lover and a wider audience of anti-fascists, continues with an exhortation to "study crying and the cause of crying, misery and the cause of misery, hate and the cause of hate, fear and the cause of fear, crime and the cause of crime, nervousness and the cause of nervousness, and study to know greed and fascism (because they are one and the same thing), in all of its hundred million disguises." Some people betraying such qualities have been seduced by fascism's ability to sound "soft and sweet and tender, sentimental, and moody, loving and kind," but in truth, "fascism would like for you to think that all of the world's troubles are your own personal fault. Fascism would like for you to weep and hang your head and get so mixed up in your thinking that you'd walk into one of its own churches looking for some kind of a personal salvation."[13]

Indeed, they discuss fascism not as a set of principles governing a state but as an emotional state—or, more nearly, an emotional imbalance. The fascist creed wasn't present only in nations led by avowedly fascist governments: Germany, Italy, Spain, and Japan. It was a mood, and a way of acting, that existed in greater and smaller pockets everywhere, manifest in dispiriting behavior that just about everyone encountered virtually every day: carelessness, bullying, the denigration of self and others. Fascism worked by exploiting vulnerability, and virtually anyone could fall victim to it.

In these letters, fascism resembles nothing so much as an abusive partner. It can make people believe they are wholly responsible for the dire state of the world. Later in the four-page letter, he describes still sometimes feeling as if "all of the world's ills and evils would have been eradicated and cured twenty years back if it had not been for the birth of W. W. Guthrie who mixed things all up." Implicitly, he suggests that in other circumstances, his predilection for feeling shame, its origins so poignantly traced in *Bound for Glory*, might have led him down the fascist path, or made him especially vulnerable to it.

Yet for all of his commitment to the messy power of emotions, the besotted Woody Guthrie writing these letters maintains a strong faith in a kind of clear-headed sense of agency that, in his attraction to Marjorie Mazia, occupies space that, for other couples, might be taken up by the allure of deep brown eyes or a dulcet voice. Bucking conventional gender associations, he saw Marjorie's smartness as embodying the "scientific" outlook through which he believed socialism would bring about a better world. There are echoes of the *Folksay* experience in these sentences— both Marjorie's quick-thinking intervention in his clumsy embarrassment and in the celebration of *organization* and *planning*, words that span the otherwise divergent arts of dance and labor activism. When he praised Marjorie's organizational skills (in contrast to his sense that he himself was "a pretty empty and disorganized person"),[14] he echoed his awe of Sophie Maslow's ability, expressed in the *Dance Observer*, to make her body do her will's bidding: "All she had to do was notify it." At the same time, he meant her ability to act effectively in concert with others, whether in a dance piece, in the performance of daily routine tasks, or in a group of workers consolidating their power to demand fair wages and working conditions. According to this logic, tidying your apartment was an anti-fascist act, a blow struck at Hitler and Mussolini. Even involuntary and non-human phenomena contained vital resources with organizational properties—features that might also be dubbed *reparative*. Marjorie's tears were oil for lubricating the engines of the Allied forces' planes and tanks. As we've seen, snowflakes falling outside Woody's window kept the sidewalks clean for anti-fascists to go about their lives' daily tasks; they also ensured the waterways of the world continued to accommodate Allied ships and boats.

This link between politics and intimacy took its most concrete form in the word *union*. Labor songs were Guthrie's bread and butter, and the term was on his lips constantly as he sang songs like "Union Maid," "Union Prayer," and "Gonna Join That One Big Union." But as he and Marjorie grew more intimate, the term became a conceptual thread link-ing their love, their sex life, and wider bonds between the people that made up collective groups, including labor unions ("people knowing people," as he'd put it in the *Dance Observer* essays). After several months, it would emerge at the center of their relationship's lingua franca. No term in Guthrie's lexicon has as much range, potency, or alchemical potential as *union*.

This word resonated with such intensity precisely *because* it spanned the labor movement and the realm of social relationships—in particular, the celebration of collapsing individual boundaries in relationships, be they between friends, family, fellow union members, or lovers. It was the same principle that resounded through the Carl Sandburg poetry from *Folksay*, and in Guthrie's own writing on the lessons learned from the dancers. Unionism, as a creed, was not totally new; indeed, decades earlier in the twentieth century, the Industrial Workers of the World had brought a quasi-religious fervor to their aspirational vision of humanity as "One Big Union." For Guthrie, unionism was a form of faith because the word itself had the capacity to unite realms generally considered distinct, such as emotional life and the fight for better working conditions. Some of his songs made the intensity of this commitment especially clear, as in "Union's My Religion":

When I seen my union vision
Then I made a quick decision;
Yes, that union's my religion;
That I know[15]

Or in "Good Old Union Feeling":

HAVE YOU FELT THAT UNION FEELING IN YOUR SOUL? IN YOUR SOUL?
HAVE YOU FELT THAT UNION FEELING IN YOUR SOUL?
IT'S WROTE DOWN IN THE BOOK OF AGES
AND IT'S CARVED IN THE SOLID ROCK
IT'S THAT GOOD OLD UNION FEELING IN YOUR SOUL[16]

Songs of this sort suppress the details of specific labor battles in favor of a more passionate exhortation to a state of faith. As Mark Allan Jackson points out, Guthrie wrote both types of songs, the specific and the general, during this era that Michael Denning has called the "Age of the C. I. O," in reference to the Congress of Industrial Organizations, then a more progressive, desegregated federation than the American Federation of Labor.[17] Using all capital letters when he published the lyrics of "Good Old Union Feeling" in his slim 1947 volume *American Folksong*, Guthrie tries to summon all the dynamism the medium of print can supply. *Union* here names, essentially, a congregation joined not only in conviction but in song. Empowerment came not from shucking off the influence of other people, but from welcoming it—by actually *embracing* the need for other people. It was socialism writ large, but Guthrie's emphasis on the emotional dimensions also tapped into a counter-strain in American life and culture dating back at least to nineteenth-century utopian experiments and reaching forward to 1960s hippie communes and happenings. When Guthrie wrote of ending "slavery, thievery, and loneliness," he was referring not only to the authoritarian cruelties of fascism but also to capitalism's predilection for distancing people from one another. Collectivism combined emotional and political needs.

Most significantly, the word *union* expressed his broad belief in seeing the world through the lens of relationships rather than the singular individual. It embodied the fundamentally *social* nature of his socialism, as well as the assumptions that brought intimacy to the forefront of his politics. Guthrie mentions loneliness several times during the first year of his correspondence with Marjorie. Certainly, his situation over the course of the fall and winter of 1942–43, waiting for Marjorie to make good on her promise to leave her husband, was a deeply lonely one. He even expressed doubts that she *would* leave him, occasionally inveighing against her angrily or claiming not to care should she decide to stay with Joe.

But in a letter that rounded off their first year of knowing one another, as he prepared to ship out to the Atlantic theater of the war, he turned this personal loneliness into a disquisition on the principle of union and the emotional dimensions of resisting social injustice. "This loneliness can be for love of a comrade or sweetheart or it can be the emptiness that comes from not knowing enough friends, not associating with enough people, just not wide awake—just not 'unionized' in your thinking."[18] He continues, "There is high rent. Bad housing. Lack of nurseries, lack of toilet facilities, the problem of commuting in bad weather, but give a person the right union and the lover of his or her choice and not wind nor weather nor mansions nor shacks can stop them." *Unionism*, in all of its senses, is chiefly useful as a weapon against loneliness and isolation, which are the customary emotional states of capitalist cultures, defining freedom as freedom from the influence of other people. As he puts it:

> But one of the worst things about capitalist society is that it teaches us to "go it alone" to get "independent" and to "hit the top" and to "retire early" and to not waste our time and money socialising [*sic*] or unionizing or thinking and planning in a good union way. This thing of "unionism" is the only lure and bait that any religion has really held out for anybody and their best slogan has been "love thy neighbor"—(work and think and plan along with your fellow worker)—this, as you rightly said in your good letter is the little thing that makes that little clicker click inside you and send you out to dance or to plow or to run a machine—this is the end of that bad old personal emptiness that catches so many of us on the grounds of love and courtship. The best part about the union hall is that it teaches you how to be free to talk and think and to hear that you are some good to somebody, some use, some help to the people of the world. A sweetheart can help to tell you this. A fellow union member can too. But if you don't hear it sung, talked, danced, acted, spoken, and over and over and over—you get to thinking you don't count for much.

Here, again, is the principle of helping "people know people," as he'd put it when writing about his work with dancers in *Dance Observer*. Fundamentally, the notion of *union* finds a revolutionary resource in closeness between people. The collective space of the union hall provides conditions for people to initiate intimacies with one another, whether they be between comrades or lovers. And the purpose of art—or, more nearly, performance—is largely the same: to make people available and open to one another, canceling such feelings as "that bad old personal emptiness." Guthrie also puts sexual intimacy on this continuum of feeling, with a porous border between what is and isn't sexual—and with a loose depiction of how the erotic dimensions of these feelings work according to gender. This was an early sign of something important in the offing: understanding sexuality as a realm of political struggle.

Every couple develops its own language, in which words and phrases that have mundane or utilitarian meanings for others take on loaded significance, whether they be pet names or references to shared, private experiences. However, instead of retreating into one another, Marjorie and Woody made their language a medium for better understanding and negotiating the political chaos of the moment in which they met. They used terms like *planning, organization,* and *union* in ways that erased the distance between the local and the global, the personal and the historical, the emotional and the theoretical, the physical and the cognitive, the micro and the macro. Their love gave them a language, and a set of feelings, with which to bridge the conventional oppositions of these arenas. As the war progressed and wound down, Guthrie would become more interested in sex, and writing about sex, as a particular version of this language.

Chapter Five

BODIES OF GLORY

O NCE THE CPUSA and others on the radical left had thrown their support behind the war effort in 1941, Guthrie joined in with a ven-
geance. He wrote songs like "Beat Mister Hitler Blues" and (with Pete
Seeger and Millard Lampell) "Round and Round Hitler's Grave." In "The
Sinking of the Reuben James," he memorialized the casualties aboard an
American destroyer sunk by German U-boats before the US had officially
entered the war. And in "Miss Pavlichenko," he sang gleefully about the
female Russian sniper who had reportedly felled over three hundred Nazi
soldiers.

In June 1943, despite having just been awarded a grant to support the
writing of his follow-up to *Bound for Glory*, he signed up and shipped
out to serve in the war with the Merchant Marine. His friend, folk singer
Cisco Houston, and Houston's pal and fellow communist Jim Longhi
were alongside him on the SS *William B. Travis* as it steamed across the
Atlantic. A week into the journey, a German submarine fired a torpedo
that hit one of the ships the *Travis* was accompanying. Watching it sink,
folded in the middle, served as a terrifying introduction to the reality of
war. That night, Longhi and Guthrie discussed their fears; Guthrie began
talking about his mother and the atrocious fires that riddled his childhood. He mentioned her illness and told his fellow sailor, "I'm beginning
to suspect that I have it too." Longhi scoffed, asking him why he would
think that. "Just feel queer sometimes," Guthrie responded.[1]

The ship sailed into the Mediterranean in support of the Allied invasion of Sicily. One night in September, as they shuttled troops between
Palermo and Tunis, Guthrie and his shipmates were jolted awake by a

deafening blast and a sudden heave of the vessel. This time, they had struck a mine. Although shaken, Guthrie, Houston, and Longhi volunteered to search the lower hold of the ship, where water was gushing in, for possible casualties. They found one seriously wounded crew member and carried him above; other searchers found a dead sailor. As the boat lurched toward the Tunisian shore, the men on board wondered whether the U-boat would come back to finish the job. Guthrie and his friends led them in song; at one point, he stood at the rail yelling "God bless the Red Army! They'll finish off the fascist bastards!"[2] Fortunately, they managed to dock and disembark before the damaged ship finally slid underwater.

After some months back in New York, where Marjorie had rented a house for them in Coney Island, and during which Guthrie undertook the most productive studio sessions of his life, the trio returned to the war-torn Atlantic aboard the SS *Sea Porpoise* in May 1944. Amid the constant tension, he wrote letters to Marjorie—sometimes as many as three in a day. If his body was feeling off-kilter or "queer," it was nonetheless also fueling a newly explicit mode of written expression, meant to substitute for the lack of her physical presence. He missed sex, he missed the allure and comfort of her body. He masturbated regularly, having done so since childhood; military literature called it "harmless and childish," he wrote, and he felt no shame about it, he assured her. He wrote her letters detailing his fantasies about her, and her body, what he'd like to do, what he'd like her to do: letters that he knew, all told, she'd rather not receive, though she told him not to worry; it was only that she wasn't able to reciprocate in similarly graphic terms. She later told him that she could only express such feelings through the art of dance. "I'm glad you want me to write. . . . I'm sorry I can't . . . but I can do other things and I will and you will have to watch and feel through my medium."[3] But while he was writing he could almost feel her there:

My mind only wants to draw you nearer and closer. And you make me the luckiest and happiest man in the world when you move your body with mine, when you close your eyes and open your mouth and roll your belly and your hips, when you spread your legs apart slow and easy and let me put my mouth and tongue on the hairs of your womb. . . . To touch your lips with my lips and lick my tongue in the hole of your vagina absolutely boils every drop of blood in my body.[4]

Across five thousand miles of ocean, with U-boats lurking beneath the dark, frigid waves, erotic fantasies like these were surely a vital method of enduring the looming threat of well-aimed torpedoes.

Often, he filled the pages of his letters with much more mundane stuff: long, granular descriptions of the daily routines necessary to maintain the new ship, the SS *Sea Porpoise*. Little episodes struck him as remarkable, like one he described in a letter from June 1944. At the time, the *Sea Porpoise* was moored in Belfast Lough, the crew getting ready to take reinforcements over to the fierce fighting against the Nazis in Normandy. On deck one day, he heard a bunch of shipmates arguing and laughing loudly and went over to investigate. One of them was holding a copy of a book by Erskine Caldwell called *God's Little Acre*. Caldwell was the author of *Tobacco Road*, the novel whose theatrical adaptation had initially brought Will Geer, and consequently Woody Guthrie, to New York. The book had a number of sex scenes, more suggestively raunchy than explicit, but it portrayed poor, white Southern characters as sex-crazed boys and girls, barely able to control their lusty appetites. Like *Lady Chatterley's Lover* and *Ulysses*, the book had been brought up on obscenity charges and, banned by the New York City's Vice Commission. Caldwell had even been arrested at an author's event.

The guy was reading a passage out loud, maybe the part where a man shocks his daughter-in-law by telling her about his penchant for concealing himself in places where he can get a glimpse of her "rising beauties," that is, her breasts. The sight, he informs her, makes him "feel sometime like getting right down on my hands and knees like these old hound dogs you see chasing after a flowing bitch. You just ache to get down and lick something."[5] The more this sailor read, the more everyone howled and demanded a night with the book. There was something desperate and childish about the whole thing—the fight over the little volume, as if for scant resources; the forced laughter; the sense that they might get caught behaving badly, doing something forbidden. It was like that other time, when they'd been learning hand signals, and a number of the crew started to make obscene gestures, miming sex through hand motions, that kind of thing. "I sometimes wonder how many more wars we will have to fight before we get over our silly ignorance about the human body," he wrote in a letter recounting the shipboard incidents.[6] Couldn't adults be open about love, lust, body parts? Talk about them freely, minus the coyness and euphemisms?

A year later, the war was over, but he'd been drafted for a short term in the army. Perhaps because of the continuing, deep exposure he had to an intensely homosocial environment, the cultural dimensions of sex were still on his mind. A couple of months before heading home from his base in Belleville, Illinois, he wrote to Margie that he thought sex should be honored, taken seriously, studied: "I wanted [sex] to be intellectual, and beautiful, and scientific."[7] Scientific, for him, meant rational, level-headed, and munificent. Certainly, sex should be explored with wonder, and not emptied of pleasure. He continued, "There was and still is a wildness that I would like to feel, a self forgetfulness, a more daring and thrilling, surprising something."[8] But it shouldn't have to turn adult men into drooling, desperate boys trying to quell their embarrassment with loud, aggressive laughter.

"You know, there is something that I want to tell you about," he wrote Marjorie, telling her that he had tried to write about it "several times" but that he "couldn't get up the courage." "The subject is masturbation. All sex books are full of it."[9] He went on from there.

When journalist Joe Klein published the first major biography of Guthrie, in 1980, he included a long excerpt from the sexually explicit letter Guthrie wrote to Marjorie from the *Sea Porpoise* in June 1944. A passage covering two full pages in the book, by far the book's longest direct quotation from the singer, contains sentences like these:

> To slip the end of my penis up to your hairs while they are so wet and oily, and to feel the head of it enter into your little hole, mama, that warm feeling that is your very life bathes one all over, and your very electricity and magnetism runs all through me from end to end.
>
> [...]
>
> Your heat gets hotter as my penis goes farther and farther. Your organs inside your belly squeeze tight around my rod and I can feel your inner womb as it fits like a glove over the end of my penis. This is the most peaceful and beautiful feeling of life to me and I only want it to be as beautiful and as good to you.[10]

Suddenly, a mass readership knew what only a small circle of insiders had previously known: Woody Guthrie loved sex, and more to the point, loved filling up pages with sexy words and sentences.

Few students of Guthrie's work have taken this writing seriously, with a couple of important exceptions. For scholar Bryan Garman, Guthrie's sex writing reflects his deep intellectual and poetic connection with the nineteenth-century bard of the body, Walt Whitman.[11] An earlier, more pointed defense came posthumously from his close friend Will Geer; just before the publication of Klein's biography, Geer told mutual pal Ed Robbin, in an interview for Robbin's book *Woody Guthrie and Me: An Intimate Reminiscence*: "People used to say [Guthrie's sex writing] was part of his disease. That's nonsense. Like most poets, Woody was deeply, passionately sexual in his life and in his work."[12] When Geer and Guthrie met in Los Angeles in the late 1930s, they bonded over their shared affection for Whitman. Geer himself was, like Whitman, bisexual, and while there is no evidence that he shared this information with Guthrie, it is clear that some measure of shared openness about sexual matters helped to bring them together. A Guthrie song titled "Walt Whitman's Niece," never recorded by its author, narrates in hilariously veiled terms a visit the two made to a brothel together.[13]

Yet most commentary about Guthrie attempts to purge the sexual content from his important writing by attributing it to the decline of his health; all too easily, the cognitive effects of Huntington's become a convenient, potentially able-ist way to account for a part of his work that runs against the grain of the conventional Guthrie image, whether that be the "ramblin' man" or the labor hero. It is true that, as we will see, Guthrie began to write erotic letters to women other than Marjorie in the mid-1940s, eventually landing himself a jail term on obscenity charges in 1949. It is true that *some* Huntington's research has associated compulsive sexual behavior with the condition, at least insofar as neurological conditions often lead to a reduction in inhibition. Yet the connection remains disputed, and it is imperative, especially for anyone sympathetic to Guthrie's politics, to be wary of the ableism of understanding the association as automatic. But in general, responsibility for the diminishment of Guthrie's sex writing lies with long-unchallenged preconceptions about the singer and his Old Left, Popular Front context. Guthrie's unsolicited erotic letters to women other than Marjorie and his 1949 obscenity arrest are cited as evidence for conclusions like the one made in the *New York Times* review of Joe Klein's biography, which called the erotic writing "obviously nutty."[14]

Guthrie's sexual proclivities did take him outside the boundaries of his marital commitments. He has been frequently dubbed, with much justification, a "womanizer." But philandering, however hypocritical and inimical to the spirit of his writings on intimacy, is by no means the end of what sexuality signifies in his work as a writer. He took sex seriously, and while a phrase like "sexual politics" would not have been familiar to him, or just about anyone else in the 1940s American left, the connections he made between intimacy and the political in his writing led him to explore sexuality as a domain of struggle and liberation, even as he also, clearly, wrote erotic material because it gave him pleasure. In his postwar writing, especially his novel (not published until 2013), *House of Earth*, he would try to reconcile these two strains.

With few exceptions, such as Emma Goldman, the left tradition that spoke to Guthrie saw sex, and pleasure more generally, as an indulgence and, quite possibly, a distraction from class conflict and revolutionary politics. In the mid-1940s, leftist writers and folk musicians remained fairly muted about sex. They believed progressive activism had much more important matters to address; chances are scant that one would hear anyone speak about it seriously at a meeting, much less refer to it as "intellectual" or "scientific." There was no CPUSA or People's Songs subcommittee on access to contraception, the right to choose abortion, or the clitoris. Nor was there an FDR cabinet position overseeing any of these matters.

For the most part, radicals still maintained a strict split between private and public matters. To men and women trained in Marxist thought in particular, the topic of sex reeked of self-indulgence, a plunge inward into individual desires and drives rather than a reach outward toward collective ones. At the same time, during the Popular Front era, much of the American left touted their commitment to conventional marriage, monogamy, and Christian values. Indeed, the CPUSA's flaunting of a wholesome "Americanism," and the American Popular Front movement as a whole, helped stifle long-running conservative attempts to associate the Left with sexual behavior deemed suspicious, like homosexuality. Well into the 1940s, virtually every issue of the *Daily Worker*, for instance, contained articles related to a brand of domesticity that looked, essentially, no different from the one touted in publications owned by wealthy publishing magnates. The women's magazine of the CPUSA,

Woman Today, "contained love stories, beauty hints, and homemaking advice"; it was by no means "feminist or for the liberation of women."[15] Even as some women and men looked to the Soviet Union for a more enlightened view of gender, the official line of American communists subordinated such concerns to the undoing of capitalism, refusing to explore links between, say, the celebration of private life and the celebration of private property.

Clearly, judging by the sexy letter that Klein quoted, Guthrie had a utopian view of sex. It extended his valorization of intimacy; it was quite literally an embodiment of the principle of *union*, at least between two people: two bodies become one. Although the idea of sex as a force of personal and collective liberation is often associated with the 1960s, it has a deeper history in the US, extending well before Guthrie's time; for example, it's present in Whitman's work, and in the writing of nineteenth-century utopian sex radicals that helped form the poet's ideas.

From this tradition, Guthrie inherited some intuition about sex as an arena in which people could act out their political principles. At the same time, his sex writing is very much of its moment, the mid-twentieth century. Sexual discourse—putting sex into words—was taking on new significance and value in a nation traditionally deemed Puritan. Sex, once considered something people *did*, was now the basis of *sexuality*, a domain of knowledge and study, with its own terms and its own truth to tell about the person to whom it belonged.[16] At the same time as Woody's letters began to heat up, sexologist Alfred Kinsey was touring the US interviewing thousands of men about their sexual pasts and proclivities, hoping to contribute to the social good with a sexual account of men in America, based on information long kept repressed. Earlier in the letter to Marjorie in which he touted an intellectual, scientific view of sex, Guthrie mentioned how common it was for his fellow soldiers to write about their sexual feelings to their wives. He was caught up not in some private indulgence but in an increasingly broad cultural assumption that there was something innately good—meaning both physically healthy and emotionally whole—about discussing sex openly, putting it into words, without coyness or euphemism; in his letters and notebooks, one encounters references to penises, vaginas, outer lips, and so on. (The clitoris, however, does not make an appearance; indeed, broad acknowledgment of it would have to wait for the women's movement of the 1960s and '70s). He believed that shame was a political problem, so announcing (as he did) his freedom from shame about masturbation in a six-page disquisition addressed to Marjorie might be considered an act of empowerment.

In that same letter, Guthrie mentioned "sex books"; Marjorie, while being interviewed by Joe Klein in the late 1970s, boasted that her husband voluntarily read sex manuals, which were touting sexual pleasure and communication as the key to connubial happiness. Books like these were changing intimacy, making it a more discrete, identifiable realm, giving it a vocabulary at a time when the word *relationship* wasn't yet widely used to refer to two people's sexual and emotional involvement. None of these books remain in Guthrie's archive, but he may have had such volumes in mind when he told Marjorie in a 1944 letter that he had learned "how to love a home partly because of your books on the shelf."[17]

As Guthrie was growing more invested in putting sex into language, he was also trying to figure out what to do next. While home between Merchant Marine tours in April 1944, he met a cranky, ambitious record company owner and recordist named Moses Asch, who, until laying down an album of children's music by Lead Belly a few years previous, had produced mostly Jewish liturgical music. In a much-retold story, at their first meeting, Guthrie introduced himself by saying, "I'm Woody Guthrie," to which Asch replied, "So what?" Nevertheless, the ornery Asch agreed to give Guthrie some studio time, inaugurating one of his most significant professional relationships since his work with Alan Lomax, Sophie Maslow, Marjorie Mazia, and Joy Doerflinger.

Over the course of six days in April and May, as Asch ran the disc-cutting recording machine, the songs came gushing out: 163 in all, all one-take recordings. Old ballads about gangsters followed tender love songs—or wry rejections of heterosexual suitors—sung from a young girl's perspective. His own compositions mixed in with songs so old they had no origin—at least no humanly accessible one. If *Dust Bowl Ballads* documented a particular crisis, this was an encyclopedia of folk culture, the product of over a dozen years playing dances, labor rallies, radio shows, and all manner of impromptu performances.[18] A crack ensemble accompanied him on many of the songs: Cisco Houston smoothing the songs' rougher edges with his tenor harmonies, Sonny Terry extending their musical reach with a wailing harmonica that brought out new intricacies in the simple tunes.

But none of the songs showed any sign of the thinking he had been doing about love, sex, and intimacy writ large. (He would, after the war, begin to write more lyrics with a personal turn, like the gorgeous "California Stars," later set to music and recorded by Billy Bragg and Wilco.) At times, the lesser-known and unknown material from these years can seem like the creation of a different artist. The ballad-blues tradition didn't accommodate the type of language and meditation that appeared in the letters to Marjorie, where he could declaim the "intellectual" and "scientific" side of sex. At the same time, he was frustrated with the response to *Bound for Glory*. He felt reviewers had pigeonholed him because he was a musician. The book tried to convey a critical worldview about "bad politics" and "racial barriers," he wrote to Marjorie, but "I've not been at all satisfied with the reviews about the book because most of them come down to [*sic*] heavy on the rambling and gambling of a wild hobo with a guitar."[19] He began making more attempts at long-form prose narrative, a series of literary endeavors that eventually led to his most concentrated, sustained, successful piece of non-personal writing on the politics of intimacy, the novel *House of Earth*.

Before he got there, he began at least four other books in the same hybrid autobiographical-fictional vein as *Bound for Glory*, using himself, his past, his present, and sometimes Marjorie as the raw materials. (He would eventually manage to finish one book begun during the war, titled *Seeds of Man*, in 1954). Mostly, he just wrote compulsively. Between Merchant Marine tours and then just after the war, he would go over to fellow Almanac Singers veteran Lee Hays's apartment to use his typewriter, tap out a dozen or more pages, then leave them there. "I used to find pages tucked in my dictionaries, and my encyclopedia," Hays said years later, "Woody always reminded me of water over a dam, just an unstoppable creation."[20]

His ambition wasn't to become a novelist; he wasn't seeking to make a splash on the literary scene. He was an avid, broad, happily undisciplined reader, and had no comprehensive sense of the contemporary fiction scene and where his work might fit in it. Nonetheless, *House of Earth* intervenes in a still-extant, belittling strain of American cultural representations of the people among whom he'd established his reputation: destitute, rural white folks. It does so even as it clearly draws from his relationship with Marjorie, through which emerges a detailed, emotionally brimming account of a few momentous days in a struggling couple's life together.

During the Depression and in its aftermath, well-known representations of poor whites ranged from the "comic" caricature (Al Capp's *Li'l Abner*) to the sympathetic but highly sentimentalized (Steinbeck's *Grapes of Wrath*). Harvard-educated journalist James Agee's *Let Us Now Praise Famous Men*, which no signs point to Guthrie's having read, made its author's struggle with realist representation across class lines its centerpiece; the innovative but often tortured abstraction of Agee's writing meant that the book fell into obscurity for almost two decades. Erskine Caldwell was ostensibly a Popular Front ally, an advocate for economic justice, but as we have seen, Guthrie was disheartened by the juvenile way his shipmates responded to Caldwell's representations of his characters' sexuality. On the whole, Caldwell's work sensationalized poverty as a form of moral and sexual depravity, as when, in an article for the *New York Post*, he claimed to have seen a destitute mother neglectfully choosing sleep over nursing her hungry babies, who lay "before an open fire . . . neither a year old, sucking the dry teats of a mongrel bitch."[21] Caldwell's writing perpetuated tropes through which eugenicists had attempted to establish scientifically that poor white people were genetically inferior and did not deserve the entitlements of their whiteness. Sexual deviance was one of these, a sentiment Steinbeck put in the mouth of one of the Okie-hating Californians of *The Grapes of Wrath*: "These goddamned Okies are dirty and ignorant. They're *degenerate, sexual maniacs*."[22] *House of Earth* stands out as a rejoinder to these artistically impoverished representations, which the Popular Front embrace of a wide swath of representational modes may have encouraged.

The novel *House of Earth* is Guthrie's most extended and adventurous treatise on sexuality, gender, and intimacy. It picks up on the ideas that his correspondence with Marjorie kindled and runs with them, yielding a moving, charmingly quirky portrait of a man and woman working out a life together amid challenging economic, environmental, and personal conditions. Intriguingly, it revisits the scene of his initial emergence: the desiccated landscape of the Dust Bowl, a dozen years after he and first wife, Mary, had watched a thick cloud of dust engulf their hometown of Pampa, Texas, and seven years after he had recorded *Dust Bowl Ballads*. What impact this setting could have on the postwar Left was unclear. A couple of years earlier, he had tried to write *Ship Story*, a novel that, though written in the third person, served as a barely veiled account of his meeting Marjorie, their developing relationship, and his service in the war. But focus proved elusive. Somehow, the older setting provided firmer ground for his intellectual and artistic explorations of sexuality.

The protagonists of *House of Earth* are Tike and Ella May, a childless, married couple living at a subsistence level in the north Texas plains. At all times, they face the threat of a dust storm or snowstorm. In either case, their ramshackle house fails to keep the elements outside out. In their personalities, they are opposites: Tike is spontaneous, jokey, lusty, while Ella May is brainy, articulate about politics, and good at planning. In a reversal of conventional gendering, he is the body and she is the mind. (Presumably, the name Ella May is a tribute to Ella May Wiggins, a singer-songwriter and labor activist murdered during the Gastonia textile worker strike in 1929; Guthrie once called her the "pioneer of the protest ballad").[23]

They share a dream: to build their own adobe house, out of the land on which they live. It is not merely a pragmatic strategy for living in their climate; the planned house represents independence from capitalism, from the repairs they must constantly perform, lining the pockets of purveyors of building and patching materials. The house also represents a connection to the land in which capitalism is not the intermediary; without making explicit his debt to the culture of his displaced indigenous neighbors in Oklahoma, Guthrie sees the adobe house as signifying not ownership but the de-commodification of land.

The book is filled with detailed descriptions of the weather, the land, and the characters' feelings. Temporally, it has a hazy, disoriented feel, embodied in the sentence that begins one of the four chapters: "Things that hurt and things that feel good. This is how the year went. This is where it went. These things, and not a clock on the wall, make a year."[24] It is obviously far less edited than *Bound for Glory*.

Fundamentally, two events occur in the novel: in the first half, Tike and Ella have sex, and in the second half, Ella gives birth. That these are the narrative's major events—both described in sometimes excruciating detail—indicates how physically focused the novel is, marked, it would seem, by Walt Whitman's influence and the still relatively new presence of dance in Guthrie's personal life. Indeed, the first description of Ella May could be Woody describing Marjorie: "She woke Tike up out of his dreams two or three times a day and scolded him to keep moving. She seemed to be made out of the same stuff that movement itself is made of."[25] At one point, Guthrie describes Ella May's laugh in a register familiar to those who've encountered the singer's 1944 radio broadcast or the iconic poster it inspired: "This laugh was not a laugh that made fun of a slim lady for being slim, a fat lady for being fat, or an ugly person for being ugly, it was not a laugh of this kind, not of the kind that makes fun of you because you are you."[26] In the first half, Tike accidentally pokes Ella in the breast and in the second half, a year later, the painful bruise is still there. Thus do "Things that hurt and things that feel good" constitute the passage of time.

In *Tobacco Road*, Caldwell lampoons his characters' misuse of modern commodities like the car as well as the land on which they farm as tenants, which the hapless Jeeter Lester makes arid by planting the same crop over and over. In contrast, in *House of Earth*, Guthrie is careful to avoid any suggestion that his protagonists' woes come from anywhere but capitalism; he is also, again, wary of presenting them as simple primitives who long to get "back to the land" in some ahistorical, nostalgic sense—that is, as salt-of-the-earth types like those familiar from Steinbeck. No aspect of the book is more representative of this measured approach—or Guthrie's astounding twist on comedy in this genre—than the way the sex scene integrates erotic desire, ideological commitment, and the couple's desire for the adobe house, embodied in a Department of Agriculture pamphlet on how to build one. Thus, the brochure's arrival in the mail amid a typical day of drudgery sparks Tike's libido, and his first task is to seduce Ella into perusing it, despite her tearful dejection about the decrepit state of their house. He slips the booklet into her pocket before beginning to caress her.

> Tike's hand felt the nipples of her breast as he kissed her on the neck from behind and chewed her gold earrings between his teeth. His fingers rubbed her breasts, then rubbed her stomach as he pulled the letter out of her apron pocket. "Read th' little letter?" . . .

"Department of Agriculture," she read on the outside.

"Uh-hmm."

"Why. A little book. Let's see. Farmer's Bulletin Number Seventeen Hundred. And Twenty. Mm-hmm."

"Yes, ma'am."

"The Use of Adobe or Sun Dried Brick for Farm Building." A smile shone through her tears.

"Yes, Lady." He felt her breasts warmer under his hands.[27]

But their foreplay, a hybrid of discursive and physical interaction, hits a dead end when Ella points out that to make use of the pamphlet's instructions, they would need to own their land, and they don't. The mood shifts, Ella asking in Steinbeck-inflected tones, "Why has there got to be always something to knock you down? Why is this country full of things that you can't see, things that beat you down, throw you around, and kill out your hope? . . . Why can't we own enough land to exist on, to work on, and to live on like human beings? Why can't we?"[28] Subsequently, they disrobe, make their clothes into a little bed on the barn floor, and commence their tryst. However, they continue to discuss the clay house and fantasize about it. Indeed, what makes the scene so long is that it contains so much articulate conversation: to call these pages a sex "scene" as if isolated from the rest of the narrative would be mistaken. At one point, in the midst of the act, they actually look around to make sure they haven't lost the pamphlet, and examine one of its pages:

She moved under him and talked with her eyes on the shingle roof. "How long?"

"How long to build one?"

"Yes."

"I don't know. Gover'ment book tells. Where's th' book at? Didn't mess aroun' an' lose it already, did you?"

"No. It's here. I had stuck it in my apron pocket and it fell out."

He looked at the book at her elbow. "It's fell out there, yeahh. It's okay. Ahh. It's turned to page five. Ain't no readin' on th' page. Just some pictures. One, two, three, four, five, six, seven pictures. Guys a makin' th' bricks. Gosh. Look what big ones. We could have our walls two feet thick if we wanted to. Whew."[29]

Strewn in with rib-nudging allusions to length and "big ones," the printed material through which the state administers social democratic policy here plays a stimulating role more commonly associated with pornography; *House of Earth* surely provides as erotic a representation as any piece of text produced by New Deal bureaucrats is ever likely to receive.

A few pages later, the progressive, modern quality in Guthrie's view of sexuality surfaces, despite the novel's rustic setting, when both lovers enjoy satisfying, simultaneous orgasms. For a reader of sex manuals like Guthrie, this happy ending to the tryst was very much of the time. According to historian Jessamyn Neuhaus, "The marital sex manuals of the 1920s and '30s aimed to correct faulty male sexual technique, with a view toward increasing female pleasure. Though they relegated the 'awakening' of female sexual pleasure to the domain of male skill, leaving men firmly in charge of that pleasure, these manuals made female orgasm central to 'successful' intercourse."[30] In contrast with the tone of these tracts, Neuhaus writes, the later manuals of the 1950s tended to blame wives who didn't enjoy sex for their own plight. Ella and Tike experience the ideal sexual outcome—mutual orgasm—in a way that suggests their potential to realize all of their ideals.

All told, this scene provides a thumbnail sketch of the fantasy driving the novel: that of a world in which sexual desire, articulate intimacy, and utopic, anti-capitalist political longing are fully entwined and mutually aroused, mutually experienced in the body and the mind. Guthrie's isn't a dreamy idealism, though; the hints to realizing these goals are contained not only in the literary language of the novel, as spoken by its characters, but in a document authored by an anonymous social welfare–minded government official, or team thereof. There are further passages of conversation in the scene, but again, these aren't moments in which the characters pause from sex. Indeed, *House of Earth* suggests that people have their best, most important conversations *while* having sex. Perhaps most strikingly, rather than refuting representations like Caldwell's by making his poor whites pure and innocent, as Steinbeck did, Guthrie makes their sexuality an integral part of why they are compelling characters in both political and literary ways.

The aphrodisiac pamphlet doesn't disappear in the second half of the book, either. It continues in its role as a fetish object; they continue to pass it back and forth, "smeared and soaked with his sweat and hers" and at one point, hallucinating as she goes into labor, Ella May imagines herself in an adobe house whose walls are papered with the pamphlet.[31] But the main preoccupations of the later part of the novel are Ella May's giving birth and the appearance of Blanche, a trained nurse who appears virtually without explanation (though we do learn that she has attended nurses' college) and is almost instantaneously swept into the dynamics of the couple's relationship. We learn little else about her background; for Guthrie, clearly, portraying characters' relations holds more importance than accounting for the singularity of any individual. It's as if everyone who steps into this world is automatically intimate with everyone else in it.

Predictably, the lusty Tike is sexually drawn to Blanche and speaks openly to Ella May of this attraction. There is a hint of autobiography here. In the fall of 1945, as Guthrie served out a brief postwar term in the army, and around the time he and Marjorie were to marry, he became involved in a steamy correspondence with a woman named Charlotte Strauss; he was open with Marjorie about the exchange, writing, "Charlotte has caused me to wake up, to shake up, to feel naturally highly attracted to her in the most sexual manner. This comes out of the best feeling that I have ever had, being asked to help a person, feeling like she needs you."[32] Essentially, Guthrie manipulated his apparently sincere commitment to helping people in need into an opportunity to indulge his own pleasure, without regard for those with whom he was already intimate, those who now depended on him. In the novel, Ella May indulges Tike's attempts to, as he phrases it, "put a little sexy fun into the situation," as she might a misbehaving child.[33] Blanche, however, rejects his advances in a way that leaves Tike to "fry and boil," feeling his body "turn hotter and hotter" in silent humiliation; his boundarylessness is as damaging as it is obnoxious.[34] Later, as the baby is being born, he sulks over being waved away by Blanche, who "laughed and thought that he was the one that needed the bed and the treatment and not Ella May."[35]

Blanche's entrance into the novel does nothing to break the intimacy of its tone; she fights and, at times, flirts on an equal footing with the people who, in a novel more committed to realism, would be called her clients. What she is really doing by teasing Tike is keeping him from interfering in the long labor process.

That Guthrie makes her one of the novel's three main characters (there is one additional character who shows up very briefly) suggests that he is imagining the care work that nurses and midwives do as a kind of professional intimacy for hire. She is there to do work a doctor both would and wouldn't do, a kind of couples' therapist as well as an expert in childbirth: she "had been the one to carry healthy feelings between wife and husband many times before, in her hospital training and in a dozen or so actual births that she had been on."[36] She "could perform most of all the things that a doctor could perform, but she was not called a doctor."[37] She "had gotten used to this business where her patients carried all of their troubles and hopes to her just because she had educated her hands to take a baby from the stomach of a woman."[38]

Notably, Guthrie doesn't rely on the traditional heterosexual dyad to bring his characters through their crises, or at least this particular one. Their romance as a couple doesn't make them self-sufficient. They need intervention, they need a Blanche, a caregiver who personifies something more like an *ethic* of care, her technical skills in midwifery couched in a broader commitment to being present for, attuned to, human vulnerability. Guthrie's portrayal of the character was one of the early instances of a growing concern of his: people who devoted their work lives to administering to others' intimate needs—especially nurses.

From a worker's perspective, the portrayal of Blanche has its problems. He depicts her work as a calling, and her as someone who finds personal fulfillment in that work, rather than as a worker deserving fair compensation for her labor. The character of Blanche echoes Guthrie's depiction of a sex worker in a long poem titled *Niagara*, begun in 1944: this figure, too, is glorified, but only for her openness to sex, and not as a laborer who performs her job to earn money with which to subsist. Such were the limits, at this point, of Guthrie's ability to wed his labor politics to his interest in sexuality and intimacy.

Nonetheless, of all three characters, Blanche most resembles the maternalism of the "Woody" of *Bound for Glory*. And yet, this generalization of maternal qualities beyond literal mothers doesn't dilute the literal mothering portrayed in the book, in an extended, vivid scene of that other kind of labor, giving birth. The novel moves toward its conclusion with what is surely one of the longest and most graphic depictions of childbirth, including the management of its physiological aftermath, to have ever been written by a male author, replete with graphic descriptions of the discharge that follows the couple's son into the world: "three or four large pieces of meaty organs, ropes of intestinal tubes, burst bags of water . . . work their way out from the outer lips of Ella May's womb." *House of Earth* ends with this birth and Ella game for a fight to purchase an acre of land on which to build the house of earth for the new baby, which Tike calls their "grasshopper." More specifically, it ends with him doing what Woody Guthrie likely would have done in that same situation: singing a song to the baby.

When *House of Earth* finally appeared in 2013, shortly after the centennial of Guthrie's birth, many reviewers treated it as a curiosity or, at best, an unwieldy showcase of the same linguistic gifts (if not the same themes) on display in Guthrie's songs. The book is certainly oddly paced and eccentric in its depiction of its characters. It was likely written in a couple of frenetic spells of inspiration. But at bottom, it is an ambitious and clear-headed attempt to bring together the personal and the political, the intimate and the historical, in a more concentrated and explicit manner than in *Bound for Glory*. In addition to its subversion of stereotypical depictions of rural poverty—whether salacious or saintly—the novel is about needing help, aid that its protagonists receive from both a distant government bureaucracy and a professional care worker whom they admit into their private life, otherwise penetrated only by dust and snow. Again, the conventional, sealed-off form of intimacy, for Guthrie, could not suffice.

Chapter Six

STACKABONES

B ACK DURING THE WAR, on February 6, 1943, in a Philadelphia hospital, Marjorie Mazia gave birth to her first child with Woody Guthrie, a daughter they named Cathy Ann. Just days after her birth, Guthrie signed off a brief letter of greeting to his new child, "I love love love you so much," in defiance of the stereotype of the repressed mid-century American male. In April of the same year, as the couple had agreed the previous autumn, Marjorie left her husband and their home in Philadelphia to settle in New York permanently, moving in with her parents in Sea Gate, Brooklyn, between Gravesend Bay and Coney Island Channel. The neighborhood was, in fact, a gated community where, in the 1930s, orthodox Jews had overwhelmed a population that had once posted "No Dogs or Jews" signs on the streets.[1] She suggested they make the Coney Island neighborhood the site of their first home together.

Initially, Guthrie was less than thrilled. He took the two months' delay in Marjorie's return to New York personally. The idea of living near the Greenblatts and their new-world shtetl inspired mixed feelings. Aliza, a poet, was warm and engaging, always happy to drink coffee and exchange ideas about verse, but Isidore's hostility to his daughter's as-yet out-of-wedlock relationship with an economically insecure, fairly weird gentile remained unambiguous. For some years, he refused to interact with Woody at all.

Her lover's complaints frustrated Mazia. Given their precarious finances, moving near her parents was the practical choice for them, she believed, and, as she told him bluntly in a letter, Guthrie's unwillingness

to face their situation suggested hypocrisy: "Take and give and try living like the real masses. . . . You have to live like they do to understand
them and maybe you did in the past but you certainly didn't since I['ve]
known you. . . . There is such a thing as home and family and budgets
and jobs and that's what people are really thinking about and doing."[2]
They looked around in Flatbush, near Prospect Park, but, he wrote to
Will and Herta Geer, "It was too bourgeoeise [sic] for us, too formal,
too restricted."[3] Marjorie worried that neighbors would mock her for
wearing shorts, he reported.

So, he acquiesced, and in October 1944, Marjorie took out a lease on
a one-bedroom apartment on the first floor of a row house at 3520 Mermaid Avenue, two blocks from the beach. A few weeks later, while home
from the war on leave, he found himself seduced by the neighborhood.
He acknowledged to the Geers that in Coney Island, "the atmosphere is
so loose and limber and relaxed, that everybody comes here in the spirit
of a vacation, a rest, a breath of open air, or to look at the sea and brood
about the war, yet, it is bright and open and the air here is working people, kids, families."[4]

On November 13, 1945, Marjorie and Woody were married, while he
was on a two-week furlough from his six-month spell in the army. The
ceremony at the Manhattan City Clerk's Office was a testament to the
impact of dance on their lives; Sophie Maslow served as witness, and a
handful of other dancers filled out the wedding party.

By the time he was back for good from the service, a few weeks later,
he had settled into the neighborhood contentedly. In every way, Coney
Island was distant from the stony-faced, work-focused crowds of midtown. The beach was just footsteps away. Salty fresh air blew in from
the ocean, reminding him of the vastness of the planet. People came to
the neighborhood to ride rollercoasters, play on the sand, swim, splash,
and eat the renowned hot dogs from Nathan's—in short, to be happy.
Laughter and delighted screams comprised the area's ambient sounds.
As a further bonus, the local headquarters of the CPUSA was two blocks
down the street. And, despite his father-in-law's hostility, Guthrie was
fascinated by the Jewishness of the neighborhood.

Of course, he had three children from his first marriage, now living
in El Paso, where Mary had moved soon after Guthrie settled in New
York. He sent them money each month and maintained an especially

close relationship with his daughter Gwen. But Cathy came into the world at a distinctly different, more stable time than when his other children had been born. He was now far more attentive to this family's needs, less likely to strike out suddenly on a journey. As Will Kaufman writes, "Many of Guthrie's private and public writings betray his unease, guilt, and longing for the stable domestic space that often undercut his wanderings."[5]

By the war's end, he was ready to explore child-rearing as another avenue of intimacy where openness to others might flourish and people might liberate themselves from social and political constraints—thus picking up on concerns begun in *Bound for Glory*, honed in correspondence with Marjorie, and extended in *House of Earth*.

On Mermaid Avenue, they gave Cathy the bedroom and slept on a convertible couch in the living room. They lined the walls with the toddler's prolific drawings and paintings. Space was sparse but filled with the basic elements of domestic happiness. Marjorie was phasing herself out of the Graham Company, having founded a dance school, catering mostly to children, in Sheepshead Bay. She also taught classes at her old school, the Neighborhood Playhouse on the Lower East Side.[6] Woody's professional prospects were uncertain, as always, but promising. By all appearances, the present offered an opportunity for a degree of stability that he and Mary had never enjoyed—or, more nearly, that he had never been willing to provide for her. The novel element in this intimate arrangement was, of course, Cathy—or "Stackabones," as her father called her, because she had felt like a stack of bones when he'd first held her. As he settled into Coney Island and Mermaid Avenue in the winter of 1946, she was turning three.

He had already spent a few idyllic months there while on furlough, getting involved in childcare to an extent unthinkable in his first marriage. He changed his daughter's diapers, made her bottles of formula, and played with her while Marjorie rehearsed and taught. He spent afternoons dispensing advice to his mother-in-law about the poetry she was writing in English instead of her customary Yiddish. He cleaned house and massaged his wife's weary dancer's legs. When he looked at her, he saw her in familiar terms of radiance, resiliency, and stamina:

Marjorie is small in size. Her hair is thick, shiny, curly, and sparkles when she shampoos the big city soot out of it. Since the day she was born twenty nine years ago she has kept on dancing, except for a few weeks here and there of busted ankles, blistered feet, bones and muscles out of joint, and ligaments and gristles pulled out of socket. Even when her body was too bruised and broken, her face, her eyes, her mind has gone on dancing.[7]

Elsewhere, he wrote: "Just how much I love them I will never be able to make plain."[8] From this vantage point, the war against loneliness had ended in victory.

When Cathy started nursery school, he walked her there in the mornings, carrying her on his shoulders, singing the songs she requested, as a delighted crew of neighborhood kids trailed behind. Or he'd walk behind her as she greeted strangers on Mermaid Avenue, and made observations about the people, the gulls, the images on the new television inside the Hubba Hubba Coffeeshop. She seemed naturally acclimated to the world into which she'd been born, saturated with dance, song, and (through both her father and her grandmother) poetry. When he brought her to Marjorie's studio, the adult students gazed at her as she made up dances, transfixed by her free physicality. He felt much the same way, finding inspiration not only in her intuitive movements—much as he did with Marjorie—but in her equally exuberant, inventive play with narrative and language:

> She dances to a hundred wolves, elephants, robbers, ghosts, mean mans, good mans, in her imagination, and plays each of them off against the other, like Shakespeare's people. I try to stay within hearing range of her, but try not to let her know that I am straining to catch her words. I curse at myself for not having a moving camera and a recording machine, a television set, and all, as I follow her along the sidewalk. . . .
>
> I just wonder what my books and papers are going to say that will give me one half the feelings that these loudmouth kids do.[9]

He painted the words "Cathy Says" in big letters on the cover of a new composition book and acted the stenographer, writing down the clever, funny, or just plain weird things that came out of her mouth.

Her creative energy seemed to inspire him to experiment aesthetically. "Watching kids is the highest form of art in the world," he wrote in an unpublished essay.[10] He began painting more, on or over the edge of abstraction, daubing paper with swirling forms strikingly similar to what abstract expressionists like Jackson Pollock were doing across the East River in Greenwich Village.[11] He wrote little pieces with titles like "Scrodging Around" and "Rug Wearing Out" that featured surreal images like "I must be that space between the salt and pepper shaker."[12] He expressed, in particular, a new willingness to adopt "wild lines with free beats and freer rhythms," a phrase that resonated with contemporary developments in urban bohemia such as bebop, jazz, and the early rumblings of beat literature.[13] He wasn't toning down his political commitments, particularly to the labor movement and, increasingly, to racial equality. But in a significant portion of his work, he was moving away from the transparency of social realism, the artistic style that was the mainstay of Popular Front culture and theory.

This was happening in tandem with his new domestic situation. He treated his young daughter less as a student or observer than as a participant and collaborator. In the long hours the two spent together in the apartment, he inevitably picked up his guitar and made up songs for her, often using her words. "When these days come on which I am left entirely alone in the house with Cathy, Miss Stackabones, I'm whipped, I'm outwitted, out run, out classed, and out maneuvered. My mind leaves off where hers begins. My ideas stop where hers start in. My brain is no match for her."[14] She was picking up language with astonishing speed, and as the hours and days passed, he grew fascinated with her relationship to words: her unguarded facility with them, her delight in absurdity and sound over sense. In this era before easily operated home tape recorders, he started writing down the more striking observations she made and the clever phrases she used, noting her attunement to sound in snatches of speech like "SAM SAM HOW DID YOU GROW / HOW DID YOU GROW I DON'T KNOW" or her fascination with how words operate in lines like the following:

Take Mommy
By Miss Stackabones
Take mommy

Take mommy
Take mommy if you can
Take mommy
Take mommy
Take mommy if you can.
Take daddy
Take daddy
Take daddy if you can
Take daddy
Take daddy
Take daddy if you can.
Take a choo choo
Take a choo choo
Take a choo choo if you can
Ride a trolley
Ride a trolley
Ride a trolley if you can.
March 22, 1946
Cathy Bones[15]

Not infrequently, he would put the most striking parts of her chatter on top of simple melodies and sing the results back to her. He ended up with songs about bathing, blowing bubbles, and the endless quest to know "why" things were the way they were. He also wrote some Hanukkah songs with his mother-in-law, who had also taken up writing verse and music for children.[16]

In Guthrie's back-and-forth with Moe Asch, producer of his marathon 1944 recording sessions, he was developing some plans for musical projects that sounded more obviously political, and he was also trying out prose narrative ideas that would eventually find their form in *House of Earth*. But he had no intention of cordoning off his new domestic life from the world of leftist ideas and principles through which his work had long percolated. He wrote to the *Daily Worker*, where he still published regularly, that in their work as the media organ of the Communist Political Association (as the former CPUSA now called itself), they needed to be "warmer, funnier, livelier, and more personal." He painted a somewhat fanciful verbal picture of their forefathers as he urged the newspaper to pay more attention to matters many radicals, men in particular, still deemed private, bourgeois, apolitical at best:

> We need to read back through the letters of Marx and Engels and Maxim Gorki who were great and deep thinkers, but first of all, warm and fun having people, real humorists. No pen could bite, laugh, cry, sing and laugh, like the pen of V. Lenin. No man could out joke Karl Marx, no one could see the personal side better than Gorki. Nobody hated stiff necked intellectuals, put-ons, uppity experts any more than these three men. . . .
>
> We need more colums [sic] and words about the house and home, actual things that take place a million times a day.[17]

Writing and recording songs for children was one way to put these ideas into practice, ideas already present, in particular, in his literary writing projects. He even submitted at least two articles about child-rearing to magazines during this period, though neither was accepted. Guthrie's endeavors in kids' music came very much from a local, domestic situation that was fertile for it. And he had a real knack for writing it. But this turn in his songwriting did not just erupt spontaneously from his own creativity and love for kids. Indeed, it was very much part of his immersion in leftist politics. Earlier radicals had viewed the family unit as an object of critique, an inherently counter-revolutionary instrument in the maintenance of private property and, to some extent, gender inequality. In the 1930s, the CPUSA began to promote children's culture and cultural institutions.[18] The party's attitude toward the family shifted, essentially alongside the formation of the Popular Front in alliance with liberals in the Democratic Party. A more Americanized radical left, according to scholar Paul Mishler, "came to recognize that the revolutionary socialization of children best took place in the context of their families, not in opposition to them."[19]

In the wake of fascism's disastrous rise and hard-won military defeat, the relationship between childhood, power, and social hierarchies was becoming a broad area of concern. Indeed, a sea change was taking place in the overall emotional environment of the middle-class family. Experts in child-rearing had eschewed post–World War I recommendations that parents stress adherence to rules and limit the overindulgence of emotional expression. In this not-so-distant past, authorities saw the cultivation of a strong will as necessary for, among other things, resisting the temptation to masturbate, an activity that, it was said, could lead to improper sexual development and insufficient ambition. Parents, went the teaching, ought to dole out physical affection sparingly, lest the child fail to separate from them and cultivate their independent strengths. By the time of the Second World War, however, prominent voices such as Dorothy Baruch and Benjamin Spock favored "permissive" parenting: letting the child's emotions and curiosity take her where they would, and even accepting the fact that children experience sexual sensations. Guiding this approach, Henry Jenkins writes, was the principle that "learning was motivated by sensual pleasure and experimentation."[20] This body of work operated by "teaching children to respect and trust their own internal responses to an unjust world."[21] According to such thinking, the child would develop a strong sense of individuality and avoid the destructive effects of being inculcated with guilt. These ideas reflected core principles of Popular Front anti-fascism—a position rendered poignantly in the title of a popular 1943 book on the early stages of parenthood, Margaret Ribble's *The Rights of Infants* (a book addressing "the feeling life of a baby.")[22] In the words of scholar Julia Mickenberg, by the mid-1940s, "the popularity of what came to be called 'permissive' or 'progressive' parenting signaled the decline of an authoritarian relationship between parents and children and a widespread desire to make imagination, free expression, cooperation, and commitment to social justice hallmarks of American childhood."[23]

Guthrie expressed his version of this theory in an essay that served as the liner notes for what would be his second collection of children's songs, *Songs to Grow On: Work Songs for Nursery Days*, released by Asch on his Disc label in 1947. (The first collection of kids' music, *Songs to Grow On: Nursery Days*, was released in 1946.)[24] He portrayed the family unit as a space where hierarchies can be either reinforced or broken down. He designed his songs, he wrote, to upend power relations within the home. "Let your kids teach you how to play and how to act these songs out," he writes, before begging, "Please, please, please don't read nor sing my songs like no lesson book, like no text for today. But, let them be a little key to sort of unlock and let down all of your old bars."[25]

With Marjorie developing a dance curriculum for children, ideas about the body made their way into the songs' lyrics and rhythms. Indeed, they were tapping into a long-standing European tradition of kinesthetic theory, dating back to the early nineteenth century. In particular, Émile Jaques-Dalcroze's highly influential theory of "eurhythmics" held that to teach children to be aware of movement was to teach them to be fully realized human beings: "Mind and body, intelligence and instinct, must combine to re-educate and rejuvenate the whole nature," Dalcroze wrote in his major collection of essays, *Eurhythmics, Art and Education* (1921).[26] There were echoes of this theory in one of the volumes about children and movement that Marjorie kept on her shelves at Mermaid Avenue, Elizabeth Waterman's *The Rhythm Book* (1936). According to Waterman:

> The present-day child needs experience in forming well-synthesized patterns, for his world both in school and in the community is a confusion of unrelated patterns. If his own reactions are not to run off in all directions at once, he must know how to select, evaluate, and relate what he considers essential to form his own organic unity of expression.[27]

Waterman, the English translator of the work of Rudolf Bode, one of Dalcroze's most influential disciples, portrayed the aim of her dance pedagogy as nothing less than teaching children to make their bodies bulwarks against the entropic conditions of modernity.

It is not hard to see how ideas like these, whether they reached Guthrie through reading or just by conversing and living with Marjorie, would open up yet another channel for his ideal of "organization," traversing the realms of socialism, labor activism, and here again, the comportment of the body. A child with a strong sense of rhythm was not a quasi-mechanical being, not the "rhythmically obedient" subject that Theodor Adorno, a philosopher and refugee from Nazism, decried contemporaneously as the product of both fascism and market-driven pop music; rather they were able to adapt to challenges and irregularities more effectively because they were so well attuned to the condition of equilibrium.[28] Thus the description for the "Young Folksay Series," from Asch's Disc Records, "planned and supervised" by Beatrice Landeck, a musicologist and educator associated with the progressive Little Red Schoolhouse in Greenwich Village:

By stimulating the imagination and creativeness of the listeners, children are introduced to a new world where they too might make music.

In this way, through the actual experience of singing and dancing and dramatic action, of playing and listening to music and creating one's own, children will have the music they need to grow on. It will belong to them and they will derive from it the spiritual enrichment necessary for calm living in a chaotic world.[29]

A booklet announcing the Young Folksay Series, in which Guthrie's children's albums appeared, featured a two-page spread of photos of Marjorie and Cathy doing stretching exercises together on the beach—at once loosening their bodies and sharpening their responsiveness to a "chaotic world."

Guthrie had written elsewhere: "You must overmaster your wildness before you can portray your life to others. The body itself is the dance, the people are the music, and the world is your stage."[30] The children's music advanced his ambition to make kinesthesia into a broad social theory. He longed for organization—of people, of bodies, of sound—convinced it could be a structure through which justice and equality could be shaped, not just left to their own devices. And there was the matter of his own body, which people close to him, such as Lee Hays, noticed as incessantly restless.[31] A former grammar school teacher once recalled, "He would get something in his hand like a ball or something and just kept [it] going constantly. . . . It looked like he had rhythm in his hands."[32] It could affect his playing, and indeed, he still needed Marjorie around him for help regulating his tempo and rhythm. In the essay for *Work Songs to Grow On*, he described her role in the recording process:

I liked having Marjorie there to help me. She tells me to sing it slow and plain, to vision Stacky Bones in my mind.

It's hard for me to sing slow enough. I've nearly lost my old knack for singing slow since I've come to New York where you sing so fast.

Marjorie is smart enough to know all of this, and smart enough to slow me down, to get me to take it greasy, easy, and to say my words plain. I think our records will help you and your family to talk a little bit slower when you hear them.[33]

Guthrie could write about overmastering wildness and taking it slow, and these well may have been the fundamental intellectual principles with which he went about composing and performing his kids' songs. (A more disciplinary attitude does drive certain songs, like "Clean-O," a song designed to get kids to take baths.) Yet there is another strain in these songs that suggests that part of the genre's appeal—his approach to the genre at least—*was* that it allowed him to indulge a kind of wild-ness and *dis*order more culturally permissible in children's bodies than in adults'. The breakneck pace of "The Car Song," for instance, contradicts his stated commitment to "take it greasy, easy"; it is worth listening to the recording alongside one of its many, notably slower cover versions to appreciate the near-punk-rock energy Guthrie brings to it.

These songs suggest that one form his intimacy with his daughter took was through the body or, more exactly, kinesthesia. One could attribute this to a "childlike" personality, a penchant for acting like a big kid, as Marjorie told Joe Klein, but it seems vital to also mark how this rela-tionship may have been therapeutic for someone with an emerging kin-esthetic illness, someone already deeply attuned, from childhood, with the frailty of seemingly vital adult bodies. A song like "Pick It Up," for example, puts a fun and comic spin on bodily disorder:

> I drop my thumb, pick it up, pick it up
> I drop my thumb, pick it up, pick it up
> I drop my thumb, pick it up, pick it up
> And put it back with my fingers.
> [. . .]
> I drop my head, pick it up, pick it up
> I drop my head, pick it up, pick it up
> I drop my head, pick it up, pick it up
> And put it back on my shoulders.[34]

Or there are songs about aimless movement, of which there is no better example than "Dance Around," the first verse of which runs, in its entirety, "Dance around and around and around and around / and around and around and around / and around and around and around and around / and around and around and around." Here, choreography is anarchy; dance is as far it could possibly be from a model of organization.

A similar passion runs through "Howdidoo," based on Cathy's charming penchant for wanting to greet and shake the hands of everyone they would encounter in their walks around the neighborhood. The line "You shake it up and down, howjidoo?" celebrates this form of physical, interactive salutation, but at the same time it celebrates *shaking*—albeit in this case, enjoying a shared rhythm, and forming a bond of intimacy through the rhythm of synchronized shaking. Another song more indulgent of the absurd is "Put Your Finger in the Air," the lyrics of which command the listener to perform what might otherwise seem like a random or impulsive movement, and several of its verses celebrate this purposeless gesture in absurdly distended stretches of time: "Put your finger in the air, and leave it about a year," goes one verse; "put your finger on your cheek, and leave it about a week," goes another.[35]

Finally, there were songs built almost solely out of rhythm and repetition, like "Grassy Grass Grass (Grow Grow Grow)," "Swimmy Swim," and "Rattle My Rattle." These were lyrically minimal, repeating the same words over and over, sometimes sans guitar, to the sole accompaniment of percussion. These songs look forward to Marjorie's own percussion-heavy album of children's music, released by Asch on Folkways in 1951, *Dance-A-Long*, and it's all but certain that Marjorie herself provides much of the percussion on the tracks. Indeed, these songs stand as a paean to the night she and Woody met, their relationship initiated by their search for a shared rhythm.

With these songs inviting families to bring pleasurable movement into their households, Guthrie extended the ideals discovered that night into another intimate realm: the relationships between parents and children. It was another way that bodies could break down barriers between people, a principle acted out rather than confined to abstraction.

But the kids' songs also suggest the possibility of a nascent set of concerns that were even more local and personal. It's curious that Guthrie's immersion in this musical idiom, which further developed the preoccupation with bodies he'd developed through Marjorie and the dance world, took place not long after his first recorded remarks about something unruly in his own body—that is, his wartime comments to Merchant Marine shipmate Jim Longhi about his "queer" feelings, and the fear he expressed that he was afflicted with his mother's condition. Whether Huntington's chorea had a direct effect on his artistic choices, of course, can't be verified as empirical fact—especially if, as seems likely, that effect was unconscious. Yet the discussion of children's music is so resonant in relation to the dyskinesia of Huntington's; it hinged on making the body both ordered and flexible, while at the same time aiming to open a space for disorderly, undisciplined movement. Perhaps, led forward by knowledge that was felt rather than articulated, he was opening a space for himself, and the subtle changes taking place in his own body. Indeed, at the same time as he was recording the kids' songs, he was also working on an "adult" project that suggested he had a foreboding sense of both his own future and the Left's.

Chapter Seven

TWO GOOD MEN
A LONG TIME GONE

T HEY WERE IN THE DISC RECORDS STUDIO on West Forty-Ninth Street, with Moe Asch running the machine. Marjorie was beside him, helping keep time, as she'd done when they recorded the kids' songs a couple of months earlier. This song was called "Old Judge Thayer." He'd written it in the style of "Froggy Went A-Courtin'," its cast a congress of animals, indicting the corrupt ways that powerful men dealt out so-called justice to the downtrodden. Verses played slow, choruses faster. About two-thirds of the way through, as he took the song into the chorus's refrain—"Old Judge Thayer take your shackle off of me"—he felt the song's tempo careening out of control and stopped, abruptly, looking at Margie.

"I thought you were gonna give me the beat," he spat out, aggrieved.

"Listen, honey," Margie began. "I tried to—"

"I just keep getting faster and faster!"

Now she was mad. "I gave it to you, but you didn't take it . . ."

"Well, how can I when you quit?"

"I don't know what to do while recording." It was a fair point.

Muted behind the glass, Moe urged them to get on with it.

"Alright," he said, then in mock anger at Moe, "and *hold the phone*!" They both broke into laughter.[1]

He could still find a joke when he needed it, ease the tension in a room, but something was wrong. He'd get a little blurry, lose focus. And then he'd get moody. Or thoughts of Natanya, Margie's colleague back in

Coney Island babysitting Cathy, or some other younger woman would intrude.

He believed it was the drinking. For years it hadn't mattered; he'd written most of *Bound for Glory* with a bottle of wine at his side, at least until Marjorie showed up. But there were also the troubles he couldn't explain. Even back in 1945, just before the couple married, Guthrie had written to his future bride describing "confused states of mind, a kind of lonesomeness, a nervousness that stays with me no matter how I set myself to reading, painting, or playing my guitar. Without trying to make it sound too serious, it never does get quite straight in my head."[2] Then again, perhaps his confusion was only natural, considering that the world itself was still sifting through the chaotic aftermath of the war.

After the military defeat of the Axis powers in 1945, the factions making up the Popular Front lost their common enemy. Fighting fascism was no longer the glue binding communists, New Deal Democrats, and ideological points in between. In the spring of 1945, with Nazi surrender looming, Guthrie got a taste of what the postwar future held for the more radical precincts of the Popular Front when the Merchant Marine leadership forced him out due to his history of associations with the CPUSA. He was subsequently drafted into the army the very day Germany surrendered to Allied forces, to his family's longtime, dark-humored amusement.

Now it was 1946, and while the new, ongoing children's music recordings reflected his pleasure in his new domestic environment, Guthrie was trying to figure out how his voice fit into the postwar cultural landscape. Rather than recording more traditional songs, or topical songs, he and Moe Asch decided this precarious moment might be a ripe time to take a look backward at the history of the American left and labor movement. In particular, they wanted to commemorate heroic responses to state violence and persecution. As early as January, Guthrie had drawn up a list of figures and events from this history involving violence, injustice, and martyrdom that he thought would work well as topics for ballads: the arrest and execution of Sacco and Vanzetti, the Haymarket Square bombing, the "Bloody Sunday" picnic massacre in Everett, Washington, the Scottsboro "Nine," Joe Hill, Tom Mooney, Mother Bloor, and Apache leader Mangas Coloradas. But, at Asch's urging, he was also learning more about the Sacco and Vanzetti case, in which two recent Italian immigrants to the Boston area, both committed anarchists and labor activists, had been convicted of armed robbery and a double murder; the pair were executed after a trial riddled with irregularities. The more Guthrie learned, the more doubtful he was that he could do justice to the arrest, trials, and protests in a single song of no more than four-and-a-half minutes.[3] The twentieth anniversary of the two men's executions would take place on August 23, 1947. By March, he had decided to concentrate on a full set of songs about this miscarriage of justice whose wounds remained raw for so many leftists around the globe. Asch encouraged this approach and told the singer he wanted the record out in time for the Christmas shopping season.

Guthrie's early 1946 letters to Asch, posted from Brooklyn to Manhattan, exude enthusiasm and optimism. He reported having "lots of things cooking" and boasted that "we've not yet touched on the bulk of my best things"—an audacious assertion from someone who had already recorded the *Dust Bowl Ballads*, the Columbia River songs, "This Land Is Your Land," and a host of other landmark compositions.[4] At times he missed his rambles, whether abroad or in the US. But to Asch and his associate at Disc Records, Marian Distler, he described acclimating to the rhythms of a quiet but vibrant domestic life for a productive artist: reading, writing, listening to music, and taking care of the lively Cathy while Marjorie began to withdraw from active performing with the Graham Company and devote the bulk of her time to dance lessons for both children and adults.

He wrote elsewhere of feelings that were harder to describe, a sense of gratitude for life marked by his recent past, witnessing and participating in events so essentially incomprehensible as the vast destruction wrought by world war. In a piece called "The Debt I Owe," he wrote:

> I walked around the streets here of Coney Island and I look in at every window, windows of the stores, windows of the houses, in the doorways and steps, and I feel this debt I owe. I walked home tonight from a movie that showed people on the Waterloo Bridge in London during a couple of air raids, and all through the movie, this feeling ran through me. You see, I've seen that Waterloo Bridge in London. I've seen their Waterloo Railroad Station while the Buzz bombs, those Nazi rocket bombs, were jarring the rocks, the concrete, the iron works, and tonight I feel my terrible debt plainer than I could see it ever before.

The feeling is a crazy mixed up whirl, a world of fallen wreckage, a garbage heap, a tangled, wild sort of a salvage yard, a vision called up by a loose blown paper, a curb stone of gum wrappers, struck matches, empty paper cups, the smell of trash cans, the looks on every face, the ways that people hump, stroll, saunter, and crawl along the sidewalks. It comes over me like a mist rising and or a fog falling, like a danger bell ringing out here in the channel.[5]

It was a perplexing feeling, this "crazy mixed up whirl," the warmth of gratitude mingled with waste, destruction, the all but impenetrable otherness of strangers. None of it made sense; it was larger than what a single individual could grasp. All he could do was feel it. But he had passed through it all, survived to live in this world, in these surroundings. He was both thankful and melancholic. He wrote about seeing Marjorie and Cathy cry periodically, and wishing he had this "gift and clean talent" to give full expression to his emotions, to experience the catharsis of releasing them to the world without shame. But he couldn't. And in truth, he noted, writing didn't offer real catharsis either. He wasn't as devastated by his experience of war as many veterans suffering post-traumatic stress disorder. But his words display the same disconnect between comprehension and experience with which Freud and others after him have described the dynamics of trauma.[6]

The first couple of years after the war could certainly have spun the heads of anyone trying to assess the nation's political climate. On the one hand, the massive conflagration, fought on three continents, was over. Hitler and Mussolini were dead, the concentration camps were liberated, and war criminals awaited reckonings with international tribunals. Initially, membership numbers in the Communist Party/Communist Political Association continued to swell. In the months after military conflict ceased, labor unions flexed their muscles as massive strikes rocked major industries, including automakers, steel producers, and maritime workers. To some, the Left seemed to be on the move, finding its footing in the postwar era; such, at least, was the attitude among some of Guthrie's closest colleagues in the music world. On New Year's Eve of 1946, Guthrie's protégé and former Almanac colleague Pete Seeger convened a meeting of politically minded musicians in order to found an organization called People's Songs, tasked "to make and send songs of labor and the

American people through the land."[7] An ancillary organization, People's Artists, worked specifically to link together a network of venues and promote bookings for affiliated performers. The newly discharged Guthrie, appointed as a board member, wrote typically gushing accounts of the first few hootenannies sponsored by the group in New York, featuring Alan Lomax and artists like Huddie Ledbetter, Sonny Terry, Brownie McGhee, and Seeger. He also hailed the effort to collectivize musicians' professional concerns: "I saw these Peoples Songs raise up storms of stiff winds and wild howls of cheer from the people in their seats, and saw also, that almost every chronic headache was eased and made quieter. I mean your headaches about writing, singing, copyrights, fees, pay finances and money."[8]

But other signs portended a darker political atmosphere. In response to the wave of labor actions immediately after the war's end, Republicans and many Democrats in Congress passed the Taft-Hartley Act, which substantially limited the legality of strikes and required union leaders to sign anti-communist pledges. Winston Churchill's "Iron Curtain" speech made the tenuousness of the peace in Europe clear. Franklin Roosevelt's former vice president, Henry Wallace, resigned his post in the Truman administration, citing its increasing conservatism and hostility toward the Soviets. In November 1946, the GOP secured control of both houses of Congress for the first time in fourteen years. A revivified House Un-American Activities Committee became a standing congressional committee. The headiest days of McCarthyism remained in the offing, but anti-communist, anti-left forces were already creating a mood of suspicion, paranoia, and fear of public humiliation. They targeted not just people with avowed leftist sympathies, but, in the wake of the war, those who deviated from behavioral norms regulating gender and sexuality.

As President Truman joined Republicans in casting the wartime ally Soviet Union as a menace to democracy, many Americans also became preoccupied with what they considered new domestic enemies. Propelled by the proceedings of the House Un-American Activities Committee, they located those enemies in the Left, casting suspicion on everyone from professed admirers of the Soviets to enthusiastic former New Dealers, searching out those deemed to have been, in a shockingly insidious phrase, "pre-mature anti-fascists." The Republicans' takeover of Congress initiated, in the words of Frederick Siegel, "a psychodrama in which senators and representatives felt free to spin out their wildest fantasies of homosexuality, intrigue, and treason, all of which were said to lie behind the New Deal." A significant number of Democrats made common cause; Truman, writing in his diary, even singled out Woody and Marjorie's meeting place, bohemian Greenwich Village, as a locus of "national danger."[9] Robert Cantwell identifies this era with a "new posture of permanent alert that read subversion into almost any form of deviance, but especially deviance from the emergent political, commercial, sexual, and family norms."[10]

Woody Guthrie, grieving the recently deceased president Roosevelt, whom he saw as having nudged the country leftward with his sponsorship of the New Deal, wrote an elegiac song to former first lady Eleanor titled "Dear Mrs. Roosevelt," poignantly featuring a line that acknowledged her late husband's physical disability: "I could see he was a cripple / but he learned my soul to walk."[11] When Henry Wallace announced he would run for president as a Progressive Party candidate in 1948, Guthrie rallied behind him enthusiastically as FDR's heir. He was delighted to play at concerts and hootenannies sponsored by People's Songs. He wrote excitedly about singing before ten thousand people at a Pittsburgh rally supporting striking Westinghouse workers.

The work on the Sacco and Vanzetti project would open up a new channel for this energy, but it would also test what impact a story so crucial to the old(er) prewar Left's identity could have in the new, postwar era. The case remained a rallying point for protests against the limits of American democracy and unequal treatment under the judicial system. There was a wealth of literature devoted to the story of the Italian immigrant anarchists' lives in the Boston area as workers and organizers, their arrest on charges of robbing guards carrying the payroll of a shoe company in South Braintree, Massachusetts—based on dubious and often contradictory eyewitness testimony—and, in particular, their trial, considered a sham by many. After the conviction, the judge, Webster Thayer, boasted at his country club, "Did you see what I did to those anarchist bastards?" Both in the US and abroad, their story had attained the status of legend. A reader picking up a random issue of what scholar Barbara Foley calls the "principal organ of the American cultural left" at the time, the journal *New Masses*, would more likely than not encounter some reference to Sacco and Vanzetti.[12] Many of the most renowned leftist authors of the generation preceding Guthrie's had written books and essays about the case. There were polemics, novels, plays, paintings, and verse by John Dos Passos, Upton Sinclair, Ben Shahn, Edna St. Vincent Millay, Eleanor Mabry, James Thurber, and others. If nothing else, undertaking this record meant an opportunity for Guthrie to propel his own name into the company of this illustrious group.

And yet, as the case became more historically distant, it also began to signal a sense of loss, an idealized memory of a once-unified movement now facing persecution and fragmentation. A 1947 editorial in *New Masses* written to mark the anniversary of the executions conveys the particular resonance of the case for leftists twenty years on, a shift from indignation toward melancholia:

> It is difficult to convey to those who did not themselves experience it the tremendous impact of those last few weeks of the battle to save Sacco and Vanzetti. Looking back over the years, it seems to us that not even the struggle in Spain—though of course its effects were more profound and lasting—so stirred the nation, roused so many people from all walks of life in common effort.[13]

The anonymous writer aches for a lost past, and the prose, while explicitly focused on the era of Sacco and Vanzetti's execution, seems in equal measure to lament the passing of the Popular Front and offer a "stirr[ing]" and "rous[ing]" sense of common purpose across various ideological lines. When the editorial subsequently declared Sacco and Vanzetti examples of a "type that has become virtually extinct," a type whose love for humanity drove political struggle, it was essentially grieving the Left of the late 1930s and wartime.[14]

Thus, the decision to write and record an album about Sacco and Vanzetti posed a question: Could Woody Guthrie, in the mixed-up whirl of war's aftermath, make the story of "Two Good Men," as he called them in one song, speak to a new historical, political, and emotional environment?

Guthrie had been prepping—although by no means steadily—for nearly a year by the time he went to Disc's midtown office to record in its little back room studio. The existence of so many textual resources concerning the case made the project a different kind of challenge than he had faced with his other song suites, the *Dust Bowl Ballads* and the Columbia River songs. And Asch, son of well-known Yiddish novelist Sholem Asch, had a personal connection to that literary tradition: his older brother, Nathan, had written an odd short novel, *Pay Day*, set against the backdrop of the case. Asch had also devoured *Boston*, the left literary warhorse Upton Sinclair's epic novel about the trial and execution. Woody wasn't likely to make it through that two-volume tome; the singer read widely, but often not very deeply. Instead, Asch gave Guthrie three pamphlets on what the singer referred to as "Sacco and Vanzetti's murder frame up": a mass printing of the long letter Vanzetti wrote to Massachusetts governor Alvan T. Fuller on the eve of the execution; a tract by the Sacco-Vanzetti Defense Committee, presumably *Facing the Chair: The Americanization of Two Foreign-Born Workingmen*, ghostwritten by John Dos Passos; and, most influentially, Vito Marcantonio's *Labor's Martyrs: Haymarket, 1887, Sacco and Vanzetti, 1927*.

Guthrie being Guthrie, what he really needed to get the project under-way was an emotional connection to the case. From late spring until early autumn 1946, when he had time, he fired up his empathic capacities and tried hard to identify with the men, to understand how they *felt* as immigrants, radicals, outcasts, and accused criminals. In March, as Marjorie toured with the Graham Company for the final time, he set aside a note-book to fill with preparatory material; it provides a fascinating window into his creative process at this moment of his career. He drew dozens of images of the men, wrote and discarded verses, and compiled long lists containing dozens of titles for potential songs. He worked at a narrative that envisioned their departure from Italy (relying on poetic license to imagine that they had made the trans-Atlantic journey together, when in fact they had met in Massachusetts) and their arrival in the United States, picturing them as migrants who shared a common, essential experience with the "Okies" he had described in the *Dust Bowl Ballads*: "I saw the same vision that you did and all of us dust bowl families saw your same vision. It is the one big union we all saw. It shines just as bright over your Italy as it does over the prairies and flatlands of my dust bowl."[15] It wasn't a complete stretch: in one of his published letters, Sacco himself described his childhood home as perched on a "vast verdant prairie."[16]

Upping the intensity, he subsequently tried to imagine the feelings of the pair as they discovered the reality beneath the veneer of the American guarantee of opportunity for all. He transformed this encounter with wide-scale economic and social crisis into images that drew from his pre-occupation with bodies. The bodies he imagined the two men encounter-ing were sick, crumbling: "You saw faces against walls, an eye gone, an ear missing, no teeth, open boils, sores of the syph and you heard there was no known cure. There was no cure known. No cure for the people. No cure for the streets."[17]

The first breakthrough into actual songwriting came in June. Sitting in front of a blank notebook page, he found an oblique but tender point of entry. Rather than beginning by narrating the men's childhoods, their respective voyages to the United States, their arrest, their execution, or any particular event whatsoever, Guthrie wrote out a simple lullaby ad-dressed to Sacco's wife, Rosa:

Go to sleep
Go to sleep
Sleepy sleepy
Little baby
Rosa Rosa
Rosey Rose
I just want to
Sing your name.[18]

If, in one way, it was an indirect start to the men's stories, in another, nothing made more sense for him than first establishing an intimate con-nection with a female figure, in a musical genre synonymous with child-hood; such were the currents of his life since Marjorie and Cathy had entered it. His role as toddler Cathy's caretaker would have made it an especially available gateway into the material. The most pressing human rights issues of the case, the seeds of passion in the wealth of materials on the case, had yet to surface for him. He needed to move into the men's private world first, and he needed a song that would make him feel per-sonally connected to them. He did so by putting himself in a maternal position, as he had in the first chapter of *Bound for Glory*.

Eventually, these lines turned out to be more than a warm-up exercise; they evolved into a song called "I Just Want to Sing Your Name," addressed to the two men as well as Rosa. It would be the most beautiful song on the album—unhurried, simple, and unguardedly warm.

As the summer of 1946 passed, more children's songs got written and recorded, but the Sacco and Vanzetti songs still weren't coming. So, in the fall, Asch agreed to bankroll a trip to Boston so Guthrie and his pal, fellow musician and Merchant Marine shipmate Cisco Houston, could tour the main sites of the case: Plymouth, where the pair lived; South Braintree, the site of the shoe factory where the payroll master and security guard had been shot to death; Bridgewater, where Sacco and Vanzetti had been arrested onboard a streetcar; and Dedham, where they had been tried, convicted, and sentenced at Norfolk County Courthouse. It was here that Judge Thayer openly proclaimed, in reference to Vanzetti: "This man, although he may not have actually committed the crime attributed to him, is nevertheless morally culpable, because he is the enemy of our existing institutions."[19]

On November 4, four days after returning from Boston, Guthrie wrote to Asch and Marian Distler (addressing them as "Dear Friends and Comrades"), informing them that the trip had failed. He and Houston had no car and spent most of their time and energy negotiating public transport to get around the largely suburban locations. These were going to be the "dozen most important songs" he had ever written, he explained. But "I just feel rushed, and I don't want this album about Sacco and Vanzetti to feel rushed, to smell rushed, to taste rushed, nor to sound like something rushed." Trying to mitigate his patrons' disappointment, he attempted a suggestive joke about women not liking things rushed. He needed more time, he said, and he needed a reliable car so he could cruise the sites at his own pace. Guthrie didn't mention his well-established history of carousing with Houston. But that possible pitfall poked through toward the end of the letter, as his cursive handwriting began to lose its shape. "I'm drunk as hell today, been that way for several days. . . . I refuse to write these songs while I'm drunk and it looks like I'll be drunk for a long time." By the end of the second and final page, the script was all but illegible, snaking clumsily around a drawing of a man with a bottle at his mouth.[20]

Recorded details of the research trip are scant. Perhaps there was just little left to see in those parts, nearly two decades after the events. Indeed, one of the songs eventually written and recorded, "Vanzetti's Rock," would be about the absence of any markers of the story in the men's home of Plymouth. Instead of any commemoration of the laborers in that colonial town, Guthrie and Houston found clumps of roaming tourists, vacationing salesmen and managers taking smiling pictures of their families next to the famous boulder, oblivious not only to the tenuousness of the rock's origin story but also to the more real, more recent history that the town had seen.

Limited to public conveyances as they were, they also might have sat on a streetcar in Bridgewater, just as Sacco and Vanzetti had been doing at the time of their arrest. In fact, that moment became a crucial one for Guthrie, knocking the case into a different register than the treatment it had received from other writers—different, too, from the register in which he was accustomed to writing.

At trial, the uniformed cops who arrested the men testified that when they saw the defendants upon boarding the trolley, the two men had "looked guilty." The officers soon discovered that the pair were concealing weapons and a pack of radical literature. The event became a lynchpin of the prosecution's case, a piece of evidence under an established legal category known as "consciousness of guilt."

This concept struck a nerve. The phrase was still ringing through Guthrie's head years later, well after he had abandoned the project following the recording sessions in January 1947. The implication that the men had somehow *condemned themselves* spoke, in some murky way, to his mood: the "crazy, mixed up whirl" settled into feelings of vulnerability, alienation, and loss.

In the minds of most of the defendants' supporters, as well as in their own trial testimony, this supposedly suspicious response from the men resulted from their reflexive assumption that the police had come to arrest them for their radical activities. As Vanzetti would put it six years after the trial, in a failed last-minute petition to the Massachusetts governor for a stay of execution: "The only guilt we were conscious of was the guilt of being Radicals in danger of arrest, detention, and torture or death."[21] In his assessment of the case for the Sacco-Vanzetti Defense Committee, communist activist and theorist Max Shachtman put it bluntly: "The consciousness of guilt attributed to Sacco and Vanzetti was nothing but a healthy consciousness of the class struggle and the methods of the enemies of the working class." [22]

For Shachtman, what appeared on the faces of Sacco and Vanzetti as consciousness of guilt was a *social* phenomenon rather than the manifestation of the men struggling psychologically with their individual consciences. For workers, to become aware of their subordinate, exploited place in the class structure *was* to become aware of themselves as they were viewed by the ruling class: as problems. And as anarchist labor organizers, Sacco and Vanzetti saw the policemen's eyes seeing them as criminals and traitors. Moreover, as Italian immigrants in the 1920s, they were deemed racial outsiders by the white gaze.

Guthrie concurred with Shachtman's view, expressing his perspective in a more existential fashion in his notebook. What the "two good men" were guilty of, he wrote, was the very fact of "getting caught and locked up and asked those questions in the Brockton jail house."

> I would look guilty and I'd feel guilty right now, tonight, this very night, here in Coney Island, in the 24th mailing zone of Brooklyn, if two or three deputy sheriffs would walk in here at my door and find something to take me to jail for. I'd feel in my soul a sort of an odd kind of a guilt, that guilt you always feel a dozen times every day, that guilt you feel inside you, that guilt that you don't talk too much about, I mean, that kind of a guilty feeling you have when you hear the sirens blow on a fire engine and when you remember those paper matches you tossed somewhere in your house and you stand there shivery and shaky on your bones and wonder if it is your house that is burning down. There's ten different kinds of little halfway careless things that you do every day and more than one time a day that you are guilty of and you always know it. I'd just wonder which one of my mistakes I was being arrested and jailed for.[23]

Directly after this passage, he put the matter succinctly: "The feeling of being arrested is itself a consciousness of guilt of some sort." For Guthrie, the notion of "consciousness of guilt" was yet another instance of how institutions of power manipulate feelings and vulnerability—not unlike the operations of fascism as he had described them in his wartime correspondence with Marjorie. In the modern era, he suggests, a degree of guilt permeates people's lives, as they conduct internal deliberations about how they might have caused harm, even ones about "little halfway careless things." Law enforcement protects the empowered classes by exploiting this sense of guilt, a form of vulnerability and attunement to one's social being. He doesn't go so far as to suggest that the police and legal system *create* guilt. But to be confronted by the authorities is to see—and feel—oneself being looked at as guilty. The specific charges don't matter, he goes on to argue; the police can always find another charge to apply, one that will stick because everyone feels guilty about *something*. While guilt and shame are not equivalent, Guthrie's contemplation of "consciousness of guilt" resonates with his view of shame's deep entrenchment, again a theme in his wartime letters to Marjorie. That he would make this point by referring to human-made fires, the source of so much childhood trauma, lends particular poignancy to this passage.

As he worked to compose the songs, then, the Sacco and Vanzetti case provided him space to think about something like "the feeling of being arrested." It allowed him to pinpoint a sense of wrongness—one that felt, erroneously, self-generated—that opened up people to exploitation. Yet this material was not the sort of stuff that went into works celebrating the martyrdom of legendary figures, at least not in the way he had written about people like Pretty Boy Floyd, Jesus Christ, Jesse James, and Lyudmila Pavlichenko. It wasn't an issue that fit easily into settings provided by an idiom that went back to Joe Hill and the *Little Red Songbook*. Here he was plumbing the relationship between state power and the most intimate depths of psychological being.

The response to the songs from critics, scholars, and even friends suggests that his hesitancy might have reflected ambivalence toward the quality of the material and the performance of it. Charges against the songs include: they are too "polemical" and insufficiently "poetic" (biographer Ed Cray); they "lack direction" (Pete Seeger to Cray); they are "superficial and forced" (biographer Joe Klein); they do not represent "Guthrie at his best" (*New York Times* music critic Robert Shelton); they are "weak, unenthusiastic, and unconvincing" (critic Wayne Hampton).[24] Listening to the 1960 album, or to the 1996 Smithsonian Folkways compact disc, it isn't hard to hear likely sources for this dissatisfaction. Each song's purpose in relation to the others is unclear. Although Smithsonian Folkways rearranged the song order for the record's 1996 re-release, it remains difficult to discern each song's individual role in the work as a whole. Details from the case, and from the two men's personal lives, are repeated, arbitrarily, across songs. Several lack memorable lyrical refrains or musical hooks; the song with the most memorable refrain, "Two Good Men," is the only song to have been repeatedly recorded by other artists. The songs can sometimes feel bloated by information, weighted down by the details of the case, to the detriment of Guthrie's usual economical directness and proficiency at turning clever, memorable phrases. Smithsonian Folkways archivist Jeff Place believes Guthrie is at times reading freshly composed lyrics off a sheet of paper, a supposition to which the comparatively flat vocal delivery of some of the songs lends support.[25]

At the same time, however, the record's naysayers are also hearing their own investment in a particular, preconceived version of Woody Guthrie. And while some songs may lack some of the immediate verve that percolates through older, more familiar tunes, or the clearer coherence of *Dust Bowl Ballads* and the Columbia River songs, they nonetheless reflect an artist struggling with the challenges of his time, with the way the "crazy mixed up whirl" at the time *felt* to him. And however much the goal of the project had been to rally the Left with a sense of its history, the defining feelings of Guthrie's struggle, as rendered by the struggles sometimes evident *within* these songs, were grief and shame.

Back in 1940, the younger Guthrie had been steered by Alan Lomax into the heart of Popular Front anti-fascism. He had then followed his left comrades, be they communists or Democrats, into a full embrace of military intervention in Europe and the Pacific. There was a mass of people whom he could imagine himself addressing. In a number of the postwar Sacco and Vanzetti songs, he doesn't explicitly describe grieving this unified configuration. But like the *New Masses* editorial pining for the days of "Communists, Socialists, liberals and others" fighting in unison, some of the songs remember the Sacco and Vanzetti affair, despite the tragedy, as a time of leftist mass motivation. The opening song on the CD version, "The Flood and the Storm," describes a global revolutionary "spirit" arriving in Boston to kindle the work of men like the two anarchists, and devotes four verses to the massive worldwide demonstrations sparked by their executions:

> *The world shook harder on the night they died*
> *Than 'twas shaken by that Great World's War.*
> *More millions did march for Sacco and Vanzetti*
> *Than did march for the great War Lords.*
> *More millions did pray, more millions did sing,*
> *More millions they did weep and cry*
> *This August night in nineteen twenty-seven,*
> *When strapped there in that chair they did die.*[26]

Just below the surface-level language of tribute, however, lies a melancholic implication: at that moment, in 1947, conditions made it impossible to marshal such a grand response in defense of the principles of justice. This song, like a few others, has no chorus or refrain. But in the fragile atmosphere in which the Left found itself in 1947, perhaps that absence served to convey the fear that there were no mass choruses left to sing.

Loss and loneliness also permeate the song "Vanzetti's Rock"; here, he uses the research trip's failure as a conceit through which to render the ephemeral quality of working-class history (especially as compared with triumphalist national history), describing tourists visiting Plymouth Rock, whose "tourist map don't show you" Sacco and Vanzetti, and longing for a time when statues of the two men will stand in the town and "trade union workers" will come to visit them.

Again, the most compelling of the bunch is the song that came out of Guthrie's early entry point into the project, the lullaby to Rosa Sacco, Nicola's wife. Like the earlier version, "I Just Want to Sing Your Name" foregrounds Guthrie's own emotions ahead of the facts of the case or the men's lives, turning the failure to find a narrative into the motive force of the song.

> *Oh Sacco, Sacco*
> *Oh Nicola Sacco*
> *Oh Sacco, Sacco*
> *I just want to sing your name.*

Oh Rosie, Rosie
Oh Miz Rosie Sacco
Oh Rosie, Rosie
I just want to sing your name.
I never did see you, see you
I never did get to meet you
I just heard your story, story
And I just want to sing your name.
Hey, hey, Bart Vanzetti
Hey, hey, Bart Vanzetti
You made speeches for the workers, workers
Well, I just want to sing your name.[27]

Edward P. Comentale writes that this song "may be the most avant-garde moment of the collection, if not Guthrie's entire career."[28] With glorious economy, the song does precisely what it says it wants to do: sings the names. There's a sensual quality to the singer voicing his desire, essentially, to feel his mouth forming their names. He lingers, tenderly, over the names of Nicola, Rosie, and Bart, eschewing, for the most part, details of the events. Indeed, he makes this preference clear: although "I just heard your story," nonetheless "I just want to sing your name"; "You made speeches for the workers," but rather than relaying what you said, "I just want to sing your name." Redemption, the song hopes, will come more from the act of singing itself than from the information the song conveys. The act of singing produces intimacy; singing these historical actors' names reanimates them through the warmth of feeling in Guthrie's lungs, vocal cords, and mouth. Plymouth may lack statues or plaques commemorating the martyred men, but history is nevertheless recorded through this affection more than through reportage or narrative description.

The phrase "consciousness of guilt," which so jolted Guthrie from the drama of the Bridgewater streetcar arrest, doesn't appear in any of the songs. But his interest in the self-blaming mind-set, and the relationship between personal and political vulnerability, hadn't abated by the time he went into the studio. These concerns run through the remarkable and odd song "We Welcome to Heaven," another example of the turn away from narrative storytelling—indeed, from any content explicitly associated with the facts of the case. The title of the song promises something elegiac yet triumphant, the men released from their torment on earth (after impoverished lives before their convictions, they spent seven years in prison, six on death row) into the immortal status of angels for the Left. But the lyrics, from the opening lines, plunge listeners into the sentiment Guthrie described when writing about "consciousness of guilt." Rather than celebrating the men's ascension, reassuring them and us of their achievements despite their execution, he becomes preoccupied with describing the woeful, all-pervasive feelings of shame and self-denigration in the world they have just escaped.

We welcome to heaven Sacco and Vanzetti
Two men that have won the highest of seats
Come, let me show you the world that you come through
It's a funny old world, as I'm sure you'll admit
If you wear rags on earth you're a hobo
If you wear satin, they call you a thief
If you save money, they call you a miser
If you spend money, you are on relief
If you work hard, they say you are lowly
If you're a loafer, of course, you're no good
If you stay sober you're known as a sissy
And if you drink liquor it goes to your head
If you are fat, they will call you a glutton
If you stay skinny, they call you a runt
If you laugh, they'll call you an idiot
And if you cry, they will ask you to stop.[29]

There are several more verses, all continuing in this vein: maintaining that below heaven, here on earth, one's fellow human beings will make virtually any personal characteristic the object of ridicule and stigma. The song puts aside the work of Sacco and Vanzetti as revolutionaries and organizers, their highly suspicious arrest, their subjection to the whims of a biased trial judge, and so on, in favor of a litany of derogatory epithets that mortals heave at one another. In his bleak depiction of the world to which humans are doomed, Guthrie had zeroed in on the common currency of prejudice, of hate motivated by the fear of difference: intolerance for deviation from the norm in categories ranging from class to bodily appearance to sexuality.

We are back in the world of feelings—not the nurturing, maternal feeling of "I Just Want to Sing Your Name," but insult, dejection, shame, and, perhaps most notably, *stigma*. Indeed, the song offers no reparative voice at all, not even, say, the cathartic solace that blues songs can offer their own singers. It is not a world in which we can produce a narrative with a beginning, middle, and end. It is a world in which we are, at worst, stuck, with only the possibility of martyrdom as solace, and at best, caught up in a "crazy, mixed up whirl."

It is definitely a world in which loneliness has yet to be defeated.

This strain of existential lament is not a tack much associated with Popular Front culture. It seems antithetical to the idea of union; or, it seems to lament the failure of that notion, with its depiction of people isolated by dejection at the hands of their fellow human beings. Indeed, the bullying voices the song depicts aren't very far removed from the blustery ones then making political capital by haranguing "pre-mature anti-fascists" during sessions of the newly permanent House Un-American Activities Committee—what Victor Navasky, in his history of the postwar Red Scare *Naming Names*, calls "degradation ceremonies." As Navasky points out, the work of HUAC "was not to legislate or even to discover subversives—that had already been done by the intelligence agencies and their informants—so much as it was to stigmatize."[30]

The question, though, was whether seeing stigma in a broader, more critical fashion might open opportunities for new forms of affiliation. In a couple of years, as his life veered away from family and toward clinics and hospitals, Guthrie would direct his increasingly lagging energy toward exploring these possibilities.

And, Guthrie had Cathy to help him work through this world of feeling, where things didn't always make sense or have structure—and they didn't have to. Who knew where this could lead him and his work in the coming years?

And then, an event both horrifyingly shocking and uncannily familiar ripped his new, settled life open at the seams. It was February 10, 1947. A week earlier, he had finished—or at least moved on from—the recording of the Sacco and Vanzetti album. Four days earlier, the family of three had celebrated Cathy's fourth birthday. That night, he played at a jubilant union rally in Elizabeth, New Jersey, where Phelps Dodge workers were celebrating a victorious settlement after a prolonged strike.

When he got home to Mermaid Avenue at 11:30 p.m., a terrifying sight greeted him: their convertible couch's mattress, partially burned, strewn in the yard. At the front door, he found a note. "Come to Coney Island Hospital immediately," it read in full, in Marjorie's handwriting. A smoky smell came from under the door. As he was headed back out, a neighbor appeared, her eyes red and face pale.

"Cathy got burned a little," she said.

He arrived at the hospital at midnight. The Youngs from upstairs were there. Marjorie said she'd gone out for five minutes, just to get milk at the store across the street, and returned home to find Arthur Young, a sixteen-year-old upstairs neighbor, cradling Cathy in a blanket out front. He'd heard her banging on the door, busted it open, found the blanket and wrapped it around her. Her entire body was covered in burns. The Youngs moved the furniture, clothes, musical instruments, and papers out of harm's way. Firefighters threw the smoldering mattress into the yard; it had ignited, they said, when a radio's wiring had short-circuited.

He was afraid to see her in this state, but then remembered how much affection she'd shown toward someone the neighborhood's bullies had branded "the ugliest person on our street."[31] She'd adopted his position on the political uses of stigma.

In the hospital room, swathed in padding, she was still laughing and joking, telling stories about school, calling everyone by their names. Something bad had happened, she conceded; she'd burned her pink dress. Stunned by her apparent nonchalance—the burns had likely destroyed enough nerve endings to free her from pain—he held her hands and held back his terror at what was unfolding. More people arrived—Aliza Greenblatt, Sophie Maslow, the favorite babysitter, and her boyfriend.

Cathy's voice got softer and softer. Then she was gone.

Marjorie and Woody left the hospital in silence, holding hands, the others trailing behind them watching their small, stiffened frames.

A few days later they entertained a long-scheduled party at a local nursery school. He sang some of the songs she'd given him words for. She would have been there, dancing around and around.

Chapter Eight

"THE WHOLE WORKS"

T HE GRIEF THROBBED THROUGH HIM as the weeks after the fire passed. For months after the calamitous event, he was still including her name when signing off letters from the Guthrie family.

He still had to produce a coherent version of himself for other people, responding to their condolences and genuine concern. He also longed to find some meaning in the event. He and Marjorie weren't religious, but they needed to make sense of the tragedy in the terms through which they understood the world. Less than three weeks after the fire, in response to a letter of condolence from Pete Seeger and family, Guthrie wrote that they had left all her artwork up on the walls of the little apartment, insisting that its presence still made their lives "brighter." Despite her tender age, he memorialized her as a fighter for social justice who had revivified his own progressive commitments. He concluded the letter, "She had the real spirit of a Peoples Dancer and of a People[s] Singer and if I ever display any signs of either spirit it will be because of what Cathy taught me with great pains and patience during her trip here."[1]

He composed a batch of similar notes, saving the last response for Arthur Young, the upstairs neighbor who had valiantly entered the apartment and grabbed Cathy. It took the form of a long poem titled "For Arthur Young Upstairs," in which he lauded the teenager's bravery in this incident as a sign of his willingness to be a great historical actor; Arthur had reacted to the fire, Guthrie wrote, "the same as you saw the whole world burn down." He compared the boy's effort at rescue to the actions of brave soldiers in the big battles that had recently brought

The Guthrie family in Oke-mah, Oklahoma, ca. 1924: (L to R) Woody, Nora Belle, Charley, and George.

Woody and first wife Mary on the front steps of their Los Angeles home with children Gwen, Sue, and Bill, 1941.

Will Geer, Guthrie's close friend for almost thirty years, as stereotypical hillbilly Jeeter Lester in the stage version of Erskine Caldwell's novel *Tobacco Road* (1940).

ALAN LOMAX

Authority on American Folk-Lore . . . Archivist to the
Library of Congress . . . Commentator and Artist on
"Columbia's School of the Air"

Promotional document for influential Library of Congress archivist Alan Lomax, who helped spur the growth of Guthrie's career in the early 1940s.

Guthrie and Burl Ives relax in Central Park after performing on the radio variety show *Forecast*, August 1940.

(L to R) Sophie Maslow, Frieda Flier, and Marjorie Mazia in the Martha Graham Dance Company's *American Document* (1938).

One incarnation of the Almanac Singers: (L to R) Agnes "Sis" Cunningham, Cisco Houston, Guthrie, Pete Seeger, and Bess Lomax (Alan's sister).

Tony Kraber and Woody Guthrie (with guitar) performing with Sophie Maslow's New Dance Group as part of the *Folksay* premiere, Humphrey-Weidman Studio Theater, New York City, March 1942. Guthrie met Marjorie Mazia while rehearsing for this production.

Woody Guthrie with Marjorie
Mazia, publicity photograph,
ca. 1942.

Woody Guthrie and Marjorie Mazia Guthrie, honeymoon, November 1945.

Children have a natural musical and rhythmic aptitude... DEVELOP IT... for health and balance

Cathy Ann Guthrie, three, and Marjorie in a photo spread for Disc Records' series of albums for children, *Songs to Grow On*. Many songs encouraged kids' awareness of their bodies.

Guthrie playing music with his third wife, Anneke Van Kirk, ca. 1952.

Look Away, June 1953. Monochromatic rendering based on original full-color painting, 42 x 26 cm, by Woody Guthrie.

Southern White, June 1953. Monochromatic rendering based on original full-color painting on two-page spread, 42 x 52 cm, by Woody Guthrie.

Southland Tourist, March 1951. Monochromatic rendering based on original full-color watercolor, pen, and colored pencil on artist's pad, 45 x 30 cm, by Woody Guthrie.

Woody with his and Marjorie's kids, (L to R) Joady, Arlo, and Nora, on the lawn of Greystone State Hospital, 1959.

down fascism. He also expressed particular gratitude to the Young family for preserving the things the Guthries held precious: Cathy's toys; Marjorie's dancing notes, books, and memorabilia; Woody's papers. While this might seem a petty concern after the loss of yet another loved one's life, the poem makes clear that he saw in such objects the sign of continuing struggle and hope, especially now that the Youngs had marked them with their courageous spirit:

> *You saved Cathy's life as far as I am concerned*
> *And you saved Marjorie's life as far as she is concerned*
> *You saved whatever whittle and spark of whatever life ever*
>   *was alive in me*
> *[. . .]*
> *I owe every minute of my life, owe my life every minute to*
>   *folks like you.*[2]

In subsequent weeks, he continued to manage his personal grief by framing it in broader terms. He saw it in the context of labor struggles, blaming the fire on cheap wiring in the radio, connecting it to work he had done in support of the strike by the Phelps Dodge workers, and claiming that a growing anti-labor sentiment, embodied in the Taft-Hartley Act, deserved blame for her death.

He took to the road, hoping the distance would help. In California, he arrived at the home of his old singing partner Maxine Crissman looking stricken and unkempt. Her own young daughter waddled into the room. He reached for the girl, but she cowered away from him. "I had one like that," he blurted.[3]

Whether because of Cathy's death, early Huntington's symptoms, the political climate, or (most likely) all three, 1947 was a watershed year for Woody Guthrie, initiating a period of struggle that would last through his permanent hospitalization in 1956. Publicly, very little creative work would emerge from this period; he found it difficult to finish projects, to organize them into a suitable condition to present to publishers and record producers, more than a few of whom were hesitant to work with leftist artists during the new Red Scare. Sadly, there were to be no more major recording sessions, no promised sequel to *Bound for Glory*, no more work with the dance world aside from playing at Marjorie's studio and the occasional revival of *Folksay*. Privately, however, he would still create remarkably compelling, challenging work in songs, writings, and visual art.

His best work from this time reflects his difficult situation: being a leftist artist in a time of conservative political retrenchment, while suffering from puzzling "queer" feelings in both his body and mind. Caught up in these challenges, his insight into them necessarily limited by the lack of a clear assessment of his health, the work often represents and acts out his confusion. It embodies the personal and historical opacity of the moment of its creation.

Guthrie maintained his commitments to collectivism through the late 1940s and into the 1950s, in defiance of both external persecution and internal rifts among communists, particularly over the Stalin regime. And yet he spent hours and hours alone with his notebooks, writing in a state of intoxication sometimes literal and sometimes figurative, recording thoughts that might have scandalized many of his fellow former Popular Front radicals. He was experimenting with form, moving way beyond the conventions of traditional balladry and topical song that had earned him what was, at the time, a considerable reputation, albeit one largely confined to folk music circles.

A lot of the newer work was about sex and shame, and in hindsight, it anticipated future leftist ideas about the locations of "the political" and the possibilities of affiliation. It was impossible to stay an old leftist—the Popular Front was cleaved apart, and anyone who openly espoused socialist or communist principles would face dire consequences to their livelihood. One had to either leave the country or repackage oneself into something more anodyne, as Pete Seeger and Lee Hays did with their new folk-singing group, the Weavers. But Guthrie, who had already been exploring the social and personal dimensions of shame in his work, took his politics in adventurous directions that would take most of the Left—or what remained of it—a couple more decades to comprehend. In particular, he was concerned with turning shame into knowledge and resistance.

Guthrie faced many setbacks in these years: among them, an embarrassing yet illuminating arrest on obscenity charges that saw him sentenced to jail and a treatment center for sex "deviants." He would *feel* increasingly off, alienated, and different, and he would experience these feelings in a society that enforced its values by dividing the normal from the abnormal or "deviant." He began to feel there was something wrong with him personally, in his being. He reacted with anger and introspection, suspecting that his society might be invested in making him feel these feelings. He began to sense that the "normal" was less a common-sense ideal than a way of maintaining the power structure.

On October 5, 1949, Woody Guthrie stood before a judge in the Federal Building on Washington Street (now Cadman Plaza East) in downtown Brooklyn and pleaded guilty to charges that in February of the previous year, he "did wilfully [sic] knowingly deposit and cause to be deposited for mailing and delivery in a post office box located in Brooklyn, New York, an authorized depository, certain non-mailable matter, to wit: a hand written letter enclosed in an envelope, which letter was obscene, lewd, and lascivious in that it solicited a meeting for immoral purposes and which letter is unfit to be set forth in this instrument and to be spread upon the records of this Court."[4] The charges—based in a set of laws established in the nineteenth century known widely as the Comstock Act—stemmed from three sexually explicit letters he had mailed over the course of ten days to a northern California woman named Mary Ruth Crissman, the younger sister of his former singing partner in the late 1930s on Los Angeles radio: Maxine Crissman, aka "Lefty Lou from Old Mizzou." Across the explicit scribblings, Guthrie smudged cerise paint in the quasi-abstract expressionist style with which he often adorned his notebook writings. Between them, according to Maxine, he inserted newspaper clippings with stories about grisly murders. Alarmed, Mary Ruth took the letters to LA to ask Maxine for advice. Maxine called the police.

During the initial investigation, the District Attorney engaged a psychiatrist who warned the Crissmans to consider Guthrie a crazed killer who might show up at any moment to kill them in the cruelest way imaginable. Indeed, for a time, investigators placed Guthrie on the list of suspects in the brutal killing of Elizabeth Short, the victim in the notorious "Black Dahlia" murder of January 1947—a case that had been spawning tabloid headlines in Los Angeles and beyond for many months. The investigation into Guthrie's letters moved back to New York when the charges became the provenance of the federal government, the act of mailing "obscene" materials the crime at issue. Jim Longhi, of the Merchant Marine days, agreed to act as his defense attorney. In Guthrie's first court appearance, on August 2, 1949, he pleaded not guilty, but then reversed course in October. On November 30, Eastern District Court Judge Harold M. Kennedy sentenced Guthrie to six months in prison. At some point, whether in an effort to reduce jail time (on December 22, his sentence was reduced to time served) or comply with a court-ordered mandate, he agreed to be evaluated for admission to a new rehabilitation program designed to treat sexual "deviance." Once the probation department and a court psychiatrist had determined him not to be among "the psychotics and mental defectives," the court granted Guthrie entry into the Quaker Emergency Services Readjustment Center, run by a psychiatrist named Fredric Wertham, who would later gain notoriety for his 1950s campaign against the supposed ill effects of comic books on children and adolescents.

Guthrie had sat in jails a few nights in his life, usually after being picked up for vagrancy or trespassing: crimes, that is, of unsanctioned movement or lack of movement, infractions that threatened the sanctity of privately owned space. He could associate such offenses with the outsiders and renegades who populated the music he loved and the songs he wrote; he could even write their spirit into an anthem like "This Land Is Your Land," in which the peripatetic narrator, in a verse many renditions censor, rebuffs the command of a "No Trespassing" sign. But this encounter with law enforcement didn't match any such narrative. In the first days of 1950, just after leaving prison, he wrote in a notebook:

> While I was in the West Street Jail [Marjorie] told all of our friends and neighbors I was out west. Everybody asks me how things are out west. I don't know what to tell them.
> I never do know.[5]

For years Guthrie had sung of the depredations that law enforcement and courts directed against poor people. He had made legends of outlaw figures he viewed as brave rebels against that persecution, like Jesse James and Pretty Boy Floyd. He had romanticized his own flouting of police authority in his songs and in *Bound for Glory*; this tack was an essential part of his work and persona. But this particular predicament, ending in a Brooklyn jail cell and a Manhattan sex deviance clinic, allowed no room for ready-made romantic myth. Shame muffled its conversion into a story.

The problem wasn't just his individual shame, but also the stigma of his designation. The remanding to therapy defined him less as someone who had committed a criminal act than as a sick person, in need of treatment and, as the name of Dr. Wertham's clinic put it, "readjustment." Entering the treatment program suggested that something in his very being posed a threat to a normal, healthy citizenry—people requiring protection from the shameful, compulsive tendencies of his ilk.

It is certainly possible that emerging symptoms of Huntington's disease played a role in Guthrie's behavior. Research into the illness has long explored connections to sexually aggressive and inappropriate acts; indeed, the very first case given this name, recorded by a Long Island doctor named George Huntington in 1872, involved two brothers, with wives, "who are constantly making love to some young lady, not seeming to be aware that there is any impropriety in it." The pair's symptoms were so advanced that their walking was severely impaired, making them appear drunk, yet they "never let an opportunity to flirt with a girl go past unimproved. The effect is ridiculous in the extreme."[6] While it is clear that the illness (like many neurological conditions) causes a loss of inhibition, early twenty-first-century medicine disputes any innate connection to sexual misbehavior. Indeed, research made available by the Huntington's Disease Society of America—an organization that Marjorie Mazia Guthrie founded in 1968—notes that *hyposexuality* is more commonly reported among those with the condition.[7]

It would be a mistake to collapse all of Guthrie's interest in sexuality into disease pathology. As we've seen, he took sex seriously as a realm of political exploration and awakening, a passion on display in his wartime letters to Marjorie and the novel *House of Earth*. As the years passed, he became increasingly preoccupied with writing about sex in the form of letters addressed directly to specific women, whether sent or not. In 1947, in particular, he began filling more notebook pages with long accounts of sexual fantasies about specific women who moved through his and Marjorie's life on Mermaid Avenue. It's not clear how many women he actually mailed letters to. But he likely didn't expect the state to intervene in this intimate realm of his writing.

For Lee Hays, Guthrie's aim in such scribbling was to "duplicate the sex act in rhythm much as musicians have written pieces of music to that end."[8] Sex as writing, writing as sex: it was, to Guthrie, a genre of its own. One day in August 1947, for example, he was sitting at home in front of a 1946 memo book he'd recycled as a journal, fantasizing about Natanya Neumann, a young dancer friend of Marjorie's and one of the women helping them with their new baby, Arlo, who'd been born on July 10. In the pages of a 1946 datebook he was using as a journal, he started to scrawl a loosely rhyming poem, beginning: "I now hold here in my hand the hottest pen of natural man and I try to call my nerve up here to sing my warmest song / I now squeeze my song to Tania off the end of my slick pen that will burn and blaze and jump seeds in the skin of girls and men."[9] If Guthrie wasn't literally masturbating as he wrote this, as seems highly possible, he was certainly constructing an analogy between pen and penis that equated writing with sexual arousal. He seems to have experienced it as a sexual act in itself. The letters to Crissman, which are inaccessible or destroyed, likely looked something like this unsent note to Neumann. Several other examples of this type of writing exist both in private holdings and in the Woody Guthrie Archive.

To his discredit, he didn't always leave these scribblings in his notebook. Mailing them, unsolicited, made them amount to what we would today call sexual harassment, a breach of consent. Clearly, neither Guthrie's openness to sexuality and femininity nor his powers of empathy extended to imagining what it would be like for Mary Ruth Crissman to receive such letters, out of the blue. He was, apparently, unwilling or unable to think critically about gender and male privilege in these contexts. Such was the limit of his sexual politics.

Equally disturbing is the report about the newspaper clippings, despite his claim in a written statement that "I did not try to frighten her nor to Blackmail her, nor, in the least way to bring violence nor destruction to her property nor person."[10] Notably, nothing in the indictment mentions such clippings, and the account of them seems to come solely from Maxine Crissman. Guthrie's oft-stated belief that sexual repression leads to violence would not undo the damage caused by the clippings, but it seems possible that this is the message he was trying to communicate with them. These ideas went back to wartime, when he linked Nazism to sexual repression. In his unfinished novel *Life's Other Side*, begun during the war, a stand-in for Marjorie avoids sexual assault by convincing a would-be rapist that fascism has driven him to become a sex criminal. But the fall of European fascism didn't put a stop to these thoughts, which he linked explicitly to "newspaper headlines" in a stirring essay, "My Best Songs," written in early 1947.

Still, it seems curious that all of these factors would warrant investigators using the letters to tie him to the Black Dahlia murder, one of the most notorious sex crime cases in American history. Indeed, the circumstances of his behavior toward Mary Ruth Crissman do not explain his being charged by the US government with obscenity (under laws initially designed by nineteenth-century anti-vice crusader Anthony Comstock in part to repress the flow of information about contraception and abortion)—that is, writing words literally deemed unspeakable, even in court and legal documents—rather than, say, making threats. The prosecution, much like Guthrie, was evidently unconcerned with either Crissman herself or matters of consent. Charges of this nature seem mismatched with the punishment and treatment demanded of the singer: initially, six months of incarceration, as well as therapy in a state-of-the-art psychiatric clinic whose patients, in the vast majority, were men (many of them, like Guthrie, veterans and working-class) arrested for having sex with other men in public.

Historical conditions likely help explain the way Guthrie was treated for this incident—specifically, postwar political panic's reach into matters of sexuality. According to those caught up in the increasing anti-communist hysteria, homosexuals, communists, and homosexual communists were all undermining American imperial might and security; the radical left threat was, in this view, necessarily a threat to heterosexual masculinity. The two forms of deviance, the one sexual and the other ideological, became widely linked in popular discourse.[11]

Despite the clear fact that sending the letters was a breach of his commitment to treating others with empathy, his jottings about his prosecution were unequivocally unapologetic. He cast himself as the victim of repressive attitudes toward sex and class-based standards of propriety, as demonstrated in remarks found in a notebook from October 1949, before he changed his initial non-guilty plea to guilty:

> Judge & Sex
> My judge can't even say the word, sex, without thinking the word, maniac. I'd ought to be up on that judging bench looking down at him.
> Obscene
> That word obscene means, of the low and common people. I think my words talk more for the common people than my probation officer does. He can't force my people to talk the kings old rotten English.[12]

Although the experience would mainly yield only fragments of writing, he viscerally felt that the charges reflected class warfare, criminalizing him for being a vocal representative of "the low and common people." And in an odd, clumsy way, the obscenity conviction was the culmination of several years of his exploration of sexuality—its open expression and representation—as a threat to established orders of class and even race. The treatment of poor rural white folks' sexuality as pathological had served as the background against which the articulate sexual encounter between the fictional protagonists of *House of Earth* stood out. After a draft of that novel was completed, Guthrie's writings—generally confined to notebooks and journals—suggest that he had begun to see himself as a kind of sexual dissident, even if his reasons for doing so do not always seem pure of selfish motive, or demonstrate much consideration of their ramifications for Marjorie. Nonetheless, by 1947, his writing on sex begins to show a sense of embattlement and defiance, of external pressure bearing down on him, that rarely surfaces in the more effusive, idealistic eroticism of his wartime letters to his wife or *House of Earth*.

For instance, as the pages written to dancer-babysitter Natanya Neumann continue, they take a surprising turn:

> Your own people will sing loud yells about Woody Guthrie being two sex maniacs. But if I took the other road these same several yellers would scream that I'm a queer. I fully aim at this time, dear lay man and lay woman, to walk up and to run bare back down both of these trails

and to get my soul known again as the two, both, the sexual maniac, the saint, the sinner, the drinker, the thinker, the queer. The works.

The whole WORKS.

It's not till you have called me all of these names that I feel satisfied.[13]

In this passage, an increasingly common preoccupation surfaces: his belief that, in the world as we know it, people compulsively stigmatize and shame their own kind. But here, instead of assuring audiences that, for instance, he hates a song that shames them for being or looking like who they are, he insists that he *wants* to be called the bad names as well as the good ones; he *welcomes* stigmatization by forces he considers twisted and suspect. What came off as dreary abjection in parts of the Sacco and Vanzetti project becomes angry and defiant.

It is all but impossible to imagine any other figure associated with the Popular Front writing this way. The point of difference isn't simply the sexual content and the use of words considered vulgar—neither of which, to be sure, was a serious element of the Old Left arsenal of inspiration. It is that the passage slides toward undoing basic binary oppositions that older agitprop would have maintained, between who was good and who bad, who was virtuous and whose hands were stained with corruption or worse. Whereas an old leftist and a younger Guthrie (especially as a songwriter) would have firmly planted themselves on one side, the side of righteousness, this passage calls into question something more fundamental—a system that generates such distinct categories, that assesses and classifies people so tidily.

From 1947 onward, Guthrie's writing reveals his increasing awareness of social stigma broadly—not just in terms of class, but "the whole works." In this context, his focus on sexuality was not simply his idle obsession, or a symptom to be ascribed to Huntington's, but a lens that convinced him of the political uses and abuses of stigma, and which gave him a sense of the construction of the "normal" (even as his learning process was sometimes clumsy and hurtful).

The point of raising questions about the Crissman incident isn't, ultimately, to rehabilitate Guthrie or claim that he was treated unjustly as an individual. Instead, by illustrating how and why writing about sex could be deemed criminal and psychologically aberrant in the late 1940s, how and why it could be deemed to warrant a state response, the case helps trace the politicization of not only norms around sex but the very notions of normality and its opposite, deviance. It also helps deepen our understanding of Guthrie's response to this historical process—and how that response surfaced in his writings, even as he faced challenges regarding his health, in his personal life, and from the increasingly conservative political environment. Coming at a time that saw the emergence of some of the first activism around sexualities branded "deviant," Guthrie's sex writing and prosecution show him becoming more alert to how the policing of sex—and of intimacy—might fit into a broader arena of struggles for social justice.

In the 1930s and well into the 1940s, Guthrie and the Popular Front hoped that "the people" could plan and organize the world they wanted, and to achieve these aims they saw government as the people's instrument, whether via New Deal programs or as an in-the-offing revolutionary communist state. In the postwar years, however, one of the challenges these ideas faced was the growing power of the institutions of psychology and psychiatry. According to Ellen Herman, the postwar period saw these fields, whose nineteenth-century roots lay in philosophy, transform into "helping trades" that made them "a source of moral, cultural, and political values" and "allowed psychological experts to make extremely broad claims to authority."[14] They did so by using people's private lives as their raw material; essentially, they professionalized intimacy. In asserting what was "normal," they also gave a professional imprimatur to the association between political dissent and unconventional sexuality.

Reading Guthrie in this period, you don't get the sense that he would have signed up for participation in a "gay-straight alliance" group, had such a thing existed at the time. He makes remarks about "sissies," for example, that would be considered homophobic. You do, however, see someone increasingly aware that sexuality is political, and, in particular, that it is wrapped up in power relations with social institutions like law and psychiatry.

At times, he saw sex as under siege. He speaks this vision most volubly in an essay written a few days before Cathy's death in February 1947, titled "My Best Songs." In this piece, Guthrie reaches out to perhaps his most important literary muse: Walt Whitman, a figure whose sexuality was both flamboyant and difficult to categorize. Will Geer, himself a queer man, described Whitman's impact on his close friend: "Woody loved the sensuality in Whitman. He had the same wide, democratic feeling for his fellow men—liked to move among them, live and touch all their lives. Like Whitman, he loved to catalog the names of places as well as the bodies of men and women and all their parts."[15]

There are further points of comparison between the two. Whitman titled his most famous work "Song of Myself"; in "My Best Songs," Guthrie was indulging the same, expansive notion of "song" beyond literally sung ditties. Whitman's poem begins, famously, "I celebrate myself, and sing myself / And what I assume you shall assume." He wrote in long, free lines rather than the more orderly verse of his forebears, the Romantic poets. Enraptured by the sound of ordinary, everyday speech in the streets around *his* Brooklyn (and elsewhere), he let the words determine the poem's rhythm, rather than vice versa. He wanted his poetry to embrace on its own terms everything considered common, sinful, or even abject. He believed describing and celebrating the reality of his own body was a quasi-sacred act, a path to the soul of humanity.

Similarly, in an undated note, Guthrie once declared:

> Gain all the wisdom you can about your human body. Get all of the knowledge you can about your human body. Learn every little fact that you can learn about your own human body.
>
> Your own body is the only one thing that you can put your head to, to study for all of your lifetime. Every other form and channel of study leads on up and up to your miraculous body, anyhow.[16]

"My Best Songs" brims with similar declarations. It is an ode to the body, and to nakedness. He demands that we look beyond the songs found on record, on radio, or in live performance—what *song* meant for his compatriots in People's Songs. His real "song" is the conduct of his own life, and the essence of this song is the place where his senses interact with the world: his body. Guthrie shares Whitman's commitment to including *every* aspect of the self—"the whole works," as it were—in this celebration. Bringing the body into the piece serves as proof of this commitment. "My body is naked now, and it was born naked" is the piece's refrain. He links this salute to nakedness with a rejection of poetic artifice. "My best songs will be the ones that never rhyme," he writes, for rhyme is merely an ornament meant to hide the naked body of the poem, and nakedness is itself a divine state.[17] All told, the piece is a celebration of truth, honesty, and authenticity—and the ultimate sign of these values is a free and inviting attitude toward sexuality. As in Whitman, the body being celebrated is a sexual body.

But the divinity of nakedness is not pure. Celebrating the whole works requires embracing aspects of life his world generally considers disgusting, obscene, or abject—not just "the body" in an abstract sense, for instance, but actual bodily fluids:

> Give me the vision of my world with the true thinking true believers singing and dancing and sweating on it, rubbing bellies of creation and stuck together with the glues, foams, juices or [sic] running and wheeling love. Give me a planet where the dead leaves do not dictate it nor rule like death.[18]

Lovingly embracing substances generally considered waste, he is modeling a way to transcend that treacherous force, shame.

Whitman often addresses his verse to an unnamed "You." The effect is to bring the reader into the poem, as if the text were an intimate whisper—despite the grandiosity of some of its declarations, and despite the whirlwind tour of a huge range of American lives for which "Song of Myself" makes readers his companion. This aspect of Whitman's poetics appears all over Guthrie's writing, which shares the same compulsion to make the universal as local and personal as possible, and vice versa. However, in "My Best Songs," Guthrie's "you" bears more sinister, threatening qualities than Whitman's. Instead of hailing a companionate reader through affection and gentle persuasion, the pronoun stands in for social forces that Guthrie sees as threatening truth, honesty, anti-artifice.

> I am not ashamed of me nor ashamed of myself.
>
> I am not ashamed of me in any of my positions nor moods nor attitudes. I will fight your ugliness with my very health and beauty. I must try my level best to display my beauty, to sing and dance in my feelings, the pretty feelings, to overcome, override, and to overflow your

bogholes and wallows of neurotic fear, hate, greed. You are spreading a
worser gospel of hate than just simple race hate, you are spreading the
gospel and the sermon that I'd ought to hate and to fear and to weep
and to mourn about my only good possession, my own self. (47–48)

Guthrie declares himself free from shame, but his assertions repeatedly lapse into angry, embattled language, leaving his condemnations
of shame suggesting how closely it looms for him. At the core of this
besieged tone is his adversarial relationship with this "you," whom he
addresses not with a whisper but a sneer. The issue was, in part, class.
He was convinced that those in the upper tiers of social power cultivated
shame about the body because, as scholar Bryan Garman puts it, "as
long as individuals feared their own bodies and the bodies of others, they
could not successfully unite in the struggle for freedom and economic
justice."[19]

Despite the lines of affiliation between Whitman and Guthrie, the
works of each are marked by the differences in the historical context in
which they appeared. Whitman's declarations came at a time when, in
fact, the very notion of "sexuality" didn't yet exist. Sex was considered
a set of practices, something people *did*, not what it would come to be in
the twentieth century: an identity, a core quality of the individual comparable to gender, race, or religion. The terms *homosexual* and *heterosexual* wouldn't appear until around the time Whitman died, in the late
nineteenth century—and then largely in professional sexological journals. Legal authorities considered men (like Whitman) who had sex with
other men to have committed criminal *acts*; less emphasis was placed on
their character or some internal quality that drew them to desire and love
other people of the same gender. Indeed, in this environment, men worried less about the social and personal ramifications of showing affection
for other men.

Nearly a century later, Guthrie composed his prose-y poem in a much
different environment, in which individuals' sexual behavior was understood to reflect a deeply embedded truth of the self—in the words of legal
theorist Janet Halley, "the unedited *real thing* about us."[20] The rise of
psychoanalysis, in particular, drove this shift. In this environment, men
who desired and loved other men were internally flawed as people. The
reasons for this shift are legion and too varied and complex for anything

near a complete discussion here. But, in essence, where the boundaries of "proper" sexuality had once been regulated by the church and the legal system, new institutions had taken over this authority. The legal system still played a role, but in the wake of Freud and the debates around his work's legacy, psychiatry and psychology had become much more central to debates over what constituted "normal" sexuality.

Thus, Guthrie's question in "My Best Songs" ("Why can't I sing the most beautiful song of them of all, the doings and feelings of my un-clothed and unhid self?") isn't rhetorical. It has an answer: there are peo-ple and institutions who work actively to silence this "beautiful song." Unlike his nineteenth-century muse, Guthrie writes under the constant pressure of people invested with authority lent them by institutions, the "worlds and worlds of rooms and desks where men and women are gath-ered around in robes, coats, suits, and dresses, to say what I shall write, speak, talk, and sing / And they tell me that I am locked and barred from singing the true feelings of my nakedest skin."[21] Elsewhere he mentions a "you" poised to "burn my books . . . my films, my scripts, my papers and my handbills."[22] He refers to a "room or table rounded with censors and judges."[23] And later, when the "you" has shifted in a more Whitmanian direction, to refer to a reader-slash-lover, he remains tied up in explicitly juridical language: "Your legs can't open in a way that I will arrest and give a summons. Your thighs can't move in a way that I'll lock up behind my bars. And those rumps, hips, and belly muscles of yours, you could never shimmy nor shake them in a way which I could drag off to my chain gang. Your back, your ribs, your breasts could never cause me to latch you away in my psycho cellar."[24]

Remarkably, here he is, over two years before his obscenity conviction, writing about the threat of judges, punishment, and psychiatric institu-tions with a version of that concept he'd fixed on during the Sacco and Vanzetti project: "consciousness of guilt." He broadcasts his awareness that some of his readers will understand him to be speaking as abnormal, *as a deviant*. He is reacting to an environment in which what he does sexually is taken as a diagnosis, as who he is, by experts. The socially repressive, shaming power rarely present in Whitman but so present here takes the form of these specific penal and medical institutions. *I know what you think of me when I discuss nakedness, bodily fluids, and pubic hair*, Guthrie essentially keeps saying, *and I know where you would have me sent: the jail or the insane asylum.* Far more than Whitman, Guthrie perceives himself as living in a world in which institutions of discipline and correction are always lurking close by in the margins of his text, at the ready to target the value he places on sex and sexual expression with as much or even more intensity than they do his allegiances with communism.

Six months after writing "My Best Songs"—after Cathy's death, Arlo's birth, at least one affair, and in the midst of growing distance from Marjorie—Guthrie echoed this mood with even more bite in the "Whole Works" letter/passage written to Natanya Neumann. And here, too, he shows prescience in his language, in his exhortation to call him "queer" and a "sex maniac." It was as if he sensed that any sign of deviation from so-called normal sexuality would eventually lead to being labeled with such epithets, or their scientific analogues. In fact, the censors, prisons, bars, and "psycho cellars" of "My Best Songs" reflect an atmosphere of cultural panic around sex that had been growing since before the war, driving a sensational preoccupation with sex crimes among law enforcement and media. In 1937, FBI director J. Edgar Hoover announced a "War on the Sex Criminal," claiming that "the most rapidly increasing type of crime is that perpetrated by degenerate sex offenders" who had "become a sinister threat to the safety of American childhood and womanhood." According to historian Estelle Freedman, "public outrage over rare, serious sexual crimes facilitated the establishment of legal and psychiatric mechanisms that were then used to regulate much less serious, but socially disturbing, behaviors."[25] In 1938, for example, the Los Angeles City Council established a "Sex Bureau," a body "designed to operate, according to the press, 'on the theory that each minor sex offender is a potential major sex criminal.'"[26] Such a "theory" provided the rationale for putting Woody Guthrie on the list of suspects in the Black Dahlia case when he was under investigation for sending obscene material through the mail.

Even the most valorized and romanticized aspects of his image faced the scrutiny of this panicked environment. As we've seen, eugenic theories cast poor whites and migrant "Okies," in particular, as, in the phrase from *Grapes of Wrath*, "sexual maniacs." In the mid-century US, from a particular angle, the "rambling man" himself, so seductive a figure for Guthrie heirs like Bob Dylan and Ramblin' Jack Elliott, looked creepy and queer to many people. The notion that economic crisis and war had uprooted men's traditional economic and social roles reflected anxiety about mobility and rootlessness. According to historian Jennifer Terry, many Americans associated sex deviance with people who, by necessity, choice, or some combination of both, did not plant their private lives squarely in one place, with a partner of the opposite sex: "As social relations and families were radically disrupted, the figure of the sexual psychopath, *imagined as a drifter or shiftless man cut loose from family ties*, symbolized the dangers threatening innocent citizens in the streets, schoolyards, and parks."[27]

Some psychologists and sociologists even argued that the very urge to travel—subtly cast with sexual overtones via the German word *Wanderlust*—grew out of the same psychological "urge" as sexual perversion.[28] Seen in a particular light, passages from Guthrie's writing like *Bound for Glory*'s first chapter, in which transient men on a moving box car, some of them shirtless, administer to one another's vulnerabilities, might also feed this panic about so-called perversion, and risk attracting the wrath of law enforcement and intrusion of psychiatry. In this environment, the forlorn and homeless "wandering worker" of Guthrie's song "I Ain't Got No Home," who "go[es] from town to town" looking for employment and dodging the police, was not simply a disconcerting vagrant; he was also someone targeted by the state as prone to sexual deviance, and considered drawn to sexual practices—homosexuality in particular—in need of regulation by various authorities. Guthrie's people needed straightening out. And this mission was even taken up in the emerging "planned world" of the New Deal; panics about homosexuality, often expressed in the homophobic form of fears about child molestation, in federal camps for people displaced by economic crisis, led to the specific exclusion of so-called deviants from a range of programs and organizations, an effort that spawned the first policies specifying homosexuals as unfit and ineligible for military service. In addition, this new policy mandated that veterans identified as homosexual be barred from receiving recently legislated benefits like the G.I. Bill.[29]

Given the governmental mobilization on these issues, it's no surprise that homophobia seeped into the authorities' approach to the Crissman letters. But rather than causing a retrenchment into convention (or the more traditional leftist denial of sexuality as an arena having anything to do with politics), the combination of Guthrie's experience and this environment seems to have loosened his sexual imagination and lexicon, as manifest in passages like the following, from a letter to Marjorie scribbled while he traveled up and down the West Coast in May 1947, as he struggled to find equilibrium in the wake of Cathy's death:

> Writing a letter to you is just about the same thing as me being there licking my tongue around in your little pussy. The taste is as good. . . . I want to actually drink your juice like wine, like sodie, like rum and like the healthiest fruit juice. I want you to love me this much and in the same wild unbridled Walt Whitman way.
>
> [. . .]
>
> And if you was the man and I was the woman you'd have my same feelings and I'd have all of your womanly and feminine and motherly feelings. If I was your woman and you my man I'd do all of these curious odd and strange things just to bring you to another little ounce of good feelings.
>
> I'd kiss your pecker honey if you only had one. I'd fondle it. I'd suck it. I'd drink your pecker milk and your pecker juice lots sweeter and quicker than any vegetable or fruit's juice, lots quicker than any orange or lemon juice and lots faster than any grapefruit's juice.[30]

In this strikingly un-homophobic passage, he makes "juice" into a sexual medium that crosses gender, thus undoing the difference between male and female sexual desire.

Regardless of his intentions with the Crissman letters, which were at the very least callous and selfish, Guthrie became subject to a form of power against which the Popular Front left provided few if any tools to fight. Despite having noted to Jim Longhi his "queer" feelings during the war—his sense that something was off in his health—he did not, of course, identify as queer in the way the term has been politically reclaimed since the 1990s, nor would he warrant being called a proto-"ally." As Will Kaufman notes, he looked askance at effeminacy in men.[31] But he was treated by the authorities in the same manner as they would have treated his queer friend Will Geer had they arrested Gear for having sex with another man in a public park.

These ideas stayed in Guthrie's private writings. Despite his commitment to collective action, there was no place for these ideas in the world of People's Songs or the Henry Wallace for President campaign, two major sites of investment for alumni/ae of the Popular Front. These circles were devoting their attention to racial injustice—to overturning Jim Crow in the South as well as housing discrimination in the North; another priority was resisting the Taft-Hartley Act and preventing the labor movement from capitulating to the Red Scare.

Guthrie had long relied on his intimate relationships, his intimate life, as a space where he could experiment with ideas and modes of expressing himself. Will Geer would have been the logical person with whom he might have explored this increasing sense of himself as a sexual dissident of sorts. It's important to remember that no one really knows the details of Guthrie's and Geer's relationship—the nature of intimacy is that a great deal of it goes undocumented. And, as much as open communication might seem like the hallmark of intimacy, close bonds can be forged through silent agreements about what *not* to talk about. Guthrie may not have known, or he may have known and kept mum at Geer's request, or he may have known and decided to keep mum on his own. But the historical circumstances shaping intimacy at the time likely would not allow communication about these matters or would have required a degree of risk-taking that neither man would indulge.

But someone else from Guthrie and Geer's circles was just beginning to open up new avenues for connecting radical class politics to fighting for an end to the persecution of non-normative sexuality. In the late 1940s, Harry Hay, one of Geer's ex-lovers, was assembling the first version of what would in a few years become the first public group advocating for civil rights for gays and lesbians. Hay was a staunch communist; he was also an expert on global folk music dating back to the Middle Ages, and an officer in the LA chapter of People's Songs, under the aegis of which he offered Marxist courses on the history of music. Unbeknownst to colleagues like Guthrie, he was a homosexual. Like many gay men of the time, he lived a largely secret life behind a veil of convention, with a wife and family. During the Wallace for President campaign, Hay organized a group called "Bachelors for Wallace," in which he broached the notion that the persecution of, and discrimination against, homosexuals was a civil rights issue—that is, that these "bachelors" constituted a *type* of person whose rights were imperiled and worthy of protection, akin to the situation of African Americans.[32] This group evolved into the

Mattachine Society, widely recognized as the first gay rights group in the United States.

Guthrie appears to have gotten to the point of understanding sexual stigma as something that branded particular people inferior outcasts, but not quite to the point of seeing the way society *defined* certain people's identities through such stigma. Consequently, despite sharing a passion for folk music and a common class politics, he also could not yet see common cause with someone forging a civil rights movement based on that very stigmatization, like his former associate Harry Hay. Granted, it is unlikely that Guthrie knew much of anything about Bachelors for Wallace or the Mattachine Society, and that ignorance is itself a symptom of a cultural resistance to sexual variance that one straight man could do little to counter. But it remains striking that for all his interest in forging politically meaningful collectivity out of shame, he generally could not see past that culturally enforced stigma toward a group of people whose identities were so fully forged out of the experience of sexual shame. I write "generally" because the next great crisis of his life brought him right up to the point of doing so.

In any case, Will Geer would become the greatest, most forthright proponent of taking the sexuality in Woody Guthrie's work seriously. In the years following Guthrie's death, Geer even read sections of "My Best Songs" in public lectures and performances. In a sense, Geer's memorial gift to his friend was to offer him as an icon to sexual nonconformists, a radical whose outlines the man who asked to be called queer could only vaguely make out while alive.

Chapter Nine

"SICK IN HIS OWN HEALTHY WAY"

O N JULY 22, 1952, Woody Guthrie checked himself into Brooklyn State Hospital, at 681 Clarkson Avenue in the East Flatbush neighborhood. During his first couple of days there, from the reception ward, he wrote to his sister Mary Jo to report his optimism that he would be "miraculously healed" by "modern day medicine" at this impressive institution "with all its outlying trees and buildings." He looked forward, he said, to being an object of study. He had long wanted to look at himself "under the most scientific microscope known to man and this big hospital . . . is just the very chosen spot for several dozens of nurses and doctors to show me inside post card movies of my own dang self." After getting to watch those inner reels of film, he believed he would "even be able to help you fix your own self back if and when you each do crackup or breakdown."[1]

In his first days as a patient, the hospital gave him a buoyant sense that medical innovation was traveling the right path:

> I see them use so many of our new wonder drugs; vitamin shots, penicilin [*sic*], germ killers, and I see the doctors and nurses using new revolutionary kinds of mental therapy; love instead of hate, tenderness instead of brutality, a whisper and a handpat and a flirty little smile in the place of nightmarish screams; love in the place of hate; freedoms instead of restraints; friendships in the place of animosities and friends for life instead of enemies; this and these are all the new cures and new healings and the greatest of all is that, it makes me love myself all over again.[2]

In his optimistic view, state-of-the art treatment included not only new professional innovations like drugs and therapeutic methods but kindnesses: love, tenderness, flirting, friendliness. In the hospital that he wished to see, medical approaches were supplemented by the empathic and generous conduct of life, an environment designed to restore patients' self-regard. As always, everything came down to relationships between people; no treatment was more important than the way people treated one another.

And what was the condition needing these "new cures and new healings"? Not Huntington's disease, he assured his sister: "All the good doctors tell me that there is no connection between Huntington's Korea [*sic*], which Mama had, and my own trouble whatever my own will be named and labeled."[3] No, what he needed was treatment for a wound of the soul; he needed penicillin, or some comparable miracle of the secular world, to cure him of self-contempt. The kindly atmosphere at Brooklyn State, just six miles north of the family apartment in Beach Haven, made him confident that it would happen. Or so he told Mary Jo, in an effort to protect her feelings.

For anyone reading Guthrie's papers chronologically, his mention of Huntington's here arrives with a jolt. It is the first acknowledgment of the condition in the archive, and yet it arrives without hesitation, as if, despite its absence from Guthrie's writing, the family had known for years exactly what had sent Nora Belle Guthrie to the state hospital in Oklahoma. He softens the mention for his little sister by punning on "Korea," in reference to the Asian peninsula where the United States was currently engaged in a Cold War anti-communist "police action." He softens it even further by denying that it pertains at all to his present predicament.

The woes he faced, however, were considerable. Almost three years after his prison term and "readjustment" at the Quaker Emergency Services clinic, he was in his third public mental hospital in three months. Somehow, the most reliable, steady parts of his life had begun to unravel. His career prospects looked ever dimmer. His marriage had slowly declined as he and Marjorie grew distant, she increasingly alienated by his behavior that showed little regard for her and the kids, of whom there were now three. His anger had, for the first time, reached the point of lashing out physically at his family; sudden outbursts of intense anger are often one of the first signs of Huntington's to surface.

There was no longer any way to deny that his body was changing in substantial and frightening ways. At times, it had begun to feel like a large, alien appendage, acting independently of—and often in opposition to—his will. He went through long spells of feeling jittery. His guitar playing was suffering, the old struggles with rhythm and tempo reappearing with greater force. He had spells of cognitive confusion, too. He forgot the lyrics to songs in the middle of playing them; for a couple of years he had needed Marjorie onstage with him, prompting him with questions to keep him focused. He believed, like people around him, that he was suffering long-term effects of years of excessive drinking. Surely the hospital—or "hopey-tal," as he sometimes called it—would examine him and figure out what was wrong, and in doing so supply him with the sense of wholeness he had felt lacking for so long, perhaps since Cathy's death, or maybe since the focused years of the anti-fascist war.

Six weeks after his admission, however, his optimism had waned. He found himself wishing Fredric Wertham, the head of the Readjustment Center he'd been sent to (and also a senior psychiatrist in the New York City Department of Hospitals), could hear a fellow Brooklyn State patient, a veteran, yelling "I'm a schizo-phreeny!" while ambling down a corridor in the ward. In his outbursts and deportment, this "combat fatigue vet" ridiculed the label given him by the staff doctors' "scientific microscope," the diagnosis that the hospital tried to make his identity; in a couple of months, Guthrie would reanimate his colleague's voice in the poem "Post War Breakout":

I'm a post war breakout
I'm a post war bustdown
I'm a post war nervice [?]
And a post war hero.
I'm a post war skitzoe
I'm a post war freenyol
Post war nerve case
And a post war face history.
I'm a psykoe pathy crackdown
I'm a looney blooney breakdown
War shocky suki yaki boy
I got a long personality,

I got a medal I'm a hero
I got an id, I got an ego
I got a pocket book and no dough
Just a post war shock job.
I'm a evil minded breakdown
I'm a vulgar thinking crackdown
I'm a lascivious lewdy nude boy
I'm a great long doctor book full.[4]

Did the doctors—not just the ones here, but the head of the Readjustment Center, too—not understand that these "big names" with which they labeled patients today would, in twenty years, be obsolete, replaced by a new lexicon? To Guthrie, the doctors' misplaced faith in the authority of these "names" exemplified as well as anything how the "whole psychological process . . . helps us not a drop and it makes us ache in places we can't mention."[5]

Despite what Guthrie told his sister, from the beginning of his stay at the hospital, in the admitting doctor's statement, the Brooklyn State medical staff had been floating Huntington's as a possible explanation. Over the course of his time there, they asked him about his mother repeatedly, until finally issuing a diagnosis six weeks into his stay.

Sickness with a chronic, terminal, hereditary illness put Guthrie in yet another stigmatized position. Moreover, it did so firmly, with scientific authority, and without any of the ambiguity that surrounded his marginal past as a poor white Okie, his contested conviction as a sex offender, and his blurry experience of "readjustment." But the certainty of the diagnosis conflicted, glaringly, with the sense of total disintegration brought on by the disease's symptoms. The doctors had provided a firm explanation for something unthinkable, indescribable, utterly irrational. It didn't help him any more than the "schizo-phreeny" diagnosis had helped Guthrie's voluble colleague.

From his factually baseless reply, back in 1942, in answer to Marjorie's question about whether he could contract the condition responsible for his mother's demise ("No, only women") to his letter to Mary Jo saying doctors had ruled it out, to the continuing doubts he would display even after the diagnosis, Guthrie's response to Huntington's looks a good deal like the protective strategy commonly known as *denial*. Given his up-close experience, in childhood, of the illness's intensely destructive nature, few could fault him for this reaction. But as the disease's symptoms closed in on him, his refusal to simply accept the diagnosis served a purpose consistent with his politics: it revealed his skepticism toward how medicine treated people, toward how it stigmatized them through diagnosis, evaluative processes, and imbalances of power between doctors and patients. The written record he made of his stay at Brooklyn State shows him contesting the theory and practice of treatment in the institution, in which patients' intimate lives became the raw material of professional methods and ways of building knowledge. At the same time, he found sustenance, and hope, in the social world of the patients, the unpredictable relationships and alliances that people forged out of the regular, prescribed routes of contact. His early optimism about the hospital, which never fully left him, transformed into a nascent theory of stigma as a revolutionary force, a shared medium for building collectivity across marginalized social categories, including sexuality. In the tall stack of handwritten pages he produced while a patient, he imagined shame as a way of making individual vulnerability the forge of collective solidarity.

The pages are also the clearest record we have of how Guthrie's illness fostered his understanding of politics rather than simply destroying the beloved image of him. Combining the thick description of ethnography, the emotional avowals of love letters, and the thought experiments of progressive theory, the hospital writings comprise one of the most substantial and compelling texts in all of his unpublished writing. There is no more probing, detailed document of a time when he was undeniably sick but still able to think and write critically and lucidly. And indeed, rather than understanding his response as denial, we might take it as a more critical attempt to exert some degree of agency in his medical treatment and make some mark on the culture of treatment, to shape the meaning of being sick with a neurological disease at this historical moment.

For a veteran of the Popular Front, that moment was largely a bleak one. The "degradation ceremonies," as Victor Navasky called them, mounted by the House Un-American Activities Committee and other anti-communist crusaders were closing in on him. In 1950, the right-wing journal *Counterattack* published a pamphlet titled *Red Channels: The Report of Communist Influence in Radio and Television*, containing a list of 151 communists and fellow travelers in the arts and entertainment industry; this list soon became the basis for the Hollywood blacklist. Guthrie friends and associates appearing on it included Will Geer, Pete Seeger, Alan Lomax, Earl Robinson, and others. Sophie Maslow, though not on the list, found her flourishing career suddenly shut out by major institutions, including broadcast television.

Although never Blacklisted per se, Guthrie suspected—correctly— that he was being tracked by the FBI. Despite his ambivalent optimism about Brooklyn State as he entered it, doctors there appear to have been among the lawmen's most reliable informants. There are at least 447 pages of FBI papers concerning him, spanning 1941 to 1955, at which point a field agent reported to his superiors that the singer was too sick to be worthy of further attention.[6] His name appears numerous times in HUAC documents: as a member of the People's Songs board and a writer for the *Daily World* and *Daily Worker*, for example. And the fearful postwar political climate did affect his life both directly and indirectly. He still played concerts, still wrote songs, still made recordings and wanted to make still more. But record labels, periodicals, and publishing houses shied away from working with figures who had expressed sympathy with communism or appeared at events alongside avowed communists. According to Pete Seeger, Guthrie's 1950 offer to do another series of recordings for the Library of Congress was turned down because the new folk-song archivist—Alan Lomax having fled to the UK to escape the atmosphere of persecution—was timid about political and professional blowback.[7] If nothing else, the menacing climate left the singer isolated; his later writings exhibit a far less palpable sense of a network of radical artists eagerly at the ready to collaborate on work in support of leftist causes.

Not everything that happened in the first years of the 1950s tells a story of mounting challenges. After adding Arlo to the family in 1947, and Joady in 1948, Woody and Marjorie welcomed their last child together, Nora Lee, in 1950. Relief for the family's ever-more-taxed financial stresses came in the form of a $10,000 advance when Seeger's new group the Weavers licensed his Dust Bowl ballad "Dusty Old Dust," retitled "So Long, It's Been Good to Know You." The new cash on hand allowed them to move out of the tiny Mermaid Avenue place into a spacious two-bedroom apartment a few blocks north in a housing development called Beach Haven. For the first time in his life, he had a dedicated work area in his home. Marjorie even purchased an upright piano for the place.

Another happy addition to the family, for a time at least, came in the form of a tape recorder, loaned by Howie Richmond, owner of a music publishing organization with which Guthrie was negotiating a contract. Beginning to imagine a future as a performing family, on the model of his longtime musical idols, the Carter Family, he made tapes of Arlo singing, and of Marjorie playing piano, in addition to working on his own songs.

After the Weavers made his song a bona fide hit, he acquired management and signed on with Richmond. The Weavers' label, Decca Records, offered him an audition and signed him to a contract.[8] It seemed possible that a real professional and personal revival was in the works. He canceled travel plans and hunkered down, as best he could, telling his friend Stetson Kennedy he wasn't coming to Florida to visit after all because "Marjorie needs my help. Everybody needs my help. And I need their help."[9]

However, there were signs he needed a much more involved kind of help. His sickness wasn't yet unavoidably visible. The symptoms of dyskinesia were in their early stages, easy to mistake for the alcoholic "shakes." But the contrast is stark between, say, the 1940 Library of Congress sessions and live performance recordings from 1949 and 1951.[10] In the latter, his speech and singing sound slightly slurred and dopey. The sparkling energy and eloquence of yore, on a document like the Library of Congress recordings, is absent. Marjorie sat beside him onstage, prompting him in between songs to tell certain stories and cutting him off when he rambled too much. Sometimes she succeeded in sparking a winning back-and-forth with him. But her presence was clearly a concession to his faltering abilities, and it sometimes irked the listeners: a tape of an April 1951 performance at St. John's College in Annapolis, Maryland, reveals audience members calling out "Let him sing!" as Marjorie discusses some aspect of Woody's songwriting onstage.[11]

Non-musical writing still gushed out of him: fragmented political rants, limericks, more pages of *Seeds of Man*, the novel-memoir that he'd begun in 1946 about a trip to the Southwest with his father. His style grew more abstract in certain endeavors and more direct in others. Increasingly, anti-Black racism's entrenchment—and its effects on his fellow citizens' lives through both structural and direct violence—preoccupied his thoughts and motivated his writing, songwriting, and visual work. It was becoming more personal, more connected to his own whiteness, intersecting more with the concerns about sexuality with which he had been struggling, in his writing and in his life.

On February 9, 1951, Guthrie suffered an acute rupture of his appendix; doctors told him he was lucky to have survived. He spent several weeks in Coney Island Hospital, the same place Cathy had died, then another few recuperating at home in Beach Haven. Housebound, he had some productive weeks making some remarkable paintings about racial violence. But then the situation worsened significantly.

There was more drinking, more rancor at home. In the past, there had been spells when Guthrie seemed possessed by dark moods, but a new, grimmer phase had begun. Oftentimes, when he wasn't angry, he was sullen, remote, and unreachable—emotional states commonly associated with Huntington's disease. Finally, in the fall of 1951, Marjorie kicked him out of the house, swearing that she would divorce him. At times in the coming months, he agreed that divorce was the best path; at others, he raged against her, or begged her to take him back. He wandered, crisscrossing the continent with stops in Florida, Texas, Oklahoma, and other far-flung locales. When he returned to New York, he slept on friends' couches and in cheap hotels that catered to the indigent. He complained of a "dizzy kind of sickness" that was destroying his sex drive; he attributed it, and his general malaise, to the heavy alcohol consumption he couldn't seem to stem.[12]

At the beginning of May 1952, he rented a room in Greenwich Village, in the same boarding house on Fourteenth Street where, almost exactly a decade earlier, his relationship with Marjorie had blossomed, during the production of *Folksay* and composition of *Bound for Glory*. It was a passive-aggressive message to his wife, who had begun dating other men. Hypocrisy be damned, Guthrie was acutely jealous. The couple's correspondence and phone conversations grew increasingly contentious and heated. Then, on May 15, the acrimony transformed into something much more sinister. One evening he showed up at the Beach Haven apartment and physically attacked her, waving a pair of scissors in her face. At the first chance, she fled to a neighbor's apartment. The neighbor contacted the police, who were satisfied, apparently, when Guthrie agreed to check himself into a hospital rather than be taken to the station house. Marjorie called their friend from the days of *Folksay*, the composer and singer Earl Robinson, who agreed to drive Guthrie the six and a half miles to Brooklyn's Kings County Hospital. Compared with the precise script with which he had filled notebooks just a year or two earlier, his handwritten letters and notes from Kings County look slovenly. But he entered an Alcoholics Anonymous program at the hospital and briefly got sober, even beginning to write a song titled "A. A. Boogy."

After a three-week stay in that facility, he made the mistake of going back to the Fourteenth Street room. Despairing of his lonely situation, he started drinking again, heavily. A few days after his return, on June 14, he phoned Marjorie and threatened to commit suicide by jumping from the roof of the rooming house.

This time, she called the police immediately; they picked him up and delivered him to Bellevue, Manhattan's renowned psychiatric facility. What that (in)famous institution's resident psychiatrists made of his abject state there is not totally clear. Marjorie told biographer Joe Klein that one day Woody phoned her and said, to her surprise, that he was out of the hospital. She suspected he had broken out, and called Bellevue, where the doctors said, as she recalled it, "Mrs. Guthrie, your husband is a very sick man and we don't know what to do with him."[13] Some sources say he was diagnosed with schizophrenia, as he would be in a few years.

A month later, on July 15, the day after his fortieth birthday, he was discharged. He went directly to Beach Haven, where he fought with Marjorie about her new boyfriend, and hit another low point, striking Arlo when the five-year-old complained about being sent to bed. Humiliated, he left, met up with Cisco Houston, and drank himself into a stupor. The next morning, he checked back into Kings County. A week later, on July 22, he entered Brooklyn State Hospital on the advice of Earl Robinson's brother-in-law, Joseph Wortis, a psychiatrist who had published essays in the *New Masses* and was well-known in communist circles.

At Brooklyn State, the doctor who wrote Guthrie's admission notes described "a thin, scrawny looking white male looking somewhat older than his 40-odd years," because of his lined face and weather-beaten features. He was "constantly jumping up from his chair" and his physical movements were "jerky and athetoid in nature. . . . Many of these movements are random and purposeless. His speech too is hesitant with many jerky pauses." He was "coherent and relevant," though "rambling," and prone to becoming "preoccupied so that it is difficult to interrupt him." He showed "no psychotic trends" and "no ideas of grandiosity, persecution or reference." Still, there was, apparently, no doubt that Guthrie was ill. But with what? The doctor mentions several possibilities, deferring a conclusion:

> This is one of those cases which stubbornly defies classification. In it, it has elements of schizophrenia, psychopathy, and a psychoneurotic anxiety state, not to mention the mental and personality changes occurring in Huntington's chorea, at this patient's age. As such, examiner chooses to defer diagnosis until such time as further observation has made the picture clearer.[14]

They needed more time to determine what treatment would mean. The uncertainty left Woody Guthrie room to wonder about the same question.

He could think about it in relatively comfortable surroundings. The director of Brooklyn State, Clarence Bellinger, who died during Guthrie's stay, "was credited with being one of the most progressive directors of institutions for the insane in the nation," according to his *New York Times* obituary.[15] On a typical day, on his way to the job he'd been assigned in the dining hall, Guthrie might have walked past the room where a group of patients were assembling that week's issue of the patient-run newspaper. Or he might have stopped off on his way to watch TV; there was one on every ward. Once he got to the commissary and got some food to eat before his shift, he would have sat down among patients of both sexes. Some of them could have been eating with visiting family members. A staff member might have announced a coming field trip to see the Dodgers play at Ebbets Field, or an athletic event in which Brooklyn State patients would do battle with a team from another institution. Walking back to his ward, he would have passed a beauty salon and multiple rooms where patients trained in occupational skills. The 28-acre facility loomed large in the Flatbush neighborhood. But when outsiders visited—hospital staff offered tours to the public—they discovered a world bearing little resemblance to the gruesome one they'd seen depicted in the Oscar-winning 1948 Hollywood film *The Snake Pit*, or in journalist Albert Deutsch's popular book-length exposé of state asylums from the same year, *The Shame of the States*. What they saw looked like a beacon of enlightened progress in a field that had long been tainted by abuse, exploitation, and maltreatment. According to the hospital's annual report for 1953, the culture of the "modern, progressive" institution "gave patients assurance that every effort was being made to restore them to health, and did result in making many more patients normal, useful citizens, able to support themselves and their families."[16]

A beacon of progressivism in an area of medicine long associated with neglect and mistreatment, Brooklyn State was an environment conducive to optimism. In the ideals espoused by Brooklyn State, at least, the hospital environment was itself a form of treatment, an attempt to administer to the whole person rather than a single issue or problem. This immersive approach helped patients realize their potential to be "normal, useful citizens."

The hospital's self-description raises questions about the meaning of treatment: how to treat (by means of a total living environment in addition to directed medical treatment); what should be treated (not just specific sicknesses but a condition of spoiled personhood, of being abnormal and unable to contribute to society); and what successful treatment should look like (not just recovery but a return to normality and usefulness). Notably, at least some of the hospital's doctors believed that giving potentially incriminating information about their patients to the FBI didn't contradict their roles as healers.

Guthrie was also interested in asking questions about the meaning of treatment, usually from very different angles, and with very different results. For instance, he believed that, fundamentally, mental hospitals treated the ill effects of capitalism: "The world's best monetary system [is] still a sickly disease worse than any this hospital can ever observe or tell about. [It causes] ninety nine percent of all these socalled [*sic*] crackups and wreckages."[17] But he also refused to divorce the word *treatment* from its association with the way people treat one another, the ways they extended the reach of their personal worlds—their goals, interests, fears, desires—to include those of others. From Guthrie's point of view, treatment in a hospital was by nature about how patients were treated— not as patients, but as people—by the individuals staffing the institution. In the aftermath of his appendicitis, he had opened up a new, blank notebook and dedicated it to thoughts on this matter, as if sensing it was moving to the center of his life:

> Book #13 (Thirteen) Doctors, Nurses, Hospitals, Healing, Diseases, Sick Spells (etc.) and how our labors of love are always somehow the only true cure for any or all said symptoms and nervous breakouts and nervous crackups.
> Doctuer [*sic*] Woody Guthrie[18]

While a patient at Brooklyn State, however, he did most of his writing on sequentially numbered pages of ruled loose-leaf paper, in strikingly neat handwriting. He wrote several hundred pages, the typical combination of letters, memoirs, songs, and poems with which he filled his notebooks. It is often very difficult to tell whether he is writing to someone in particular, although at times he clearly addresses Marjorie, or the children, or Pete Seeger. When Marjorie visited each week, he would hand her the pages. When he wasn't writing, the bulk of his time was spent doing his assigned chores, playing chess, chatting with other patients, and talking to staff doctors. The institution's rules, however relaxed, did not include permission for him to keep a guitar.

Despite all he had done to her, he believed he could still be a good husband to Marjorie. On many pages, he swore allegiance and tried to convince her that his illness did not go beyond his excessive drinking. The main factor in his breakdown was alcoholism brought on by self-imposed professional pressure, he claimed early on. He had become obsessive, tried too hard to become a "champion" songwriter, poet, essayist, and reader, and lost sight of the "unplanned element which makes life so warmly worth the working and the living." He condemned his "promiscuous" sexual past, which he also blamed on alcohol. Drinking had twisted his sexuality and destroyed his libido while simultaneously bringing about a state in which "your imagination runs wild with every hideous nightmare type of sexy dream you could ever think of."[19] He knew all of this was repulsive to her, he assured her; he understood why she would go looking for another partner. He had self-diagnosed, and apologizing to her was part of the treatment.

Throughout the pages written at Brooklyn State, he declared his love for her and the children again and again, as if for the first time. When he was out of the hospital, he promised, they would start a new life, touring the world as a musical family, the von Trapps of the Left. He would write more, get published more, demonstrate that he was a representative of the general working person, not just the Dust Bowl refugee—a legacy of his early work that he still carried as a burden.

For some years now, writing had provided him not just an emotional outlet and intellectual laboratory but a kind of physical reassurance. This aspect of its therapeutic dimension was becoming clearer than ever as the weeks in Brooklyn State passed:

> I sure do feel like a psycho something this morning, though; my control feels worse, dizzier, and all out of balance. Like I'm on another drunk. Stumbly. Fally. About 1/2 blind. I feel afraid everybody will notice how bad I look and how much worse I move around. Restless. Jittery. Jumpy about anything and everything . . . tried to help stack and dry our morning dishes; but I fell around on all the men in the kitchen so bad I felt plumb ashamed of myself . . . keep craving to find me a chain and a table spot to set down and write my feelings on, but, feel all confused and all bollixed up, all mixed up; all screwed up. Hard to control my arms and my hands unless I'm here over my page putting my psycho feelings down in writing; writing is the only kind of action I really feel free and easy at.[20]

Writing provided a feeling of coordination that eased his ever-more disorganized sense of his body and mind. One day he saw a young fellow patient, a "boy," sitting at a table scratching at a piece of paper with a pencil, while a number of others stared at him. Then Guthrie looked closer. The pencil was leaving no marks. It had no lead. And yet he recognized himself in this image, understood that just the physical act of writing, beyond the content of what was written, could provide a kind of succor.

Sometimes the other patients stared at him when he wrote, the same way people gawked when he would walk the streets of Coney Island scribbling notes and observations. Some of his ward-mates came over and tried to read what he was writing. "One big fat kid teases me and says I'm stir crazy but good for killing myself like I do to write this letter I never mail. He doesn't know how correct his remarks are."[21]

He watched and listened as his neighbor, a "Mohammedan fellow," made odd sounds and movements in his sleep. He decided the man was dreaming about chasing geese.

He spent time trying to learn Castilian Spanish from another patient.

There was a hundred-year-old man living on the ward; the other patients thought he and Guthrie looked alike.

Observations like these supported his contention that being in the hospital provided him a perch as a "scholar." But every hospital patient has one main job to do: being a sick person. The job requirements include not just getting better but, more importantly, providing data, evidence, and other raw material for increasing the precision of diagnostic science and treatment, particularly for a mysterious condition, or one about which little is known, like Huntington's chorea. He was in the hospital for treatment, but being there meant being treated, over and over again, as an object of research, what disability studies scholars Sharon Snyder and David Mitchell call a "seemingly inexhaustible evaluation regimen" that reinforces the patient's sense of identification with their sickness.[22] It meant repeatedly sharing intimate details of his life, and being told over and over that his illness defined his being—because in a hospital, no matter how many clubs and activities are on offer, it does. And this made the hospital's staff a particularly valuable asset for the FBI's efforts to keep tabs on him.

Although apparently unaware that his intimacy with the doctors fueled his surveillance by a fiercely conservative law enforcement agency, he longed for a truly scientific therapy that might liberate him from having to give himself up to the institution, share his life with the doctors in a way that would confine him to what sociologist Talcott Parsons, in a book published the previous year, called the "sick role."[23] It was a category that justified the marginalization of the ill and disabled, marking them as deviant, a threat to the social order requiring containment and treatment. Perhaps conceiving of him in this manner made it easier for doctors to feed information about him to the FBI, who clearly considered him a threat to the polity.

But he didn't need to know this troubling fact to become acutely critical of the way his doctors were conducting the case. Always alert to imbalances of power, he was bent on trying to reimagine how to understand mental illness and its treatment. As it stood, the psychiatrist's relationship with their patient was a pale, deadpan parody of what he considered true intimacy. Institutional authority *compelled* the patient to speak. The doctor's role was to observe, and to perform a personally disinvested kind of listening. Supposedly dedicated to soothing the patient's innermost wounds, it was a model prone to shut down "union": the dialogic, social, boundary-shattering model of human interaction that Guthrie so prized. Hence his poem from the ward, "Psyko Story":

> *My highest ambition*
> *Is to sit down across*
> *A table and hear some*
> *Psychiatrist tell me*
> *His life story*[24]

He wasn't simply imagining turning the tables on his shrink. Guthrie felt people were as nourished, as present in the world, when they were in the position of a listener as when they were sharing deep, long-guarded parts of themselves. His psychiatrists, however, seemed to want to avoid that dynamic and escape into the abstractions of diagnosis.

Years earlier, in the autobiographical *Bound for Glory*, he'd represented these values in a section about becoming, as a young man, a kind of therapist for people in his then home of Pampa, Texas. Amused that the townspeople interpret his practice to be fortune-telling, Guthrie insists that he is simply listening closely to their plaints, essentially mimicking the work of a professional listener like a psychoanalyst or a detective. He notices details that seem irrelevant or marginal. He pays attention to the comportment of the people talking to him. He'd put these skills into practice while at Kings Hospital, just prior to his time at Brooklyn State:

> I learned twice as much (by trying to talk to three men and to get them to tell me about their own selves) as I learned by talking to the psycho-doctor in back of all the little locked doors. I played checkers and chess and all sorts of card games with three men, not to see if I could best them at any of the games, but, more to keep them talking about their own ideas and past happenings in their lives. I listened and compared their hurts and miseries and good and bad habits of action to my own and this was more what slowly proved to me that my own case was not

quite the worst in this world. I felt my own self pity, self worry, and my own pride and my own fear fade and retreat back into absolute zero.

Pacing those floors up and down both of those wards over in Kings County G Building, I talked to almost enough, if not quite enough good people, patients, visitors, doctors, nurses, healers, squealers, rocker and reelers, to have all the same healing effects on me as the finest kind of group therapy would have.[25]

As professional listeners, psychiatrists had twisted this principle, bending what they heard into conformity with predetermined templates, the "big long scientific name[s]" they used to designate patients. From the ground zero of Brooklyn State, he summed this idea up in another biting little poem, "My Voices": "All my psycho does is ask me do I hear voices / And all I tell them is yes / When anybody sings or talks to me."[26]

Listening to someone, he believed, ought to open up the world by relaxing a person's sense of where they ended and everyone (and everything) else began. But in his view, doctors listened in a way that narrowed the world, attempting to affirm predetermined categories and closing down possibility in their quest to find certain behaviors, such as "hearing voices," symptomatic. True listening was a sensory experience that grounded him even as it held out the potential of transformation. In contrast, the doctors kept asking him the same questions, with no clear aim beyond reconfirming their already held assumptions.

This distrust of professional talk therapy had political underpinnings, and led Guthrie to favor a type of treatment that today sounds frightening, but that also had the endorsement of Joseph Wortis, the communist psychiatrist who had recommended he check into Brooklyn State. In the journal *New Masses* and a book called *Soviet Psychiatry*, Wortis had criticized his own profession, in its Euro-American configuration, for its preoccupation with the unconscious and other psychoanalytic paradigms. He felt that the Freudian tradition upheld the ruling order of power by denying social and political factors in mental illness. Rather than talk therapy, he advocated a treatment called Insulin Shock Therapy (IST), which he had studied in Europe with its inventor. In the US, Brooklyn State was pioneering the use of IST. According to muckraker Albert Deutsch, Brooklyn State had "achieved a nationwide reputation for its outstanding results with insulin and other types of shock treatment." He added that "virtually every patient who is admitted gets an early chance at shock therapy, if suitable for such treatment."[27]

The process certainly looked like a horrid scene from the movie *The Snake Pit*. Doctors used insulin to induce a coma and seizures. The patient would be revived by having water poured into their nose through an elevated tube. But advocates like Wortis touted an 80 percent success rate in the treatment of schizophrenia, even as critics contested the accuracy of that figure and no one seemed able to pinpoint precisely how the therapy worked. Ideologically, both Wortis and Guthrie considered it a viable, more democratic alternative to psychoanalytic talk sessions. In Guthrie's case, though, the appeal of IST was based on mistaken presumptions, probably willful ones. He imagined it as discursive, as providing unmediated access to the unconscious. It became a sketchpad for his fantasies of what therapy might do, might be like.

Even back in his first writing from the hospital, his letter to sister Mary Jo, he'd spun a yarn about having received an insulin injection and how he found its effects fruitful: "I was delirious and talking and singing all outta my head, but I still caught up with a long list of the very best song ideas I ever so far found."[28] Nine or ten days after actually being moved to the IST ward, in a section addressed to Pete Seeger, he again (mis-)described the procedure in a telling manner:

> I was scared witless when I first moved over here and heard everybody yell and moan and groan in their comas and shocks, but, when I saw how they laff [*sic*] their heads off telling one another what you screamed about (you can't remember your own actions. Idea is for your subconscious mind to call up to plain view all the enemies, all your personal problems and trouble and to argue them out to your own soul in your own best lingo). You listen to several other guys and they listen to you, see, then you spend the next few hours telling Bill what he yelled about and he tells you what you yelled about. Your actual fight for your own survival builds up all your own personal reasons to survive and to keep on living; and the whole experience everybody tells me is the very best medicine to calm down jumpy nerves you can find.[29]

This account is largely fanciful. Patients undergoing the procedure did frequently scream and moan, but there was no discursive process to the therapy, no eruptions of speech and thus no words that patients could tell each other they had said while comatose. (In another passage in the hospital writing, Guthrie claims to have heard a patient in an induced insulin coma singing the traditional song "Wabash Cannonball," and muses that the treatment will stimulate his songwriting.) Nevertheless, the fantasy is a sharp, telling one: he imagines the therapy as a democ-ratized, do-it-yourself revision of the false listening he associates with his encounters with doctors. Guthrie imagines the pinnacle of modern treatment as an argument-dialogue with oneself, and then a processing session with one's fellow patients, after gaining quasi-magical access to the unconscious. The effectiveness of the imagined process depended on eliminating the participation of professional mediators. It was a protest against the growing authority of the field of psychology, which rested on abstractions and suppressed the fact that talk therapy was, in fact, a relationship between two people (or more, in the case of group therapy).

Six weeks into his stay at Brooklyn State, with no set diagnosis, his doctors moved him into the IST ward. As he waited for the doctors' final decision on treatment, he repeatedly expressed his desire to be given IST. But his experience of the hospital had also led him to become increasingly fixated on the possibilities of connections between patients, and the chal-lenges the hospital posed to collective ideals like those he saw embedded in the concept of *union*, as he'd described it to Marjorie nearly a decade previous.

His physical distress was intensifying. It was also becoming harder to isolate what was happening to him physically from his emotional state, which he described in highly material terms:

> Here's my funny feeling over me again. That lost feeling. That gone feel-ing. That old empty whipped feeling. Shaky. Bad control. Out of con-trol. Jumpy. Jerky. High tension. Least little thing knocks my ego down below zero mark. Everything cuts into me and hurts me several times more than it should. Everything hits me. A word or a look or an action of anybody here deals me a misery. I've not got strength to go on, nor to see things in the light they should be. No bodily (physical) pains; just like my arms and legs and hands and feet and my whole body belongs to somebody else and not to me; so ashamed of myself I want to run hide away where nobody can find me nor see how bad I feel.[30]

Pains isolated in specific parts of the body weren't the problem with this "lost," "gone," "empty whipped feeling"; rather, the challenge he faced was the disintegration of the wholeness of his being, as though his "whole body belongs to someone else." Not only could he not keep still, but he also had no firm covering to protect himself from outside, from other people—he was a walking open wound, vulnerable to humiliation by any look or attention paid to him. And even that desire for protection was part of the problem. It was as though the dyskinesia had shattered any semblance of a shell protecting him from the outside world. What he was describing was boundarylessness, and the cure would be to embrace it, but he couldn't.

He continued in the same passage:

> Worse than this, I ask myself what makes me [break my head] to try to hide my weak jitters? Why don't I break down and spill them out all over to the first person I see? Why don't I? Why?
>
> It would all be over (the worst of it) if I could cave in and fall down and tell everybody how I feel. My trouble isn't the dizzy spell nor the pains not in my [weakly] feeling, but my worst pains come because I spend every drop of my bodily strength trying to hide my trouble away so you can't see it; trying to keep you from reading it in my face, or my eyes, or in any words I'd say or in that stumbly way I walk around.[31]

These remarkable passages show that Guthrie's definition of illness itself ranges far beyond a set of symptoms, a physical state, or even, in a conventional fashion, a psychological state. He uses his feeling of fundamental disorientation to reframe how we typically understand sickness, from the perspective of the medical institution. He suggests that from the patient's perspective, illness simply cannot be removed from the web of relationships with the people one is around. Sickness is social. He continues:

> We never try to help our coal miners till our mine caves in; we never can let you help us till our pride caves in, and till our fears cave in.
>
> This business of trying to hide our weaker feelings surely surely must be in all of us. Surely I'm not the only man on this ward that hides all this as long as he can. Everybody does it; everybody tries to hide it so's you'll never guess how bad and how empty we feel.[32]

Guthrie's writing had now shifted toward the first-person plural, toward a collective sense of "us," however vexed. He had for years been interested in how stigma operated politically. Here, in Brooklyn State, he had a new opportunity to explore how it both eroded and stimulated people's capacity to enter into empowering, mutually supportive relationships. Perhaps shame was even more powerful than he had once thought.

Around this same time, five or six weeks into this stay, he began to explicitly consider an issue that had been a shadowy presence during his first go-round with therapy, three years previously, at the Quaker Emergency Service Readjustment Center: same-sex desire. Mulling over shame and solidarity in a time when the vast majority of Americans deemed homophobia far more normal than homosexuality, his writing begs the same question as did the events of 1949: How far was he willing to extend his empathy for the shamed and could it include people whose identity was bound up with their "deviant" sexual lives?

In a different time, Guthrie might have readily connected the plight of gay men on the ward with him to his own anger at American sexual mores and the institutions that enforced them. In fact, virtually no models existed that would have encouraged identification across these lines and, in theory, made it possible for him to overcome the homosexual panic that, at the core of the Left, still infused notions of masculinity. He had either never come across Emma Goldman's writing in defense of homosexuality or had rejected it out of hand. Although he surely knew the composer Marc Blitzstein, who lived an openly gay life, as well as Marjorie's colleague Merce Cunningham and his partner John Cage, Guthrie never commented on the matter. And yet, at Brooklyn State, he began, in a small way, to see matters differently.

To live in a mental hospital was to dwell in an environment suffused in talk about sex's relationship to mental health and, in particular, about nonconformist sexual practices like homosexuality. Indeed, it was likely the only place, outside of certain subcultures, that such discussion wasn't viewed with suspicion, as obscene or even, particularly in the postwar era, seditious. It was, therefore, a place that might cultivate otherwise unlikely realizations and affiliations around sexuality.

Hardly any matter had greater weight in how the patients were being assessed and how they were being asked to assess themselves. The doctors asked Guthrie, repeatedly, whether he had ever been attracted to other

men. They also asked if he was attracted to young girls, whether he masturbated, and whether he experienced sexual impotence. He reported that
he had answered "no" to all the inquiries other than the one about masturbation, which, he insisted as per usual, "is entirely natural and normal."[33]

But the matter of homosexuality permeated the hospital's atmosphere; it was, as we've seen, something psychiatrists of the time considered linked to a huge range of pathologies. "Being around a place of
this kind," he wrote in mid-September 1952, after about six weeks in
Brooklyn State, "gives me not a few, but many chances to reconsider all
my past and present thinking along the various lines of homosexualities
we hear about and see every minute around us." He does not mean that
he observes actual sexual activity taking place between men. He means it
is something people regularly discuss, regularly think about. As a result,
he thinks back to his time spent on the road, a geographical and cultural
space known for its queerness:

> Being here makes me think how many other times I've been picked up
> while hitch hiking and given the age old proposition by numerous fine
> gentlemen. The first few times I flew off my bean and said crazy things
> to the man which made him feel a good deal worse than he was feeling
> before he met me. I had no basic knowledge as to how or why he got
> like he was. I just lost most of my control and ended up feeling awful
> glad to get away from said man and on my way. I later learned that he
> is a sick man and possibly a little glad to be *sick in his own healthy way.*
> I had a lot of long talks with different ones after that and found all of
> them to be most willing to delve as deep or deeper into the subject as I
> could understand.[34]

Guthrie's hospital stay has generated a compelling, if awkward, story
of his knee-jerk aversion to gay men that is loosening its grip. Essentially,
he describes a historical narrative in ideas about what sorts of difference
deserve civil rights and protections. In Guthrie's former sense of homosexuality, men interested in sex with other men are, essentially, monsters
who cause a panic reflex and need to be immediately denounced, if not
attacked. Reflecting on such experiences from within Brooklyn State, he
notes that he now sees the gay man as sick, "and possibly a little glad
to be sick in his own healthy way." As a statement of solidarity, this is

certainly as faint as they come. Still, intimacy has opened the potential for understanding; his encounters with gay men have become notably "deep or deeper," and he has begun to occupy for them that valued position of non-professional listener.

How much this passage expands Woody Guthrie's social justice laurels may not be the main point. More salient is the fact that thoughts like these had become historically possible—and that they were being thought in what at first might seem fairly bizarre circumstances: by a sick person in a mental hospital. And truly laudable is the extent to which Guthrie was (again) able to use his own stigmatization, marginalization, and abjection to further his embrace of the so-called abnormal, of others maligned and shamed because of their difference. At this early but clearly manifest stage in the illness, he transformed being sick into a remarkable means of insight and powerful political *resource*. In the first place, it opened him up to listening, genuinely, to a type of person he would have previously deemed too frightful a conversational partner. It also produced a compelling little turn of phrase: "sick in his own healthy way." With this paradoxical, self-canceling phrase, Guthrie wants to redeem not just gay men but sickness itself. That is, he detaches sickness from the well-being of the supposedly sick individual. In doing so, he opens up a vision of stigmatization as a resilient form of difference, of dissidence. Indeed, it is not hard to imagine him using the phrase to describe himself.

There still remained the matter of his own condition's diagnosis, of doctors uttering the words that would explain the trajectory of his life and possibly reconnect him, bodily, with his mother. One day, also around six weeks into the hospital stay, Guthrie was feeling especially dizzy and jittery. He went in for a consultation with a doctor. Narrating his condition, he used some choice words to describe the process of alcohol detox.

Eventually, the doctor interrupted a long, colorful series of complaints about the damage done from being a drunk: "Don't you think 45 days is a long time to stay dizzy from alcohol withdrawal?"

People in alcohol withdrawal typically have far more aches and pains than Guthrie was reporting, the doctor added for emphasis. Then he asked the singer to walk up and down the room. Guthrie didn't record whether the doctor said anything after observing his little stroll.

A few days later, he was lying in bed when a group of doctors and nurses surrounded him. After they conferred with one another a bit, someone addressed him directly, asking, "Did your mother die of Huntington's chorea?" He answered yes.

It was a startlingly direct answer from someone who had been so consistently cagey about the matter for so long. But recording this incident in his loose-leaf pages, he still presented a cloudy understanding of the illness:

> Got me worried a bit. Wondering. Could it be that I'm taking an early stage of that same disease? Sure love to read some books on it so I'll sorta know partly what to expect.
>
> It sure does put a new light on the subject, doesn't it? Does it?[35]

It is tempting to wonder why, if he was wondering about these questions in earnest, he didn't simply ask them for more details about the disease and what they were thinking, and there are several possible explanations for why he didn't. Perhaps, because of the rarity of the condition, they simply did not know. Perhaps the environment of the institution (and of this era) was such that patients did not feel entitled to ask questions of their doctors, even basic ones of this sort.

But the all-but-absurd claim that this suggestion "put a new light on the subject" must certainly come from a continuing resolve to resist diagnosis, resist letting the physicians' language stick to him. Of course, again, who could blame someone for wanting to stave off a diagnosis with a disease as destructive as Huntington's? And yet, all of this haziness and uncertainty, all of this odd apparent resistance to knowing, is also certainly a form of passive resistance to being categorized. It is an attempt to refuse the foreclosure of possibility—not just the possibility of recovery, or life itself, but of further relations with other people that aren't overdetermined by his being someone with Huntington's. As long as he is sick in some unspecified way, he can claim adjacency to, and empathy with, a variety of stigmatized, shamed categories. But having Huntington's would make it all the more challenging to be "sick in his own healthy way."

Soon after leaving Brooklyn State, in the notebook he'd labeled "Doctors, Nurses, Hospitals," he wrote a short poem of grievance about institutions authorized to separate people from their own worlds, and confine them in isolation. It laid out a continuum between the supposedly therapeutic (hospitals) and the supposedly correctional (prisons). To Guthrie, these were now clearly all state forces of incarceration and social control:

> *Hospital Too Full*
> *I see every hospital too full;*
> *I see every jail house too full;*
> *I see every prison overloaded for hell;*
> *I see every chain gang too damned crowded;*
> *Every insane asylum packed and overpacked*[36]

The lines are simple and repetitive. But the bareness with which he describes these images also creates a sense of rising tension, of walls about to crumble. Where these institutions were attempting to isolate individuals who challenged the norms of society, he was seeing powerful masses bringing the forces of incarceration to the breaking point. The slow violence of these spaces could only go on so long. In their arrogant exercise of their power, they would create the collective forces that would destroy them.

Chapter Ten

LOOK AWAY

GUTHRIE LEFT BROOKLYN STATE HOSPITAL on September 24, 1952, his discharge papers bearing the diagnosis of Huntington's chorea. He could no longer skirt the question of his mother's illness and the source of the "queer" feelings he'd described as early as during the war. More recently, he'd suffered from episodes of rage and improper impulse control; now it was clear that these spells were early manifestations of the dementia all but certain to descend on him in coming years. No longer could he or those around him blame drinking for the slightly odd movements and speech patterns he was exhibiting. His past was rewritten; his future, in fundamental ways, prescribed.

A diagnosis of a major illness, in other words, brings with it a particular story, stamped with the authority of Western medicine. It has been understandably hard for anyone telling Guthrie's story to resist streamlined accounts of his creative output in the late 1940s and early-to-mid 1950s as a matter merely of decline. Huntington's disease can be used to explain why he wasn't putting out records, or for that matter books. It can be used to explain why work from this period is so different—the song lyrics more personal, the writings and visual art more surreal. The story this book has been telling has suggested that the illness becomes a convenient way of accounting for (and judging negatively) an unfamiliar, less accessible Woody Guthrie, and continuing the marginalization of this work, to the detriment of our understanding of Guthrie's art and politics.

But the point has not just been to counter the presumption that Huntington's and the accompanying disability necessarily resulted in work that was diminished, diluted, defective. Another story here is what the ill-ness may have *enabled*—what it may have allowed him to express that he hadn't previously been able to, when he was busy (and capable of) being the Woody Guthrie widely known and loved. In particular, his sense of having a "queer" or extraordinary body led him to become preoccupied with the body's role in determining the shape of our lives, and made it possible for him to tell certain truths in this regard.

Guthrie's work on race and racism in the early 1950s presents the most dramatic challenge to any simple narrative of artistic decline. It was riveting, cutting-edge political art addressing the cause of the most fundamental rift within American culture: white supremacism. It was also deeply, though rarely explicitly, personal, addressing his own back-ground and suggesting that he recognized something of his origins in this violent history. The work wasn't easy to look at or easy to be inspired by. But it illustrated a dramatic, newly complex, self-interrogating attitude toward racial politics, formed as much *because* he was sick as *despite* the fact that he was sick.

After Guthrie left Brooklyn State Hospital, he made a cross-continental beeline to the home of one of his most consistently reliable caretakers and advocates: Will Geer's ranch in Topanga Canyon, California, near Los Angeles. He was still downplaying the now-official diagnosis, even with his closest friends. In a letter to Pete Seeger, he continued to blame alcohol addiction for his troubles: "There are lots of kinds of chorea and nobody is plumb sure about what kind I'll most likely have, if any. . . . They say it ain't deadly or fatal, so my days in yonders hospital weren't quite wasted if they got me off the bottle."[1] Alcoholism had come to seem, oddly, like a panacea; it was a condition from which recovery was possible.

Marjorie, though, had had enough. It was now more than a decade after they'd first met at Almanac House; they had three children and had lived through an array of challenges and catastrophes, both global and intimate, together. But in the months leading up to his hospitalization, his erratic and irresponsible behavior had entered newly grave, threatening territory. Moreover, the Huntington's diagnosis meant he would never return to be being a viable partner, much less the thoughtful man of the wartime and early-postwar years. But their bond remained strong; she visited him throughout his time at Brooklyn State, making sure he and the kids stayed in touch. The couple's letters from this period occasionally reach the intensity of those from the wartime years, but they oscillate wildly between anger, avowal, and optimistic pronouncements that they will stay close as friends. Although he sometimes claimed to her that he had overcome his symptoms, he could also be more candid: "My chorea isn't kidding these days. I feel it as a nervous fluttery heart condition with a slight lack of control over my body at times. I feel it sort of steady now at all times and a bit more so sometimes than at other times. I don't [get] entirely lost nor entirely gone but partly so part of the time."[2]

Out in Topanga, he settled into a little hut on the lush, sylvan property where the now-blacklisted Geer lived with his wife and kids, curating and managing an outdoor performance space called the Theatricum Botanicum. Guthrie spent long days lazing around, punctuated by spells of writing, painting, even sculpting. In left LA circles, word spread that he had settled in the area, and a trickle of young radicals and musicians came through to meet him.

Marjorie had started dating, and she suggested he find another woman. In response, he told her he was actively looking for his next wife, and that "she must be darkskinned. She can't be blonde nor light-colored."[3] He told friends he wanted his next wife to be African American. Nonetheless, one day in Topanga, he encountered a young white woman in a barn the Geers had set up as an art studio. She was at work on a pottery wheel. Her name was Anneke Van Kirk; she was twenty-one years old, a banjo player and singer, physically robust, and living with her fiancé nearby. They began taking walks in the hills around Topanga. As Woody and Anneke spent more time together, she became disenchanted with her groom-to-be, and finally broke off the engagement. Early in 1953, Guthrie returned with her to New York and they got married.

Guthrie's stated desire to set up house with a woman of color has a creepy, fetishistic quality, suggesting he was objectifying and exoticizing Black femininity in this imaginary "darkskinned" woman. It was another instance of his politics of intimacy being both self-serving and naïve, the presumption that being emotionally and sexually intimate with a Black person was necessarily an anti-racist act. But, in a clumsy and unthinking way, it may also have reflected his deepening preoccupation with racial politics: even to probe his own place and past through this lens. After all, intimacy and sexuality were the devices, the instruments, that had for so long helped him think on a grander, more critical scale.

He was on surer ground when he wrote "Post War Junk Pile" while still in Topanga. The poem connected the decline of the Left to the persistence of racial injustice in the US. That persistence, he wrote, embodied the failure, the incomplete business, of the Popular Front era. He had risked his life in Europe as part of a global fight against fascism; part of the purpose was to destroy domestic fascism as manifest in the form of racism. But "racey hate" was "flying exactly like it ever did only a little bit smoother and a little bit worser than it ever flew before." Racism plus the decline of unions and the continuing idolization of capitalism had brought him to the edge of dissolution: "It's a big wonder I've not broke down and done a good deal worser than I've done so far," went one line.[4] He could deny the specific diagnosis all he wanted to, but his experience in the mental health system, as a person deemed sick, was now helping him frame his politics.

This poem appeared in one of the strangest, most remarkable documents that he was ever to produce. In a large hundred-page ledger apparently procured during his army days, "Post War Junk Pile" took up a page among striking images he was making with paint, pencil, and ink, occasionally interspersing a phrase, sentence, or prose poem. Many of the images featured figures in KKK-like garb. On some pages he brushed the words *Peace* and *Vote*. But throughout the book, on nearly every page, he scrawled the phrases *Southern White*, *White Only*, and variations on them, in large, graffiti-like block letters. The images and words in this notebook expanded on those featured in a group of paintings he'd made in 1951, while recovering from appendicitis. These showed acts of violence, or impending ones, performed by figures who looked like Klansmen or law enforcement officers. The victims in the images were sometimes engaged in sexual activity.[5]

Guthrie's turn to a more visual mode suggests that he found this material, this topic, difficult to narrate in words, whether in prose, verse, or song lyric. On the whole, the work has a haunted feel. It was as though he was returning to his past, his origins among Southern white people. Because he loved some of these people, he couldn't disconnect himself from a certain sense of shame about his past. Although clearly addressing racism and racial violence, issues he identified at that moment as the most challenging, the work seemed to bring to the surface deeply personal, difficult-to-express internal battles, including a sense of shame and alienation connected to his own body and its whiteness. The work also gestured toward a signal event in his family of origin—his father's involvement in the lynching of Laura Nelson and her son L.D. in 1911, the year before Charley Guthrie of Okemah, Oklahoma, named his second son after the first president from the South since the Civil War, Woodrow Wilson.

Woody Guthrie's reputation as a hero of social justice hinges mainly on his support for the labor movement, as well as his more general buoying of the concerns of a supposedly raceless "common man." In part, this is because we consider his career to have faded before a broad coalition of the Left—a new Left—made civil rights one of its central concerns. According to historian Glenda Gilmore, however, that the reigning story of Black civil rights begins in the 1950s rather than the 1930s is a legacy of anti-communist panic. In fact, radicals, with African American communists in the lead, had been fighting Jim Crow, white supremacist violence, and other forms of racism for decades. Indeed, the purview of 1930s anti-racist radicals extended well beyond voting rights and segregation in schools and public facilities, the main preoccupations of the church-led movement of the 1950s. Obscuring this deeper history "erased the complexity of a drive to eliminate the economic injustices wrought by slavery, debt peonage, and a wage labor system based on degraded black labor."[6] Over the course of the 1940s, Guthrie read about these efforts in the *Daily Worker* and talked through them with friends and associates in the CPUSA. As a consequence, he absorbed this version of the civil rights movement.

But in the work he made in the early 1950s he also brought a special purchase to the issue, a perspective shot through with his critical perspectives on sex, shame, and stigma, as honed in his experiences of the previous few years. It was some of the last extended work he was able to produce before symptoms of Huntington's made it all but impossible for him to write, paint, or play music, and it looks like nothing else of its time. And though he couldn't have known exactly when he would stop being able to work, this material does have the feel of someone struggling to bring their expressive life full circle, taking their last possible chance to attempt a reckoning with a troubling, traumatic past. In both its explicit-ness and its framing of whiteness itself as a concern, the work also has a strikingly forward-looking feel.

Against the grain of his origins, the man who began his autobiogra-phy, "I could see men of all colors bouncing along in the boxcar," had for nearly a decade made fighting racism a part of his artistic and polit-ical mission. According to Gilmore, "African Americans [of the Popular Front–era radical left] always used geopolitics to fight domestic racism," and Guthrie had absorbed this lesson, seeing a virulent, homegrown fas-cism—a direct relative of Nazism—in domestic racism and the Jim Crow laws with which the state sanctioned and enforced it.[7] Thus, he supported the far-reaching agenda of the pre-1950s civil rights movement: cam-paigns against lynching, housing discrimination, police violence, biased white judges and juries, poll taxes, and racialized economic inequality, which extended well beyond the boundaries of the South.

In postwar New York in particular, Black communists had an espe-cially audible voice in the struggles, and they were increasingly targeting what they called "legal lynching": that is, police violence and other mis-carriages of the judicial system that directly harmed African Americans. The topics of Guthrie's anti-racist songs from this era mirror many of the particular cases toward which an interracial New York left directed vibrant, grassroots efforts, even as more mainstream civil rights groups, like the NAACP, were becoming anxious about any association with rad-icals. In "The Blinding of Isaac Woodward" (which, on August 18, 1946, he sang before over twenty-five thousand at a benefit at Lewisohn Sta-dium, to "the biggest and loudest applause that I've ever got anywhere I've been"), he described South Carolina police officers' violent abuse of a Black veteran.[8] In "The Ballad of Rosa Lee Ingram," he honored a Black woman from Georgia whose sons had been executed for beating a white man they had found in the act of raping her. In "The Ferguson Brothers' Killing" he turned to a case just a few miles east of Brooklyn in Freeport, Long Island, where police had murdered two unarmed Black men who had earlier summoned law enforcement after being snubbed at a coffee shop. In "Trenton Frameup" and "Buoy Bells from Trenton," he advocated on behalf of six African American men from New Jersey accused of the murder of a white man in 1948, a song that connected the skewed workings of the justice system to those that had condemned Sacco and Vanzetti to die in electric chairs.[9]

At the same time, race wasn't exclusively a Black-white issue for Guthrie; he wanted an inclusive, multicultural nation. He condemned discrimination against Japanese Americans in *Bound for Glory*, and opposed the internment camps set up in the West during the war, at one point telling Marjorie he planned to write a "lost home song for the Japanese evacuees."[10] More famously, in one of his most poignant, accomplished, and lauded songs from the postwar era, "Deportee (Plane Wreck at Los Gatos)," he penned a set of lyrics commemorating the deaths of twenty-eight migrant Mexican workers killed while being flown back to their native country by immigration officials.

But this body of largely visual work took up the issue of Black-white race relations in an entirely different idiom. It was as though his perspective on these matters had exploded, leaving the pages strewn with shrapnel. The moral authority in the voice of songs like "Deportee" and "Blinding of Isaac Woodard" [sic] was absent; authority, in general, had vacated the work. Instead, Guthrie seemed possessed by some spectacular compulsion. In the bound volume begun in Topanga, the very repetition of the words *White* and *Southern*, and the dramatic, explosive manner in which they appeared, was the most dramatic part of the book. The words riddled its pages like scars.

It was far from obvious what the words were meant to express as they spread out over the pages of the notebook. In many instances, they appeared along with images that were clear allusions to violence by the KKK or other white supremacists. But why were the words written on a page of animal drawings by one of the Geers' young children, or at the top of "Name Wanted," a prose poem written from the point of view of a nurse in a mental hospital? Was the theme here a general sense of Southern white people as the source of the nation's racial strife? Or was he alluding to more particular, complicated feelings about his own personal origins in those liminal Southern regions, Oklahoma and Texas? Or perhaps some combination of both?

The lack of clarity suggested that the work was reckoning with the way racial violence and injustice permeated his being, in particular during the formative years in which his father's then-considerable social authority in his hometown depended on his endorsement of white supremacy, to the point, it would seem, of the murder of a Black mother and son. What he was representing was psychologically complicated, not reducible to slogans, perhaps not even adaptable to narrative.

"Me and my background are always having a fight," he wrote in 1947.[11] Indeed, writing that same year about visiting relatives still living in Pampa, Texas, he portrayed how wholly *other* they seemed, how outside their world he felt, and the determining role their anti-Black racism played in engendering this sense of distance:

> Makes me feel lots better to go around and shake hands with all of my relations every so often. But the kind of lives they live and lead look like the old trap to me. They tried to read my sign on my guitar "This Machine Kills Fascists" and nobody there could say the word fascist. They say "niggers are born according to the bible to be the beasts of burden for the white man!" The negro section is flat and low and dirty and muddy and they still call it niggertown.
>
> They spent more time in fighting and scratching each other than in reading or even listening.
>
> [. . .]
>
> If I hooked up with them I'd let myself and my ideas get pushed out the rear window. I recalled all too clear that this has long been the way things ran for us. I can see the bigger view now of the jobs that you and me work together on. We'll have to show them how to sing, dance, and make up songs and most of all how to have kids and raise them like humans. I remember now why I started walking out and down that Pampa road back in 1936.[12]

Addressing Marjorie, he could coherently, if uncomfortably, describe his alienation from his past, from a life that might have remained his had he not "started walking out and down that Pampa road." At least during a happier time in their relationship, the remedy for his ills came from familiar places: self-expression, domesticity, Marjorie herself.

The work that culminated in the "Southern White" notebook suggested that in the early 1950s he was still struggling to understand how his troubled past figured in his troubled present. Or, perhaps more accurately, he was representing in paint and ink his very struggle to look at that past, including images of lynching in which his father would have quite likely occupied the position of one of the perpetrators.

One image from the "Southern White" notebook in particular showcases the contrast between the emotional tenor of this collection and the tone of his more conventional anti-racist protest songs. Fashioned with watercolor, ink, and pencil in Topanga Canyon on December 25, 1952, as Marjorie, Arlo, Joady, and Nora Lee were celebrating Christmas over three thousand miles away, it shows a hooded figure, presumably a Klansman, raising a fist, possibly in a gesture of triumph, possibly in the act of striking someone or something; the terms *south* and *white* link it to the suite of works on the pages preceding and following it. In larger letters, Guthrie has painted the words *Look Away* across the image. The cultural reference here, of course, is to the lyrical hook of the anthem of white Southern plantation nostalgia, "Dixie." But amid the chaos of the painting, and given the violent act occurring beneath the letters, Guthrie puns. The words are not just a leftist's sarcastic swipe at what the South represents; they engage the matter of vision itself—of what people are trained to allow themselves to look at and see. It was a challenge not just to violent white supremacists, but to white people generally, raising the question of what whiteness provides the privilege to look away from. It is not demanding, paradoxically, that its viewers look away; rather, it portrays the act of disavowing responsibility and complicity—the attempt to stave off shame rather than, as we have seen Guthrie advocate in other contexts, reckon with it. This page, and the artistic corpus of which it was a part, was a particularly lucid moment of Woody Guthrie's longer reflection on what it meant—existentially and psychologically—to be white.

The sources for this reflection were deeply personal, based in events that the bonds of kinship made especially challenging to narrate or make visible. While working on his biography of Guthrie in the late 1970s, Joe Klein asked Woody's uncle Claude about race relations in Okemah, Oklahoma, around the time Woody was born there. As if channeling the racist Pampa relatives about whom Woody had complained in 1947, Claude responded:

It was pretty bad back there in them days. . . . The niggers was pretty bad over there in [nearby town] Boley, you know . . . Charley and them, they throwed this nigger and his mother in jail, both of them, the boy and the woman. And that night, why they snuck out and hung [laughter], they hung those niggers that killed that sheriff. . . . I just kind of laughed [laughter] . . . I knew damn well that rascal Charley was [laughter] . . . I knew he was in on it.[13]

This account shouldn't be shocking; it is a simple fact that many white American citizens have relatives who, across time, committed acts of violence against people of color, and/or who owned them, people considered lesser, subhuman, or even commodities, because of their skin color and origins. In a very real way, that someone of Woody Guthrie's background could have learned to alienate himself from the "Pampa road" is hopeful and inspiring.

But Guthrie never addressed this past directly. We don't know what he knew about it. We don't have his story of the murders or, more importantly, of the people murdered. It seems unlikely that he wouldn't have heard about it from relatives like Claude or from townspeople excited to re-narrate the event. He may have known and not said. Intimacy, like whiteness itself, teaches us to look away from certain things, in order to perpetuate relationships on which we believe our survival depends. Indeed, wanting to sustain a relationship can serve as a way of perpetuating broader injustices, broader violence. Guthrie's desire to protect his father—and himself—may have led him to cover up the family's implication in this crime. But intimacy seems also to have sparked him to spin out fragmented, unruly acknowledgments of his father's likely role in the brutality, ones that would come to their most powerful fruition in the "Southern White" notebook.

There *is* a document purporting to be a clear report of what happened at the Old Schoolton Bridge over the Canadian River, just outside Woody Guthrie's hometown of Okemah, Oklahoma, in the very early morning hours of May 25, 1911, fourteen months before Woody was born: an extraordinarily disturbing photograph showing the bodies of two black people hanging from the bridge, while a row of about thirty white Okemah residents, many of them well-coiffed and smiling at the camera, pose above. Thanks to their town's two daily newspapers, the townspeople would have known a particular story accounting for the event: the dead were a mother and son who had been arrested a couple of weeks earlier in the fatal shooting of a white deputy sheriff, after a dispute about some stolen livestock. To white citizens, the blatant challenge to white authority would have justified extralegal means. The photograph reinforced the meaning of the killings by representing, with pride and confidence, not the murder of two human beings so much as the construction of authority and community pride by means of the destruction of two Black lives. The man behind the camera was the town photographer, G. H. Farnum, who had taken a family portrait of the Guthrie family just a few years earlier. His photo of the lynching was an image of another type of intimacy, white civic bonds founded in anti-Blackness, in the destruction of a Black family. Indeed, Farnum, who would soon begin listing one of his professional specialties as "lynchings," turned the image into a postcard—a not uncommon practice with lynching photos. The killings thus became a commodity, the postcard purchased and sent around the country to friends and relatives, tightening interpersonal bonds among white people well beyond Okemah and Oklahoma.

But as Susan Sontag reminds us, "the camera's rendering of reality must always hide more than it discloses."[14] Accordingly, innumerable details are hidden beneath the photo's surface, and to its sides: most prominently, the identities of victims Laura Nelson, age twenty-nine, and her son L.D., thirteen. (The names appeared in the newspaper coverage, often getting L.D.'s name and age wrong.) The photo shows no evidence of the gang rape that two outlets—the Associated Press and *The Crisis*, the journal for African Americans recently founded by W. E. B. Du Bois—reported as having preceded Laura Nelson's murder. The image can't explain why L.D.'s pants are pulled down and offers no account of the fate of his younger sibling; no news accounts did either. However, an edition of a local newspaper published the day after the lynchings described the atrocity as "executed with a silent precision that made it a master piece of planning."[15]

Could Guthrie have told a different story, made the atrocity known, visible? Did his personal proximity to the event actually lead him to look away from it? One of the things folk-ballad singers do, after all, is narrate histories that aren't written elsewhere or aren't written at all; Guthrie had done so plenty of times, whether narrating the anti-establishment travails of Pretty Boy Floyd, known elsewhere as a criminal and outlaw, or recounting the details of the Gastonia strike. Yet he never *quite* wrote a "Ballad of Laura Nelson," even though history offered him a rich well of material from which to draw.

Before statehood, Oklahoma was called "Indian Territory." It was a place for the federal government to cast off indigenous people uprooted from their lands in the South. When it was opened to settlement to the non-indigenous in 1889, it became a magnet for Southern African Americans fleeing the increasingly militant and violent white supremacy of the post-Reconstruction years. Among the most eminent of these was Edwin McCabe, a Black attorney from Kansas, who saw in Oklahoma a "paradise of Eden and the garden of the Gods," and conjectured that "here the negro can rest from mob law, here he can be secure from every ill of southern policies."[16] Eventually, there were thirty-two all-Black towns in Oklahoma, including the one Charley Guthrie's brother Claude singled out for disparagement in his interview with Joe Klein: Boley, in Okfuskee County between Paden and Okemah, just a few miles from the Nelsons' farm in one direction and the Guthries' house in another. Around this time, Booker T. Washington, touring the area, called Boley "the youngest, most enterprising, and in many ways the most interesting of the Negro towns in the US."[17]

White settlers lobbied for statehood in part because it would suture Oklahoma to a nation that, in 1896, had given Jim Crow segregation the imprimatur of the United States Supreme Court. In the meantime, hostility between white and Black settlers erupted into violence. In 1896, three hundred African Americans in Perkins skirmished with white residents to prevent a lynching; the press called the battle a "race war," a term reporters also used to describe armed conflict between Black and white people following the suppression of the Black vote in Lawton. The press and civic officials cultivated anxieties among white settlers, provoking attacks on Black homes and commercial establishments. Okemah and other towns instituted "sundown" policies barring African Americans from the city limits after dusk.[18] On Christmas Day in 1907, a group of white people in Henryetta, the town neighboring Okemah, lynched a Black man named James Garden, riddling his dead body with bullets as it hung from a tree.

In the reverse order of the Guthrie family's journey, the Nelsons—Laura, L.D., and their husband and father Austin—had come to Oklahoma from Texas, presumably part of the wave of migrants who hoped it could be a region of Black self-determination. From a US Census document, we know that prior to the murders, they owned the land on which they lived, and they were literate.[19] Even these two small pieces of data suggest that they weren't willing to live in the manner in which white supremacy wished them to live.

This environment inevitably shaped the coverage of the events that led to the deaths of Deputy George Loney and the Nelsons. The untrustworthiness of law enforcement's representation of its own conduct, particularly with regard to people of color, remains a problem to this day; in the Nelsons' day, the white-owned press would have been even less likely to raise any questions about the official account put forth by white marshals. That account is wobbly, though. Articles about the events contain numerous differences and inaccuracies. They get names and ages wrong. Some report that Laura fired the gun, others that she claimed to have done it in order to cover for L.D., whom they identify as actually responsible for the deputy's death. Some report that Laura was raped before being murdered, some do not. There is at least one report that Carry, the Nelsons' toddler, was later found drowned in the Canadian River. More crucially, the journalistic accounts of the Loney incident invariably justify the arrest and seizure of the family; none suggests that Austin could have been wrongfully accused of the alleged crime that initially brought police to the family house: the theft of a cow. None attempts to portray the volatile atmosphere in which the police attempted to make the arrest. None raises the issue of how white people may well have resented having educated, property-owning Black people in their environs, or may even have specifically coveted the property on which the Nelsons lived.

For Guthrie to tell a more personal story about Laura Nelson would have been a challenge, but there are clues suggesting that she was brave and uncompromising. At some point during her incarceration in Okemah, likely knowing the risk of her eventual fate, Laura attacked the jailer in an attempt to escape. An *Okemah Ledger* article from May 18, 1911, titled "Negro Female Prisoner Gets Unruly" describes Nelson making an attempt to seize the jailer's gun, and then trying to throw herself out a window.[20] Indeed, when the *Ledger* reported on the lynching, it claimed that during this incident in the jail she had "begged to be killed."[21] For all-white Okemah, only one story could be told—the one that would lead to the spectacle on the bridge.

While there was to be no "Ballad of Laura Nelson," Guthrie continually released work that touched on the lynching in more and less fragmentary, partial ways. The first was a 1940 song called "Slipknot," a rather generic protest against lynching that Guthrie dedicated (in a note under the lyrics) "to the many negro mothers, fathers, and sons alike, that was lynched and hanged under the bridge of the Canadian River, seven miles south of Okemah, Okla., and to the day when such will be no more."[22]

A more direct, yet still skewed, reference to the Nelson lynching appeared in the songbook *Hard Hitting Songs for Hard-Hit People*, which Guthrie co-published with Pete Seeger and Alan Lomax in 1946. In the headnote to the song "Don't Kill My Baby and My Son," Guthrie presented himself as the eight- or nine-year-old son of Okemah's "undersheriff" at the time of the lynchings. One night he hears an anonymous Black woman wailing with a "wild and bloodcurdling moan" out the window of the jailhouse; subsequently, his father tells the story of the woman and her two imprisoned children. His father says they are "doomed to hang . . . with the rise of the morning wind," suggesting that she and her son are to be executed legally.[23] If the song remains emotionally powerful in its evocation of a bereft and desperate mother—a long-standing figure of attraction for Guthrie—what lingers, in a broader context, is how it creates a space of innocence, outside the racialized struggle over Oklahoma, for himself and his father.

Indeed, in the song, news of the killing comes to the youngster not from his fictional father but through the medium of Farnum's image, now a mass-produced postcard: "Then I saw a picture on a postcard / It showed the Canadian River Bridge, / Three bodies hanging to swing in the wind, / A mother and two sons they'd lynched."[24] The mention of the postcard exonerates Charley of any individual responsibility while also simply distorting the facts of what happened by referring to "two sons . . . lynched." Perhaps even more pointedly, it plays a shell game by referring to the fact of the photo's existence while erasing the prominent presence of white Okemah residents in it—despite their pride in being visible in the actual photograph. In other words, it indulges the privilege of whiteness to look away, to selectively obscure, while presumptively condemning the lynching.

In contrast, the Smithsonian Institution holds a small 1946 drawing by Guthrie that invokes G. H. Farnum's lynching photograph, but transforms it dramatically, depicting a bridge from which hangs a long row of bodies, rather than just two of them. The image may represent the undocumented (though far from outlandish) suggestion, from the note on "Slipknot," that many Black people were lynched at the Old Schoolton Bridge. But, juxtaposed with the Farnum photo, it's also hard not to see an angry fantasy, in which the hanging bodies are those of the townspeople standing on the bridge rail in the original. It's also noteworthy, in anticipation of the 1950s work, that Guthrie turned from songwriting to visual art to make this more direct representation of the Nelson lynching.

Indeed, from the mid-1940s, Guthrie's engagement with racial issues became angrier and more militant. One might argue that he came closest to writing a song about the bravery and defiance of Laura Nelson with 1945's "Harriet Tubman's Ballad," a tribute to the fugitive anti-slavery activist, celebrating her embrace of violent opposition. At some point in 1944, Guthrie picked up Earl Conrad's thin volume *Harriet Tubman: Negro Soldier and Abolitionist*, released two years earlier by International Publishers, a firm with long-running ties to the CPUSA. The book opens by referring to Tubman as a "smoldering volcano of resistance" and recounting her conversion to militancy as a fifteen-year-old after an overseer hit her head with a brick as she sought to aid an enslaved colleague in an escape attempt. Conrad's description of Tubman's belief in the necessity of violence echoes the terms with which Guthrie described unionism; Conrad calls it an *"applied* religion, a religion premised on the need for tremendous social change."[25] In each verse of "Harriet Tubman's Ballad," freedom is associated with some image of violence—even the traditional hero of emancipation and racial progress in American history, Abraham Lincoln, is rebuked for not carrying out actions that would actually "kill" slavery.

But events in the present also moved Guthrie in a more militant direction. In late summer 1949, just before he entered prison on obscenity charges, he was among the victims of an angry mob of white residents of Peekskill, New York, who attacked the audience of a Paul Robeson concert while yelling invective like "God bless Hitler!" as well as phrases more associated with the Southern regions from which Guthrie hailed: "Lynch Robeson! Give us Robeson! We'll string that big nigger up!"[26] According to Almanac Singers alumnus Lee Hays, who was riding in the same vehicle as Guthrie: "I was literally scared shitless with Woody screaming at the Fascist pigs who had us surrounded."[27] At one point during the havoc, however, Guthrie turned to his former colleague to confess his fear: "This is the worst I've ever seen, and I've seen a lot."[28]

In the aftermath, he began to manifest signs of what Earl Conrad, in his book on Harriet Tubman, called an "applied religion" of furious anti-racism. Songs poured out of him in response to what had happened. Restraint and etiquette fell away, replaced by anger and execration. "Devils of hell are on the loose in Peekskill . . . tryin' to tie Paul Robeson's noose!" he wrote. His fury generated keen phrases, such as the image of the white rioters as "fleas on a tiger's back" in "My Thirty Thousand."[29] Perhaps the dwindling chances that the songs would ever be recorded freed him to write more candidly.

Another factor in his personal life was sharpening Guthrie's views of race in the US: his deepening friendship with Southern folklorist and anti-racist activist Stetson Kennedy. Kennedy, who had collaborated on folkloric projects with Zora Neale Hurston in the mid-1940s, became renowned among white and Black leftists after he infiltrated a Florida chapter of the KKK and published a book-length exposé, *I Rode with the Ku Klux Klan* (later retitled *The Klan Unmasked*). He and Guthrie began corresponding in the mid-1940s. In 1950, when he ran an unsuccessful campaign for a Florida Senate seat, Guthrie wrote (but never recorded) a song for the campaign, a common genre for leftist songwriters at the time.

A white man who had risked his life to counter white supremacy, Kennedy served Guthrie as a model, an ego-ideal. The leaders of the Civil Rights Congress, a Black group affiliated with the CPUSA, accorded him enough respect that they invited him to sign their 238-page screed *We Charge Genocide*, in which they asked the United Nations to condemn the ongoing, routine violence committed against African Americans in the US, often by the state's own instrument, the police. As the authors of the petition put it: "Once the classic method of lynching was the rope. Now it is the policeman's bullet. We submit that the evidence suggests that the killing of Negroes has become police policy in the United States and that police policy is the most practical expression of government policy."[30] When the volume appeared in 1951, Guthrie pored over it and its appendices, which documented hundreds of particular cases, pulling out material that would go into lyrics like "The Rape of Lila Carter." He also wrote a long poem embracing the document's position, titled "Genocide."

But Guthrie was also specifically becoming more interested in subtler ways that white supremacy manifested itself—as evident in the poems and songs he wrote about his landlord, Fred Trump, in 1951. Trump, father of the forty-fifth president of the United States, owned the Guthries' new home, Beach Haven, a complex made up of 2,253 units in twenty-one buildings constructed around an array of courtyards. The project was part of an attempt to provide affordable housing for returning veterans, built with a program that allowed public assistance for private investments.[31]

Walking the grounds or staring out his window, trying to conjure inspiration, Guthrie noticed something curious: the monolithic whiteness of the residents. He described the situation in a letter to Kennedy, calling the housing project a "Jimcrow town."[32] In part, he was inspired by a fight then playing out over a similar development in downtown Manhattan, Stuyvesant Town (where the Guthries had applied for an apartment),[33] where local activists had sued the landlord, Metropolitan Life Insurance, for maintaining a whites-only policy while receiving public funding. After a number of unsuccessful legal efforts, in March 1951— the month Guthrie began his paintings of lynchings—the New York City Council passed a law "barring discrimination in all publicly assisted private housing."[34]

Guthrie wrote a number of songs about segregation at Beach Haven, including the particularly biting and poignant "Old Man Trump."[35] But perhaps even more significant about this work is that Guthrie's reaction makes evident his attunement to the problem of whiteness. Into the twenty-first century, many white people, liberals included, are unlikely to notice if a restaurant, theater, or classroom is populated entirely with people who appear to be white. Homogenous whiteness fades into the background; it is simply nothing, the norm. But Guthrie, by this time, didn't need to see or read about the explicit victimization of Blackness

to recognize the pervasiveness of racial inequality. Racism didn't only become an issue when there were incidents of violence against Black people
to write about. He recognized that racial injustice could be manifest in
everyday, unspectacular ways, including the assumption that being engulfed in whiteness was just, well, normal—just America. He had come a
long way from Pampa, and from Okemah; as part of that journey, he had
learned not to look away from, or look past, whiteness.

By the early 1950s, Guthrie's racial politics were moving in a direction
that ran against the grain of the emergent nonviolent, passive resistance
movement led by Black Baptist churches of the South. In a piece called
"India Dear," he made his ambivalence about Gandhi's philosophy explicitly clear, calling on Indians to abandon passive actions like hunger
strikes and instead "meet me as an old lover here in my pastures of violence, in under my trees of fighting blood and my group of battling
battlers." He continued:

> When you starve to death there helpless in your lost crossroad of
> ghandersville, I my own self starve to very near death over here along
> mine, but starving to death is a thing that I'll be doing only after sixty
> or seventy or my ninety two years of most violent kicking, jumping,
> shaking and shattering down every living official that brought me and
> my family to starve unto our very death.[36]

Guthrie's militant turn is present all over the fascinating "Southern
White" notebook. Although it was begun in Topanga in 1952, just after
his release from Brooklyn State, it was largely filled when he and Anneke, along with Guthrie's new protégé Ramblin' Jack Elliott, visited Beluthahatchee, Stetson Kennedy's swampy homestead in northern Florida
(about twenty miles south of Jacksonville), in the spring of 1953. They
drove down from New York, arriving to find Kennedy absent, having fled
abroad in the wake of threats from the local Klan chapter. Without access
to Kennedy's house, they took shelter in an abandoned bus on the property. For three months, Guthrie spent days playing music with Anneke
and Jack, and filling his old army notebook with angry, terse content
about the unrelenting racism and racist violence that remained routine in
the US, with little change since his own Southern youth. Amid the strange
images and repeated inscriptions of the words *Southern White* are verses

that unabashedly depict and even attempt to inhabit Black rage—as in, for example, a poem with the prescient title "Blacky Panther":

> *Blacky Panther Blacky Panther trot*
> *over my dam*
> *Trot over my dam here just soon as*
> *you can*
> *Trot out from your timber*
> *Trot over your trail*
> *Come scream for me loud*
> *Come and drum down your tail*
> *Come signal me over*
> *Come signal me please*
> *Come tell me you've broke, all*
> *my Blacks out of jail*[37]

He took up the point of view of a Black victim of racial violence in a blues lyric called "Drain the Swamp." The chorus goes:

> *Drain the swamp, don't call the cops*
> *If I don't come back in an hour*
> *Drain the swamp*[38]

These seem to be song lyrics, and they are in a mode familiar from Guthrie's songwriting. But none of this work was public. Even if he had tried to record lyrics like this, it's unlikely that a record label or book publisher would have risked right-wing ire by issuing it, although a few white and Black musicians did issue songs about racism and police violence in this period.[39] But for the most part, outside the purview of a few tiny record labels, these sentiments were unspeakable in any broad public sphere.

As we've seen, more personal matters also limited the "speakability" of Guthrie's perspective on race and racial violence in particular. And in truth, the *images* that Guthrie made in 1951–54 are the most challenging documents of his struggle to express this perspective. As a practice, racial lynching itself is a visual spectacle, designed to terrorize people of color and solidify the power of whiteness outside the closed curtains of the legal system. In the *Look Away* painting from the "Southern White" notebook, Guthrie used the "Dixie" refrain to take up the dynamics of sight in spectacles of racial violence. This preoccupation also pervades the earlier images, made at Beach Haven in 1951. Some of these paintings, including one titled *Southland Tourist*, depict people engaged in sex acts; others depict naked or topless women. All of these figures are under threat from figures coded as perpetrators of anti-Black violence: hooded Klansmen, police, marshals.

There is a political strategy behind G. H. Farnum's photo of the Okemah lynching. It depicts the killings as an orderly, civic event, of a piece with the local newspaper's description of the killings as exemplars of "precision." Not all photos of lynching from this period are as deliberately staged as this one, but many do show white communities, composed of adults and children, posing for the camera as they bond in the aftermath of having murdered Black people and left their bodies out for display. Guthrie's images undo this order, and they do so by representing the chaotic sexual dynamics of lynching that "official" images try to disavow.

Visual culture scholar Shawn Michelle Smith writes that "forbidden sexuality haunt[s] the frames of the photographs of lynchings."[40] Perpetrators of lynching often cited the protection of white female sexual "innocence" as a rationale for the practice. Sexual violence, including castration and other forms of torture, was a common practice. More fundamentally, the spectacular aspect of lynching and its representation exploits a salaciousness associated with acts of violence, of sadism. An image like Farnum's tries to sanitize these aspects of lynching and lynching images while at the same time promoting a practice steeped in sexual politics and violence. The one exception that breaks this illusion is L.D.'s half-removed pants. Clearly, regardless of whether Laura was raped or L.D. castrated, part of the sadistic pleasure afforded lynchers involved proximity to, intimacy with, the bodies of Black people; this pleasure could be easily adapted to fantasy in the minds of non-participants looking at photos or reading newspaper accounts.

Guthrie's imagery brings the salacious, voyeuristic, sexually sadistic elements of lynching much closer to the surface. We watch people—violent white supremacists—watch their victims. In *Southland Tourist*, an image that depicts a dual hanging, he depicts the victims with their hands on one another's genitals, conveying how hanging becomes a sexualized spectacle. Even the slapdash quality of the paintings works to undermine the attempt of the Farnum image's symbolism to look clean and sterile.

These images are profoundly messy and oblique. Although the crosses clearly refer to violent white supremacism, the race of the figures being victimized isn't totally clear. The curly head of one person in a painting called *These Ones Have One Out*, who appears to be giving oral sex to another figure as an ominous sheriff-like figure looks on, could be meant to represent a Black person, but it also suggests Guthrie himself, *in flagrante* in a position familiar from one of the steamier passages of Walt Whitman's "Song of Myself." In the aftermath of his obscenity prosecution, he may, in fact, be identifying his plight as someone—in his view—sexually persecuted and shamed with the experience of being a victim of racist violence. This aspect of the paintings is undeniably troubling, as it disappears the privilege Guthrie enjoyed, as a white person, not to be subject to such cruelty. Even as such an identification erases difference, however, it indicates that the courtrooms, prison cells, and hospital wards through which his struggling body had led him had also steered him toward an intersectional insight into the role the body plays as an object of control for powerful institutions, be they psychiatry or white supremacy.

The material between the covers of the "Southern White" notebook plays with nudity and spectacle, too. But what is perhaps finally most startling about this strange, troubled document is that it won't, or can't, expunge the matter of whiteness. As noted, the phrases "Southern White" and "White Only" appear on nearly every page, often scrawled in pencil, presumably after the production of the painted image—even when that image's relationship to racism is far from clear. The iterations of these phrases across the book leave the impression of someone compulsively speaking of and from whiteness, as if trapped inside it. The words appear, in a way, like stigmata, puncture wounds riddled with shame. Once again, there seems to be no pure space, no escape offered either viewer or artist. Several of these images embody the overall feeling of inextricability; the nude bodies are trapped, enmeshed, tangled within and behind the knotted branches of (Southern) whiteness. They provide a visual echo of the way Guthrie described his own feelings of being wrapped up in shame, and the shame that surrounds nakedness, whether literal nudity or that of a person openly airing their psychic wounds.

As with so much of the material in this book, these images reflect an unfamiliar Woody Guthrie. There is no simple message here, no pat slogans indicting Southern white racism. The images are not "topical" or "protest" art in any familiar form. They look nothing like the art shown at the two major exhibitions of anti-lynching art mounted in New York in 1935, one of them organized by Black communists. They don't uplift; they don't exhort. They don't even mourn, precisely. Indeed, unlike so much of the art with which Guthrie is famously associated, the response they seek from their audience is, especially by "Old Left" standards, opaque. The protest genre typically positions artist (or singer) and audience as outside the problem they address, not part of it. In contrast, Guthrie's images are not only unruly, they flirt with arousing a salacious response in their own viewers, implicating them in the very type of looking they are depicting. Like the *Look Away* image, this work is *about* looking, about the allure of sensational images. Rather than addressing the scourge of racial violence directly, the images focus on how it is mediated, on how representations of racial violence operate culturally; the images track these phenomena, not racism, as a matter of individual conscience. It is likely less valuable to translate these works into a clear message than to understand them as documents of experience—in this case, the experience of a middle-aged Southern white man sitting with the implications of his past.

Guthrie's songwriting of the late 1940s and early 1950s shows that he was well aware of the nation's continuing injustices against African Americans, faced by musician friends and collaborators such as Huddie Ledbetter, Sonny Terry, and Brownie McGhee. But this work, and perhaps even his increasing militancy and advocacy of violent resistance, indicate that he was allowing the gaping open wounds of his past, his origins, to come out from under the bandages of conventional white liberalism and air out. As an artistic practice, this tack necessarily reanimates the mystery: Did Charley ever tell Woody about playing any role in the abuse and killing of the Nelsons? If not, did Woody suspect his father was involved, or hear he was from others in Okemah? The exact contours of his knowledge of his father's involvement remain unknown, and likely unknowable. Woody never mentions his father as having been part of the lynch mob. Perhaps there remains a modicum of doubt as to whether the son knew to connect his father's ideas to what happened to the Nelsons.

Yet if Charley was involved, it is very difficult to imagine such information not flowing freely through homes, stoops, street corners, taverns, and markets of such a small community as Okemah, Oklahoma.

Even if never spoken about openly, or referred to in blurry or strange terms (as Claude Guthrie did), the event may have shaped Guthrie's relationship with his father, and hence Guthrie himself. They may well have come to a tacit agreement not to discuss it. They may have both silently believed that their intimacy would survive only by keeping the atrocity buried. In this way, a desire to sustain a relationship can serve as a way of perpetuating broader injustices, broader violence, such as those consonant with white supremacism. Guthrie's desire to protect his father—and himself—may have led him to cover up the family's implication in this crime. But intimacy may also have generated refracted unruly acknowledgments of his father's possibly direct role in the brutality, ones that would come to their most powerful fruition in the "Southern White" notebook. That those acknowledgments came in the form of these images' twisted, threatened, unruly bodies made the work particularly visceral; it also made sense, given Guthrie's growing awareness that he didn't have to look further than his own self to see the vulnerability of bodies to power, to see the world as a place of aberrant bodies broken by the compulsions of the normal, whether in the form of ableism or white supremacism.

Chapter Eleven

"EXACTLY HOW MY
OWN MOTHER SAW AND FELT"

O N THE MORNING OF JULY 10, 1953, in the midst of his sabbatical at anti-racist activist Stetson Kennedy's abandoned north Florida property, Guthrie hobbled out of the broken-down bus he and Anneke used for sleeping accommodations and began building a fire to use for making coffee and breakfast. When he tried to stoke the blaze with some gasoline, big flames shot back at him, engulfing his entire right arm. He collapsed, rolling in the dirt, unable to protect his arm's skin, which, according to his young wife, "blistered and dropped off, rather slid off."[1] Anneke and a neighbor took him to a hospital where he was given perfunctory treatment, admission notes referring to the couple as "drifters." In the following days, the arm became fetid and infected. Finally, a doctor from the hospital visited the Kennedy property and, quite likely, saved him from losing it altogether.

Informed about the incident in a letter from Anneke, Marjorie immediately addressed the potential psychological wounds it threatened to reopen. She knew the memories lying in wait to consume him: the burnt-down house in Okemah, the unclear reason as to why sister Clara's clothes burst into flames, the kerosene incident that sparked Nora Belle's institutionalization and made Charley an invalid for a year, and most recently, the devastating loss of Cathy in the electrical fire at Mermaid Avenue. As if speaking from inside his head, she wrote imploring her ex-husband not to make the incident part of a family narrative: "Lets stop it right here. . . . It was an accidnent [*sic*] and so were all the other fires. . . . And we must learn how to prevent fires . . . that is what we should be thinking."[2] She understood better than anyone the destructive role fire had played in the Guthrie family's tragic history; once again, despite the unconventional and rocky standing of their relationship, she offered him a voice of pragmatism and level-headedness.

Still, the circumstances of his forty years on earth make it difficult not to wonder whether something deeper was in play, whether conscious or not. Freud developed the notion of the "repetition compulsion" from observing traumatized patients who would put themselves in the situation that caused their trauma again and again, hoping to gain some kind of mastery of it. Considering the long train of fire-related tragedies among the people to whom Guthrie was closest, the idea seems viable. In a sense, getting badly burned was a strangely intimate act, making him experience what a host of his loved ones had seen and felt in these traumatic, life-shattering moments.

The damage to the arm was so severe as to effectively end his musical career. Although he had been noticing the decline of his guitar playing in the past few years, and now knew to attribute the problem to the chorea, the burns hampered his arm's movement to an extent that made even typing difficult. The wooden music box that had once seemed an extension of his body, slung caseless over his back as he walked through a migrant camp or subway car, had, in effect, been amputated from him.

In May 1956, police found Woody Guthrie wandering, dazed and bedraggled, on the side of a highway near Morristown, New Jersey. It's unclear what he was doing there; he told police he was on his way to Philadelphia, but he may have been trying to find his daughter, Gwen, who had recently married and moved to the area. He told the authorities he was a well-known singer and songwriter regularly cashing large royalty checks for one of his compositions (the Weavers' "So Long, It's Been Good to Know You"). Taking him for a mentally off-kilter homeless man, they checked him into Greystone Park Psychiatric Hospital, a state-funded institution in Morris Plains, about thirty miles west of where he'd met Marjorie Mazia fourteen years earlier in Greenwich Village. With its manicured grounds and stately yet forbidding buildings, Greystone would be his home for most of the following decade; he would also spend a spell back at Brooklyn State, and then at Creedmoor Hospital in Queens, where he died on October 3, 1967, at the age of fifty-five.

The three or so years between the Florida fire and commitment to Greystone have received even less attention from biographers and scholars than the rest of his postwar life, but not for lack of documentation. Although the symptoms of Huntington's continued to intensify, he kept writing prodigiously. Journals, paintings, songs, and letters track his activities and thoughts as he bounced around the continent: Florida, California, Texas, various addresses in New York, and elsewhere. At the beginning of this period, he was still with Anneke. In July 1953, just after the accident, the couple visited Mary and the kids in El Paso, Texas, then slipped over the border so Guthrie could file for a divorce from Marjorie. Anneke and he had a child together, Lorinna Lynn, born in February 1954 in New York. But by 1955, Anneke could no longer cope with his erratic behavior, and filed for divorce while also giving custody of their daughter to a friend's family.

His correspondence fell off. Some friends, like Alan Lomax, had gone abroad to maintain a low profile amid the Red Scare; others had grown frustrated with his unreliability, moroseness, inappropriate outbursts, and poor personal hygiene. He began to collate his work, pasting typescripts of his songs into large notebooks and sketchpads, as if curating the presentation of his legacy after his inevitable, impending demise. After the stress and strain of the events leading up to internment in Brooklyn State, his interactions with Marjorie could be icy, or fiery; she had a couple of boyfriends, and he alternately lashed out at them and said he wanted to befriend them. But they stayed in close contact, even as both quickly remarried. Marjorie would still share heartfelt words of support. "I stand right behind Anneke. . . . I will never be far away from you," she told him in one letter.[3] Indeed, before the marriage's demise, Anneke and Marjorie got along well, and Woody would bring his new wife along to visits with his former family.

He reentered Brooklyn State, voluntarily, in the fall of 1954. He began to express his woes in religious terms, with paeans to Jesus that, in contrast to his early song "Jesus Christ," were more spiritual than political. While back on the same ward as he'd lived in the summer of 1952, he wrote of *wanting* to be sick, with Jesus as his doctor. Clearly, it was a way to accept his condition when, as reflected in the title he gave a brief piece written a couple of months into this return visit, there was "No Help Known" for Huntington's chorea.[4] That was what he saw in the eyes, heard in the whispers, of the mortal doctors and nurses in the hospital.

Friends worried about the fate of Arlo, Joady, and Nora as their father faded from the world. Harold Leventhal, manager of Pete Seeger's Weavers (and briefly of Guthrie himself), arranged a tribute concert to raise money for the kids, an event Ed Cray calls "a last gesture of the Old Left to the singer-songwriter who had captured so many of its causes in verse."[5] On March 17, 1956, before an audience of 1,200 at Pythian Hall on West Seventieth Street, former Almanac Singer colleagues Seeger, Millard Lampell, and Lee Hays performed, along with former *Folksay* colleague Earl Robinson. Sitting beside Marjorie's new husband, Al Addeo, Guthrie watched from a side box, unable to perform himself. At the end of the performances, he rose from his seat to acknowledge their applause, his physical fragility evident.

In his notebook jottings from this period, he rarely mentions Huntington's chorea. Some friends describe noticing virtually no change in him; others say they perceived his longtime restlessness becoming less Chaplinesque, more sinister. He would off-handedly blame "my wild disease of alcoholism" for his condition, sometimes still adamantly tracing it all back to matters of ideology: "I trace and track all of my diseases and 99% of our mental breakdowns all up to the big general bill of our capitalist system, anyhow."[6] Indeed, he took to carrying around a liquor bottle as a prop, so people would think he was drunk rather than ill with a grave disease. He didn't want Huntington's disease to be the definitive quality of his body, the essence of his self. He had come up with his own version of what his mother had done when he was a young boy, disappearing her own sick body by retreating into the darkness of the Okemah movie theater. In another perverse way, the illness was reuniting them, reanimating the closeness they had felt with one another during her most challenging years.

His writing became ever more fragmented, less disciplined, and less conventional. At times, he could hit high points, "swirling and vertiginous, a joyous spew of words," as Joe Klein put it. But there were odd technical aspects. He spelled words phonetically, or simply eccentrically. He developed a habit—perhaps a compulsion or tic—that made him add a diminutive "y" to the end of words, even in seemingly inappropriate contexts, as when he referred, repeatedly, to the social problem of "racey hate." Or when he assured a friend: "I'm still whackering out one or two or five of nine of my truefacty ballad story songs every day. Getting more & more classy conscious & lots more testy and protestyius every paussing night."[7] Some aspect of the illness, it seemed, had led him to invent his own personal dialect.

But the presence of Huntington's is nowhere more apparent than in the unraveling of his once immaculate handwriting. The formerly tidy and economical script that filled the pages of his letters and makeshift journals became swollen, then unruly, then all but illegible.

What did the effort to write mean for him, *do* for him during these late years, his artistic career at an end, before Huntington's made it impossible both physically and cognitively? He found some solace in imagining how his writing would construct and maintain his work's legacy beyond his death. In March 1954, he wrote a small passage as a kind of coda in the tumultuous "Southern White" notebook:

My Words
I want you to pay a lot more attention to all my words longer and deeper and quieter and louder than I ever could
You'll get more good out of them than I did around here[8]

He knew incapacitation and death were coming, and he began to imagine how, after he died, he would figure in the memories and minds of those who would survive. But he also wasn't ready to fade; as he declared in several places, "I ain't dead yet."

Hospitals, becoming an ever-more-familiar environment, remained a topic of concern. In another postscript in the "Southern White" notebook, he wrote at the top of facing pages "I Wanted to Die" and "I Wanted to Live." The "Die" page was otherwise blank, but under "I Wanted to Live," he wrote:

I wanted to
go ahead and
live to fight
my profit system that

floods all my
hospitals too full
3/54[9]

In the fall of 1954 and beyond, he wrote a tremendous stack of plays, which essentially created loose dramatic settings for acting out the songs he used to write and sing. These works are very strange; their scale can be so massive as to be surreal, and several contain robust sex scenes. One of the oddest and longest is called "My Whore," which involves "three Soviet sisters" who are captured by Nazis; one kills herself, another escapes and becomes a guerilla, and the third becomes a concubine in order to castrate Nazi officers. He listed the cast as "THREE RUSSIAN SISTERS & A HUNDRED NAZI OFFICERS & A WOODSFUL OF GUERILLAS & A TOWNFUL OF FINE FOLKS & A CITY LOAD OF GOOD PEOPLE & A PLANETFUL OF HARD WORKERS"[10] He covered the script with his own signature—each page contains several of them—as if reminding himself he was still here and still an author.

Again, it's easy to read this description, together with the all-caps phrasing, and conclude that Huntington's had made him, as people in Okemah used to call his mother, "batty." But in truth, the aesthetic pandemonium saturating these works resembles nothing so much as the rollicking, gargantuan "Circe" (or "Nighttown") section of James Joyce's *Ulysses*, also written as a dramatic script. One person's madness is another person's modernism. As usual, the most attuned reader for material many would consider un-Guthrian was Will Geer; fearing someone might try to expunge the plays from Guthrie's legacy, Geer made a point of preserving them. He put them in a binder titled "14 Plays by Woody Guthrie" and mailed them to Pete Seeger for safekeeping.

Other plays are less extreme. One of the most notable and ambitious of these works was a project he had initially conceived as a collaboration with folklorist John Greenway, "Songs of Struggle and Protest." Written during a voluntary return stay in Brooklyn State Hospital in September 1954, the production reaches back to the eighteenth century, covering the American Revolution, Dorr's Rebellion, the property requirement for voting rights, and issues of the antebellum era like discrimination against the Irish. It includes a long passage of actors reciting quotations from abolitionist figures, including William Wordsworth, John Greenleaf

Whittier, Harriet Tubman, and finally Abraham Lincoln. He envisioned the cast as himself, Anneke, Will Geer, and an anonymous "Negro Lady." There were sexy dance numbers, political rants, and madcap staging: at one point, a woman shoots a gun in time to the song she is singing. In essence, he was imagining something not wholly unlike *Folksay*, but more surreal and absurd, and on a far more massive scale.

By 1956, the year he entered Greystone, the main purpose of writing was more private, more concerned with maintaining a sense of composure and wholeness in himself: a sense of self that would allow him to maintain his close relationships, especially with his kids and, still, despite her new marriage, Marjorie. There was also the salvation, solace, and sustenance of the activity of writing, the practice of putting pen to paper, fingers to typewriter keys. It is notable in this context that repetitive, rhythmic activities (such as dance) are often part of therapy for patients suffering from dyskinesia. In several letters and other writings from this period, he would repeat a single phrase—"Yess lord," or "Oh, lordy," for example—over and over; these incantatory documents have a haunted quality, but he was likely also, in part, administering a kind of therapy to himself, setting himself in a familiar position with his hand perched on a legal pad.

There are other signs of what the act of writing could perform for him as he began to lose the ability to form clear sentences in his mind and to perform the physical act of writing. On some of the most recent letters he received, mostly from the kids, he would write in pencil over the sender's name—sometimes his own name, sometimes phrases like "Read by Woody Guthrie on [date]." At first glance, these scribbles seem aggressive, as if canceling or erasing the name of the sender. But in the context of Guthrie's long history of exploring and experiencing writing as a physical act, they seem more like acts of intimacy, attempts to bring his body into contact with theirs, to feel them, to feel what they were feeling as they wrote.

Many of the letters from Greystone are little notes avowing his love to Arlo, Joady, and Nora. They can be incoherent at times, but in general, they remain pretty lucid. Occasionally, his old sense of humor manages to peek out:

Deare Joadsye
How am I you are fine[11]

But in letters to Marjorie, he often revisits older themes and postures:

> You tell my kids for me I do have ta stay here in my graystoney hospital
> to help my doctors all ta make alla my several thousands of sicky people
> here all feel a little bit better.[12]

And, as always, addressing Marjorie, affirming their relationship made him stronger. In one letter from late 1956, he begged off comments in her previous letter that predicted the longevity of his legacy: "You you you you are the legend legend legend not me You're my only legend I'm sure not no kind off no legend ta my own self."[13] He begged her to "guide" and "guard" him, saying he needed her more than ever. Then, as if the letter wouldn't be truly intimate without a mention of sex, he demurred: "Sex and all aint possible by me not no more sex just is not possible with me anymore."

One of the last, most reflective letters of 1956 has all the qualities of a wartime letter from 1943, with a startling lack of a boundary line between love and politics:

> But it does take a strong soul like you are Marjory to go back through
> all my communistic days and to see like I see and to think like I think
> and to feel just as much of a communist as I am and as I always was and
> as I always will be. . . . I am stickin by you just as long now as Ive still
> got myself any drop of my life left.[14]

His powerful love for her persisted, and communism, still vital to him as a motive force in all things, was the medium through which it endured.

Certainly, this letter also reflects a man in the first throes of dementia, grabbing onto a familiar word, a familiar incantation, that had given his life meaning and purpose in the past. But to write as an avowed communist from a state mental hospital was an act that, to the young New Jersey poet Allen Ginsberg, marked a historical transition in the history of leftist struggle. The same year Guthrie entered Greystone, Ginsberg, whose own communist mother had been a patient at the institution in the 1930s, published a long poem titled "Howl." One line of the poem depicted "twenty-five thousand mad comrades" interned in Rockland State Hospital, just a few dozen miles north of Greystone, "all together singing the final stanzas of the Internationale."[15] In Ginsberg's poem, the Left is sequestered and dying in the political and cultural climate of the Cold War; their musical plea to the international working class to throw off its shackles is trickling out, nearly finished. The poem's image suggests that the political establishment's response to radical dissent has become subtle and cunning: to cast it as an illness, a condition to be diagnosed and treated. The image also suggests that these hospitals target collectivity itself—the mass, *union*.

Along with his fellow members of the Beat movement, Ginsberg would soon become a beacon to a new left, one whose prototypical representative was not a union member concerned with economic justice but a white, middle-class college student dissatisfied with the conformist and normalizing atmosphere they had inherited from the 1950s. Indeed, what Guthrie might have dubbed this literary circle's "crazy, mixed up whirl" of surreal images, unexpected juxtapositions, and full-out assaults on middle-class propriety would soon inspire a young Woody Guthrie fanatic to leave behind his idol's protest-folk tradition and invent his own brand of poetic tumult, set to the sounds of electric guitars and drums. Bob Dylan subsequently became the icon of a 1960s left that prized, above all things, individual freedom of expression and boundary-shattering personal behavior.

During his time in Brooklyn State Hospital in the fall of 1952, Guthrie wrote some lines that suggest he sensed the same historical transition, and loss, that Ginsberg would shortly mark:

> *Give me new multitudes!*
> *Gotta have new multitudes!*
> *Take this lost generation*
> *And give me new multitudes!*[16]

Guthrie's "new multitudes," plural, is a phrase that opens space for leftists to renew their commitment to collectivism and union while acknowledging the homogenizing tendencies of these ideals in Old Left politics. It recognizes that, despite the claims of the "lost generation," there is not a single multitude—a claim that tended, indeed, to submerge concerns about race and gender in the movement, and to seal it off from any consideration of sexuality or disability as inflected by politics. The trajectory of his thinking, as traced in this book, suggests that these lines—later slightly revised for lyrics to a song called "New Multitudes"—are less a song of melancholy about the "lost generation" than a hopeful song about the project of reformulating the fight against inequality under new historical conditions.[17] Instead of pining for a revival of the past, of the familiar, he wanted to imagine, wanted to bring into being, *new* forms of union, like the community he longed for in the shock treatment wing of Brooklyn State Hospital. But by the time he got to Greystone, he lacked the wherewithal to extend this experiment.

But others did. The 1960s in particular brought challenges to the homogeneity that had long constrained the class-centered Left's ability to say "We." Shame—or, more nearly, a shared resistance to shame and stigma—drove insurgent movements like Black Nationalism, radical feminism, and gay liberation. Shame's inverse, pride, became a political watchword for this new politics of identity. It would, of course, be ludicrous to suggest that Woody Guthrie's ideas anticipated these movements; each has its own long, complex, fascinating history, with its own visionaries, theorists, and fighters. But he did anticipate the impact that shame and stigmatized bodies would have on the shape of left politics. Something deeply personal, rooted in trauma and bodily disability, made it possible for him to formulate these ideas when few of his Old Left colleagues were doing so.

One other aspect of Guthrie's thought is especially important in this regard: his deep and fundamental commitment to the value of diversity, writ large. At times his expression of this commitment could be clunky, like when he would grossly exaggerate the mixed racial demographics of his home state of Oklahoma (he was fond of saying it was one-third white, one-third Black, and one-third Native American), or naively racist, as when he expressed a desire to marry a Black woman. But there was a deeply personal allegiance to difference, in a sweeping range of forms: making a world where people of various racial backgrounds could thrive, and where workers could enjoy stability and pride, but also one where the fat could be fat, the skinny skinny, even the sick sick. He cultivated this allegiance to the othered and the abjected against the background of eugenics, and later, psychiatry and the study of deviance—all invested, albeit in different ways, in the maintenance of norms, of sameness at the expense of diversity.

What's finally so compelling about this intimate life is that it doesn't sit comfortably within either the Old Left or New Left paradigm. The archival writings discussed in this book show that he saw no contradiction between a commitment to working-class solidarity and an abiding belief that politics are *felt* in people's bodies, as well as in the way various authorities classify their bodies. He was a communist committed to anti-capitalist collectivism even as he considered the notion of "normal" minds and bodies an insidious instrument of political repression. Indeed, one of the most important possibilities he offers the Left as it continues to shift is his mediation of an ongoing, reified split between those who prioritize class politics and those who favor cultural politics. We should look to him to complicate our understanding of left history, and to remind ourselves that the story that history tells is always shifting with the needs of the present. We need him not as icon, but as a complicated, uncategorizable thinker, who can help us imagine how a more just world-to-come might feel.

ACKNOWLEDGMENTS

INDISPENSABLE FINANCIAL SUPPORT for this book came from a National Endowment for the Humanities fellowship for college teachers, the BMI-Woody Guthrie Fellowship, and the Haverford College Provost's Office—where I'm grateful, in particular, to Kim Benston, Fran Blase, and Marta Bartholomew.

Haverford also supported the excellent work by my student research assistants. Cole Fiedler-Kawaguchi, Amira Abujbara, Abby Cox, and Tina Le all contributed to the book in substantial ways. Many thanks, too, to English Department administrator Tricia Griffith for her help navigating the thicket of permissions.

The knowledge and generosity of a handful of skilled and dedicated archivists were indispensable to the project, and it's a pleasure to acknowledge them here: Patrick Kerwin at the Library of Congress, Manuscript Division; Tim Wilson at the San Francisco Public Library's James Hormel LGBTQIA Center; Todd Harvey at the LOC's American Folklife Center; Jeff Place, Greg Adams, Cecilia Peterson, and Stephanie Smith at the Ralph Rinzler Folklife Archives and Collections, Smithsonian Institution; and Tiffany Colannino at the Woody Guthrie Archive in its former Mount Kisco incarnation. Many thanks to Barry, Judy, and Dara Ollman for welcoming me into their home and to Barry for making his remarkable collection available to me. The biggest share of my gratitude in this arena goes to Kate Blalack at the Woody Guthrie Archive in Tulsa; the foundation of this book owes much to her insight, patience, and dedication.

I benefited from the expertise and (in some cases) unpublished research of a number of people learned in Guthrie, folk music, and the cultural and political contexts of the 1930s, '40s, and '50s. Many thanks, in this regard, to Ron Cohen, Thomas Conner, Mark Fernandez, Mark Franko, Jesse Jarnow, Will Kaufman, Peter La Chapelle, John Shaw, Timothy Stewart-Winter, and Elijah Wald.

I'm grateful to the many people who read drafts and supported proposals: Ed Comentale, Barry Shank, Charlie McGovern, Gayle Wald, Anna McCarthy, Lindsay Reckson, Robin Wheeler, Jennifer Doyle, Kyla Schuller, Pam Thurschwell, Michael Bronski, Andrew Friedman, and David Suisman. I'm *exceedingly* grateful to Peter Coviello, Will Kaufman, Mike Levine, and Jill Stauffer, all of whom read the entire manuscript at various stages of its development.

In Tulsa, huge thanks to the Director of the Woody Guthrie Center, Deana Stafford McCloud, for her support and seemingly inexhaustible good spirit, as well as for the brilliant work she does to make clear Woody Guthrie's relevance in the twenty-first century. Thanks, too, to the crew she gathers there, especially Mark Fernandez, Robin Wheeler, Lance Canales, Sam Canales, Will Kaufman, Judy Blazer, Stephen Petrus, and Jerry Wofford. I also need to thank the Oral Roberts University undergraduate from a few years ago who, at the conclusion of a delightful conversation on the brief flight from Tulsa to Dallas–Fort Worth, asked if she could say a prayer for my book, and did.

Deep gratitude to Anna Canoni and Nora Guthrie for their generosity and their unceasing commitment to their ancestor, both his legacy and his anti-fascist, anti-racist principles.

My project arrived on Joanna Green's desk in a substantially different form and it is a much better book because of her editorial guidance. Working with her has been an unmitigated pleasure; throughout the process, she has been a clear-sighted, patient, kind, and instructive mentor in the world of trade publishing. Her Beacon colleagues Marcy Barnes, Susan Lumenello, and Alison Rodriguez have been equally great to work with. Brian Baughan's copyediting was a great, late gift to the book.

This book is a product of middle age, a time when many people's lives begin to feel isolated and routinized. So I feel truly fortunate that during the construction of this book I've enjoyed the gift of invigorating, life-affirming friendships with truly phenomenal people, including John Andrews, Farid Azfar, Cristina Beltrán, Mandy Berry, Sarah Blackwood, Daphne Brooks, Matthew Budman, Ruth Charnock, Brian Connolly, Tom Devaney, Jennifer Doyle, Jonathan Flatley, Beth Freeman, Andrew

Friedman, Billy Galperin, Michael Gillespie, Sarah Kessler, Homay King, Ben Le, Joan Lubin, Dana Luciano, Sarah Mesle, Raji Mohan, Amber Musser, Julie Beth Napolin, Tavia Nyong'o, Lindsay Reckson, Marina Rustow, Eileen Ryan, Cynthia Schneider, Jesse Shipley, Stefanie Sobelle, Asali Solomon, Jordan Stein, Jennifer Stoever, Tony Tauber, Pam Thurschwell, Kyla Wazana Tompkins, Karen Tongson, Sharon Ullman, Jeanne Vaccaro, Alexandra Vazquez, Gayle Wald, Patty White, and Tina Zwarg. I wish more than anything that my beloved comrade José Muñoz were still here. And I need to single out a few people: Lara Cohen and John Pat Leary for their many kind ministrations of bourbon, banter, and karaoke in West Philly, and Peter Coviello, Kyla Schuller, and David Suisman for their relentlessly generous and joyful companionship over the past decade or so.

For five decades now, my sisters Priscilla and Frances Stadler have inspired me with their warmth, intelligence, ethical commitments, and passionate devotion to artistic expression. They are at the core of a wonderful extended family that includes Christophe Itsweire, Eric Itsweire, Russ Denney, Cecille Denney, Rene Sing, Cheryle Stauffer, Anne Stauffer, and Natalie, Scott, and Ramsay Kidder.

It is a truly absurd task to try to thank Jill Stauffer for all she has done to bring feelings of joy and well-being to my world. So, I'm left just saying here what I ought to say every day: you are brilliant, and sexy, and courageous, and good, and I love you and our life together.

None of the sustenance I enjoy as an adult would have been intellectually, spiritually, materially, or indeed biologically possible without my parents' expertise at being exactly the wonderful, loving people they are and were. This book is dedicated to my mother and to the memory of my father.

CREDITS

NOTES

ABBREVIATIONS

WGA = Woody Guthrie Archive, Woody Guthrie Center, Tulsa, OK
RRFAC = Ralph Rinzler Folklife Archives and Collections, Smithsonian
Institution, Washington, DC

INTRODUCTION: *When to Be Personal*

1. Guthrie, "Acting and Dancing," notebook, Collection of Barry and Judy Ollman.
2. Quoted in Joe Klein, *Woody Guthrie: A Life* (orig. 1980; New York: Delta, 1999), 236. My account of this incident is a slightly imaginary version of the story as told in many venues.
3. Nora Guthrie, "Woody Guthrie and Sophie Maslow," in *Making Music for Modern Dance: Collaboration in the Formative Years of a New American Art*, ed. Katherine Teck (New York: Oxford University Press, 2011), 144.
4. Ed Cray, *Ramblin' Man: The Life and Times of Woody Guthrie* (New York: Norton, 2006), 24.
5. Woody Guthrie, *Bound for Glory* (orig. 1943; New York: Plume, 1983), 40.
6. Guthrie, *Bound for Glory*, 40.
7. Guthrie, *Bound for Glory*, 136.
8. Lee Hays Papers, interview series, "On Woody," RRFAC, http://edan.si.edu /slideshow/slideshowViewer.htm?damspath=/Public_Sets/CFCH/CFCH-RRFAC /CFCH-SOVA/CFCH-HAYS/Interviews/HAYS_05_05_049.
9. Woody Guthrie, "Singing, Dancing, and Team-Work," *Dance Observer*, November 1943, 104.
10. Hays, "On Woody," http://edan.si.edu/slideshow/slideshowViewer.htm? damspath=/Public_Sets/CFCH/CFCH-RRFAC/CFCH-SOVA/CFCH-HAYS /Correspondence/Personal/HAYS_01_01_028.
11. For Denning, this phrase broadly defines "the left." See *The Cultural Front: The Laboring of American Culture in the Twentieth Century* (orig. 1996; New York: Verso, 2011), 3.
12. Denning, *The Cultural Front*, xv.
13. See Paul Mishler, *Raising Reds: The Young Pioneers, Radical Summer Camps, and Communist Political Culture in the United States* (New York: Columbia University Press, 1999).

14. Daniel Hurewitz, *Bohemian Los Angeles and the Making of Modern Politics* (Berkeley: University of California Press, 2008), 176.
15. Hurewitz, *Bohemian Los Angeles and the Making of Modern Politics*, 176.
16. Vivian Gornick, *The Romance of American Communism* (New York: Basic Books, 1977), 108.
17. Lauren Berlant, *Desire/Love* (Goleta, CA: Punctum Books, 2012), 71.
18. Woody Guthrie, "I Ain't Got No Home in This World Anymore," *The Asch Recordings*, vol. 3, Smithsonian Folkways Recordings, 1999.
19. WG to MM, 9 December 1942, WGA, correspondence series 1, box 1, folder 44.
20. "Howdy World," WGA, notebooks series 1, item 61, p. 4.

CHAPTER ONE: *"I Don't Sing Any Silly or Jerky Songs"*
1. Woody Guthrie, "WNEW," in Robert Shelton, ed., *Born to Win: Woody Guthrie* (New York: Macmillan, 1965), 223.
2. Guthrie, "WNEW," 222.
3. Susan E. Folstein, MD, *Huntington's Disease: A Disorder of Families* (Baltimore: Johns Hopkins University Press, 1989), 2.
4. Alice Wexler, "Stigma, History, and Huntington's Disease," *Lancet* 376, no. 9734 (June 30, 2010): 18.
5. Wexler, "Stigma, History, and Huntington's Disease."
6. "Woody Guthrie by Woody Guthrie," 5, RRFAC, 03-06-01.
7. Cray, *Ramblin' Man*, 44.
8. Will Kaufman, *Woody Guthrie, American Radical* (Urbana: University of Illinois Press, 2011), 10.
9. Edward P. Comentale, *Sweet Air: Modernism, Regionalism, and American Popular Song* (Urbana: University of Illinois Press, 2013), 122.
10. Earl Browder, *The People's Front* (New York: International Publishers, 1938), 22.
11. Browder, *The People's Front*, 68.
12. Hurewitz, *Bohemian Los Angeles and the Making of Modern Politics*, 152.
13. Hurewitz, *Bohemian Los Angeles and the Making of Modern Politics*, 154.
14. Hurewitz, *Bohemian Los Angeles and the Making of Modern Politics*, 176.
15. In the full, unedited draft of "Woody Guthrie by Woody Guthrie," he wrote that while at KFVD, "I took time out several times to apologize to the Negro people forthings [*sic*] that I let slip out of the corners of my mouth" (9).
16. Peter La Chapelle, *Proud to Be an Okie: Cultural Politics, Country Music, and Migration to Southern California* (Berkeley: University of California Press, 2007), 23 and throughout part 1, chapter 1.
17. Lennard J. Davis, *Enforcing Normalcy: Disability, Deafness, and the Body* (London: Verso, 1995), 35.
18. Frank G. Brooks, "The Oklahoma Sterilization Law and Its Application," *Proceedings of the Oklahoma Academy of Science for 1931*, vol. 12, pp. 52–54.
19. Cray, *Ramblin' Man*, 168.
20. Transcribed from the Library of Congress recordings as released on the box set *Woody Guthrie: American Radical Patriot*, Rounder Records, 2013.

21. Richard Reuss with JoAnne C. Reuss, *American Folk Music & Left-Wing Politics, 1927–1957* (Lanham, MD: Scarecrow Press, 2000), 140.
22. Robert Cantwell, *When We Were Good: The Folk Revival* (Cambridge, MA: Harvard University Press, 1996), 133.

CHAPTER TWO: *Choreographing the Revolution*

1. Guthrie, "Tom Joad," *Dust Bowl Ballads*, Folkways Records, 1964.
2. For vivid details about Almanac House, see Aggie "Sis" Cunningham and Gordon Friesen, *Red Dust and Broadsides: A Joint Autobiography* (Amherst: University of Massachusetts Press, 1999).
3. Uncredited interview of Sophie Maslow, Sophie Maslow papers, Jerome Robbins Dance Division, New York Public Library (S), MGZMD 361, box 3, folder 10.
4. Linda J. Tomko, *Dancing Class: Gender, Ethnicity, and Social Divides in American Dance, 1890–1920* (Bloomington: Indiana University Press, 2000).
5. Oliver Sayler, *Revolt in the Arts: A Survey of the Creation, Distribution, and Appreciation of Art in America* (New York: Brentano's, 1930), 16.
6. See Mark Franko, *Dancing Modernism/Performing Politics* (Bloomington: Indiana University Press, 1995), 27 and throughout chapter 2.
7. Julia L. Foulkes, *Modern Bodies: Dance and American Modernism from Martha Graham to Alvin Ailey* (Chapel Hill: University of North Carolina Press, 2002), 15.
8. After Guthrie's death in 1967, Marjorie Guthrie founded the Committee to Combat Huntington's Disease, which subsequently became the Huntington's Disease Society of America.
9. See Tomko, *Dancing Class*.
10. Sandburg, *The People, Yes*, in *The Complete Poems of Carl Sandburg* (New York: Houghton Mifflin Harcourt, 1970), 453.
11. "Recital Reflects Growth of Modern Dance," *Daily Worker*, March 17, 1942. Quoted in Josh Perelman, "I'm the Everybody Who's Nobody, I'm the Nobody Who's Everybody: How Sophie Maslow's Popular Front Choreography Helped Shape American Jewish Identity," in *Seeing Israeli and Jewish Dance*, ed. Judith Brin Ingber (Detroit: Wayne State University Press, 2011), 90.
12. John Martin, "The Dance: Gala Debut," *New York Times*, March 15, 1942, 8. Edwin Denby: "At every performance Woody Guthrie, the folk singer, who accompanies the piece with songs and jokes, is superb," *New York Herald Tribune*, December 5, 1943.
13. Wanda Marvin, "Reviews: CBS," *Billboard*, December 2, 1944, 12–13.
14. Guthrie, "Acting and Dancing."
15. Guthrie, "Singing, Dancing, and Team-Work," 105.
16. Guthrie, "People Dancing," *Dance Observer*, December 1943, 114–15.
17. Mark Franko, *The Work of Dance: Labor, Movement, and Identity in the 1930s* (Middletown, CT: Wesleyan University Press, 2002), 47.
18. Guthrie narrates this evening in the "Acting and Dancing" notebook.

CHAPTER THREE: *"I Hate to Describe My Mother in Terms Such as These"*

1. Quoted in Cray, *Ramblin' Man*, 175.
2. Hays, "On Woody."
3. Quoted in Cray, *Ramblin' Man*, 256. Guthrie uses the phrase "our book" twice in an undated WG to MM letter, probably from December 1942. WGA, correspondence series 1, box 1, folder 3.
4. Quoted in Klein, *Woody Guthrie: A Life*, 242.
5. Guthrie, "The Rail Roaders Cannon Ball Gazette," WGA, manuscripts series 2, box 2, folder 14.2.
6. Bob Dylan, *Chronicles, Volume One* (New York: Simon & Schuster, 2004), 245.
7. Alice Kessler-Harris and Paul Lauter, introduction to Fielding Burke, *Call Home the Heart* (New York: The Feminist Press, 1983), ix, and Paula Rabinowitz, "Women's Revolutionary Fiction and Female Subjectivity," PhD diss., University of Michigan, 1986, 4. Both quoted in Barbara Foley, "Women and the Left in the 1930s," *American Literary History* 2, no. 1 (1990): 152.
8. Nina Baym, "Melodramas of Beset Manhood: How Theories of American Literature Exclude Women Authors," *American Quarterly* 33, no. 2 (1981): 123–39.
9. Franko, *The Work of Dance*, 47.
10. Guthrie, *Bound for Glory*, 19.
11. Bryan Garman, *A Race of Singers: Whitman's Working-Class Hero from Guthrie to Springsteen* (Chapel Hill: University of North Carolina Press, 2000), 114.
12. Guthrie's version of the song appears on *The Asch Recordings*, vol. 1, Smithsonian Folkways Recordings, 1999.
13. Denning, *The Cultural Front*, 137.
14. Maxim Gorky, *Mother*, trans. Margaret Wettlin (Moscow: Progress Publishers, 1949), 212.
15. Guthrie, *Bound for Glory*, 40.
16. Guthrie, *Bound for Glory*, 39.
17. Guthrie, *Bound for Glory*, 43.
18. Guthrie, *Bound for Glory*, 136.
19. Guthrie, *Bound for Glory*, 76.
20. MM to WG, December 31, 1942, WGA, correspondence series 2, box 2, folder 27.
21. Guthrie, *Bound for Glory*, 137–38.
22. *Springfield Republican*, quoted in Cray, *Ramblin' Man*, 265.
23. Horace Reynolds, "A Guitar Busker's Singing Road," *New York Times Book Review*, March 21, 1943, p. 40.
24. Marguerite Young, "Writin' Star Rises from 'Skid Row,'" *Tulsa World*, April 22, 1943, online at https://www.tulsaworld.com/archive/writin-star-rises-from-skid-row/article_15ee4b75-d1c5-50a8-b023-7a7f0a9cb196.html.
25. WGA, notebooks series 1, item 49, p. 17.

CHAPTER FOUR: *The War Against Loneliness*

1. See Rosalyn Baxandall, "The Question Seldom Asked: Women in the CPUSA," in *New Studies in the Politics and Culture of U.S. Communism*, ed. Michael E. Brown, Randy Martin, Frank Rosengarten, and George Snedeker (New York: Monthly Review Press, 1993), 141–62.
2. WG to MM, November 17, 1942, WGA, correspondence series 1, box 1, folder 44, p. 4.
3. See Pierre-Joseph Proudhon, *What Is Property?* (orig. 1840; Cambridge, UK: Cambridge University Press, 1994).
4. WGA, notebooks series 1, item 11.
5. WGA, notebooks series 1, item 90, p. 5.
6. WGA, notebooks series 1, item 90, p. 5.
7. On Guthrie's understanding of dialectical materialism, see Will Kaufman, *Woody Guthrie's Modern World Blues* (Norman: University of Oklahoma Press, 2017).
8. WG to MM, November 17, 1942, WGA, correspondence series 1, box 1, folder 44, p. 1.
9. WG to MM, April 5, 1943, WGA, correspondence series 1, box 1, folder 47.
10. MM to WG, December 8, 1942, WGA, correspondence series 2, box 2, folder 27.
11. WG to MM, December 9, 1942, WGA, correspondence series 1, box 1, folder 44.
12. WG to MM, December 9, 1942.
13. WG to MM, December 9, 1942.
14. WG to MM, December 14, 1942, WGA, correspondence series 1, box 1, folder 44.
15. Quoted in Klein, *Woody Guthrie: A Life*, 281.
16. Moses Asch, ed., *American Folksong: Woody Guthrie* (orig. 1947; New York: Oak Publications, 1961), 33. The lyrics appear in all capital letters in original.
17. Mark Allan Jackson, *Prophet Singer: The Voice and Vision of Woody Guthrie* (Jackson: University Press of Mississippi, 2007), 24.
18. WG to MM, April 5, 1943, WGA, correspondence series 1, box 1, folder 47.

CHAPTER FIVE: *Bodies of Glory*

1. Jim Longhi, *Woody, Cisco, and Me: Seamen Three in the Merchant Marine* (Urbana: University of Illinois Press, 1997), 62.
2. Klein, *Woody Guthrie: A Life*, 282.
3. MMG to WG, May 14, 1947, WGA, correspondence series 2, box 2, folder 33.
4. Quoted in Klein, *Woody Guthrie: A Life*, 296.
5. Erskine Caldwell, *God's Little Acre* (orig. 1933; Athens: University of Georgia Press, 1995), 88.
6. WG to MMG, June 13, 1945, WGA, correspondence series 1, box 2, folder 2, p. 3.

7. WG to MM, November 5, 1945, WGA, correspondence series 1, box 2, folder 10, p. 5.
8. WG to MM, November 5, 1945.
9. WG to MM, November 5, 1945.
10. Quoted in Klein, *Woody Guthrie: A Life*, 296–97.
11. See the excellent chapters on Guthrie in Garman, *A Race of Singers*.
12. Geer interviewed in Ed Robbin, *Woody Guthrie and Me: An Intimate Reminiscence* (Berkeley, CA: Lancaster-Miller, 1979), 122.
13. The song is the first track on Billy Bragg & Wilco, *Mermaid Avenue*, Elektra Records, 1998.
14. Christopher Lehman-Haupt, "Books of the *Times*," *New York Times*, June 30, 1981, https://www.nytimes.com/1981/06/30/books/books-of-the-times-064020.html.
15. Baxandall, "The Question Seldom Asked," 154.
16. See Michel Foucault, *The History of Sexuality,* vol. 1, *An Introduction*, trans. Robert Hurley (New York: Vintage, 1978).
17. WG to MM, May 25, 1944, WGA, correspondence box 2, folder 1.
18. According to Smithsonian Folkways archivist Jeff Place, "These sessions make up the vast majority of the songs Guthrie recorded during his short career, and most every recording of Guthrie's currently available comes from these sessions." Place, "The Music of Woody Guthrie," *Woody at 100: The Woody Guthrie Centennial Collection* CD box set booklet, Smithsonian Folkways Recordings, 2012, 45.
19. WG to MM, March 29, 1943, WGA, correspondence series 1, box 1, folder 45.
20. Quoted in Cray, *Ramblin' Man*, 301.
21. Erskine Caldwell, *Some American People* (New York: Robert McBride & Company, 1935), 232.
22. John Steinbeck, *The Grapes of Wrath* (orig. 1939; New York: Penguin, 1992), 283. My italics.
23. Patrick Huber, "Mill Mother's Lament: Ella May Wiggins and the Gastonia Textile Strike of 1929," *Southern Cultures* 15, no. 3 (2009): 96.
24. Woody Guthrie, *House of Earth* (New York: HarperCollins, 2013), 106.
25. Guthrie, *House of Earth*, 8.
26. Guthrie, *House of Earth*, 60.
27. Guthrie, *House of Earth*, 12–13.
28. Guthrie, *House of Earth*, 16–17.
29. Guthrie. *House of Earth*, 34.
30. Jessamyn Neuhaus, "The Importance of Being Orgasmic: Sexuality, Gender, and Marital Sex Manuals in the United States, 1920–1963," *Journal of the History of Sexuality* 9, no. 4 (2000): 450.
31. Guthrie, *House of Earth*, 142.
32. WG to MMG, December 14, 1945, WGA, correspondence series 3, box 1, folder 11.
33. Guthrie, *House of Earth*, 134.
34. Guthrie, *House of Earth*, 138.
35. Guthrie, *House of Earth*, 190–91.

36. Guthrie, *House of Earth*, 166.
37. Guthrie, *House of Earth*, 167.
38. Guthrie, *House of Earth*, 203.

CHAPTER SIX: *Stackabones*

1. Emily Judem, "Residents Only: Inside New York City's Oldest Gated Community," brooklynink.org, November 14, 2011, http://brooklynink.org /2011/11/14/35830-residents-only-inside-new-york-citys-oldest-gated -community.
2. Quoted in Cray, *Ramblin' Man*, 264.
3. WG to Will and Herta Geer, November 12, 1944, WGA, correspondence series 1, box 1, folder 18.
4. WG to Will and Herta Geer.
5. Kaufman, *Woody Guthrie's Modern World Blues*, 66.
6. WG to Robinson family, March 3, 1947, WGA, Wolfenstein Collection, series 6, box 1, folder 17.
7. Woody Guthrie, *Pastures of Plenty: A Self Portrait* (New York: HarperCollins, 1990), 88.
8. Quoted in Cray, *Ramblin' Man*, 273.
9. "Stackabones," WGA, manuscripts series 9, box 4, folder 30.
10. "Child Sitting," WGA, manuscripts series 9, box 4, folder 33, p. 1.
11. According to Will Kaufman, painters Jackson Pollock and Willem de Kooning had visited the house on West Tenth Street where the Almanac Singers had lived before 1942. See *Woody Guthrie's Modern World Blues*, 23.
12. Untitled document, WGA, manuscripts series 9, box 4, folder 27.
13. Woody Guthrie, "People I Owe," March 13, 1946, in Shelton, *Born to Win*, 17.
14. "Child Sitting," p. 6.
15. RRFAC, box 2, folder 10A.
16. Two of Aliza Greenblatt's poems were eventually set to music and appeared on the 1960 Folkways LP *Mark Olf Sings Yiddish Songs for Children*.
17. Letter to "What's Wrong" column of *Daily Worker*, November 14, 1946, WGA, manuscripts series 9, box 4, folder 32.
18. Paul C. Mishler calls the "creation of children's summer camps in the 1920s" the "fullest expression" of "the shift in . . . practical expressions of utopianism from labor to leisure on the part of American radicals." *Raising Reds*, 10.
19. Mishler, *Raising Reds*, 38.
20. Henry Jenkins, "The Sensuous Child: Benjamin Spock and the Sexual Revolution," in *The Children's Culture Reader*, ed. Henry Jenkins (New York: New York University Press, 1998), 215.
21. Henry Jenkins, "'No Matter How Small': The Democratic Imagination of Dr. Seuss," in *Hop on Pop: The Politics and Pleasures of Popular Culture*, ed. Henry Jenkins, Tara McPherson, and Jane Shattuc (Durham, NC: Duke University Press, 2002), 188.
22. Margaret Ribble, *The Rights of Infants: Early Psychological Needs and Their Satisfaction* (New York: Columbia University Press, 1943), 2.

23. Julia L. Mickenberg, *Learning from the Left: Children's Literature, the Cold War, and Radical Politics in the United States* (New York: Oxford University Press, 2006), 16.
24. Comprehensive information on Guthrie's recording sessions and releases, compiled by Jeff Place of the Smithsonian Center for Folklife and Cultural Heritage, appears in the text accompanying the box set *Woody at 100*.
25. WGA, notebooks series 1, item 48.
26. Émile Jaques-Dalcroze, *Eurhythmics, Art and Education*, trans. Frederick Rothwell (London: Chatto and Windus, 1930), vii.
27. Elizabeth Waterman, *The Rhythm Book: A Manual for Teachers of Children* (New York: A. S. Barnes, 1936), v–vi.
28. Theodor Adorno, *Essays on Music*, ed. Richard Leppert (Berkeley: University of California Press, 2002), 460.
29. Young Folksay Series booklet, RRFAC, WG-2-10-01.
30. Quoted in Kaufman, *Woody Guthrie's Modern World Blues*, 163–64.
31. Hays, "On Woody."
32. Cray, *Ramblin' Man*, 25.
33. WGA, notebooks series 1, item 48.
34. "Pick It Up," on Guthrie, *Songs to Grow On for Mother and Child*, Smithsonian Folkways Recordings, 1991.
35. "Dance Around," "Howdidoo," and "Put Your Finger in the Air" on Guthrie, *Nursery Days*, Smithsonian Folkways Recordings, 1992.

CHAPTER SEVEN: *Two Good Men a Long Time Gone*

1. Verbatim from recordings in RRFAC, CD #87 Sacco and Vanzetti transfers—disc 1, across tracks 15 and 16.
2. Quoted in Klein, *Woody Guthrie: A Life*, 314.
3. WG to MA and Marian Distler, January 2, 1946, RRFAC, WG-4-01-22A and B.
4. WG to MA, Marian Distler, and David Stone, June 21, 1946, RRFAC WG 04-01-26.
5. Guthrie, "The Debt I Owe," in *Pastures of Plenty*, 86.
6. See Cathy Caruth, *Unclaimed Experience: Trauma, Narrative, and History* (Baltimore: Johns Hopkins University Press, 1996).
7. *People's Songs* 1, no. 1 (February 1946): 1. Quoted in Ronald D. Cohen, *Rainbow Quest: The Folk Music Revival and American Society, 1940–1970* (Amherst: University of Massachusetts Press, 2002), 42.
8. Guthrie, *Pastures of Plenty*, 161–62.
9. Frederick F. Siegel, *Troubled Journey: From Pearl Harbor to Ronald Reagan* (New York: Hill and Wang, 1984), 73. Quoted in Cantwell, *When We Were Good*, 155, 159.
10. Cantwell, *When We Were Good*, 162.
11. Guthrie, "Dear Mrs. Roosevelt," woodyguthrie.org, https://www.woodyguthrie.org/Lyrics/Dear_Mrs_Roosevelt.htm.
12. Barbara Foley, *Radical Presentations: Politics and Form in U. S. Proletarian Fiction, 1929–1941* (Durham, NC: Duke University Press, 1993), 65.

13. "just a minute" (*sic*, no author listed), *New Masses* xiv, no. 9 (August 26, 1947): 2.
14. "just a minute," 2.
15. WGA, notebooks series 1, item 52.
16. Nicola Sacco and Bartolomeo Vanzetti, *Letters of Sacco and Vanzetti* (New York: Penguin Classics, 2007), 13.
17. WGA, notebooks series 1, item 52.
18. WGA, notebooks series 1, item 46.
19. Quoted in Ralph Young, *Dissent: The History of an American Idea* (New York: New York University Press, 2015), 347.
20. WG to MA and MD, November 4, 1946, RRFAC, 4-01-35.
21. Bartolomeo Vanzetti, "Vanzetti's Petition to Gov. Fuller," http://dwardmac.pitzer.edu/Anarchist_Archives/bright/SaccoVan/defense.html.
22. Max Shachtman, *Sacco and Vanzetti, Labor's Martyrs* (New York: International Labor Defense, 1927), 31.
23. WGA, notebooks series 1, item 63.
24. Cray, *Ramblin' Man*, 299; Klein, *Woody Guthrie: A Life*, 327; Shelton quoted in Ronald D. Cohen, *Woody Guthrie: Writing America's Songs* (New York: Routledge, 2012), 57; Wayne Hampton, *Guerrilla Minstrels: John Lennon, Joe Hill, Woody Guthrie, and Bob Dylan* (Knoxville: University of Tennessee Press, 1986), 124.
25. Place, "Archivist's Remarks," liner notes to *Ballads of Sacco and Vanzetti* compact disc, Smithsonian Folkways Recordings, 1996.
26. Guthrie, "The Flood and the Storm," *Ballads of Sacco and Vanzetti*, Smithsonian Folkways Recordings, 1996.
27. Guthrie, "I Just Want to Sing Your Name," *Ballads of Sacco and Vanzetti*.
28. Comentale, *Sweet Air*, 144.
29. Guthrie, "We Welcome to Heaven," *Ballads of Sacco and Vanzetti*.
30. Victor S. Navasky, *Naming Names* (orig., 1980; New York: Macmillan, 2003), 319.
31. WG to Seeger family, February 27, 1947, WGA, correspondence series 1, box 3, folder 23. See, also, Cray, *Ramblin' Man*, 310.

CHAPTER EIGHT: *"The Whole Works"*
1. WG to Seeger family, February 27, 1947. WGA correspondence series 1, box 3, folder 23.
2. WGA, manuscripts series 9, box 4, folder 52.
3. Cray, *Ramblin' Man*, 313.
4. Criminal Case File 42202, United States District Court, Eastern District of New York, The United States of America vs. Woodrow Wilson Guthrie.
5. WGA, notebooks series 1, item 73.
6. George Huntington, "On Chorea," *Medical and Surgical Reporter* 26 (1872): 317–21.
7. John Barkenbus, MD, "The Urge to Act: Impulsivity and Huntington's Disease," Huntington's Disease Society of America, 2015, 10. https://hdsa.org/wp-content/uploads/2015/02/13090.pdf.

8. Hays, "On Woody."

9. WGA, notebooks series 1, item 52.

10. Guthrie, "The People of the United States Versus Woodrow Wilson (Woody) Guthrie," WGA, manuscripts series 1, box 7, folder 24, p. 9.

11. See, for example, John D'Emilio, *Sexual Politics, Sexual Communities: The Making of a Homosexual Minority in the United States, 1940–1970* (Chicago: University of Chicago Press, 1983), throughout chapter 3.

12. WGA, notebooks series 1, item 71. As late as 1953, he wrote a song about the case called "Judge Kennedy and Me."

13. WGA, notebooks series 1, item 52.

14. Ellen Herman, *The Romance of American Psychology: Political Culture in the Age of Experts* (Berkeley: University of California Press, 1995), 5.

15. Robbin, *Woody Guthrie and Me*, 122. Moe Asch said Guthrie was "the person most illustrative of Walt Whitman that I've ever come across," and compared both men to the hippies of the 1960s (quoted in Jeff Place, "The Music of Woody Guthrie," 43).

16. Guthrie, *Pastures of Plenty*, 226.

17. Woody Guthrie, "My Best Songs," in Shelton, *Born to Win*, 17.

18. Guthrie, "My Best Songs," 49.

19. Garman, *A Race of Singers*, 108.

20. Janet Halley, *Split Decisions: How and Why to Take a Break from Feminism* (Princeton, NJ: Princeton University Press, 2006), 119.

21. Guthrie, "My Best Songs," 47.

22. Guthrie, "My Best Songs," 49.

23. Guthrie, "My Best Songs," 53.

24. Guthrie, "My Best Songs," 55.

25. Estelle B. Freedman, *Feminism, Sexuality, and Politics* (Chapel Hill: University of North Carolina Press, 2006), 129. See also George Chauncey, "The Post War Sex Crime Panic," in *True Stories from the American Past*, ed. Richard Graebner (New York: McGraw-Hill, 1993).

26. Hurewitz, *Bohemian Los Angeles and the Making of Modern Politics*, 138.

27. Jennifer Terry, *An American Obsession: Science, Medicine, and Homosexuality in Modern Society* (Chicago: University of Chicago Press, 1999), 273. My italics.

28. Margot Canaday, *The Straight State: Sexuality and Citizenship in Twentieth-Century America* (Princeton, NJ: Princeton University Press, 2009), 98–99.

29. When the Quaker Emergency Services Committee declared "readjustment" the aim of their clinic, they chose a term that today conjures images of *Manchurian Candidate*–style mind control. In fact, the term applied generally to efforts to re-acclimate veterans to domestic civilian life; the proper name for the legislation popularly known as the "G. I. Bill" was the Servicemen's Readjustment Act of 1944. Getting over the jolting experience of having served in the war meant getting straight again, and vice versa.

30. WG to MM, May 8, 1947, WGA, correspondence series 1, box 2, folder 12.

31. Kaufman, *Woody Guthrie's Modern World Blues*, 191–92.

32. Guthrie never mentions Hay, but curiously, the earliest known recordings of Guthrie, made at the KFVD studios, ended up in Hay's possession. See Peter

La Chapelle, "Woody Guthrie's Los Angeles Recordings," *Woody at 100* booklet, 28–30. In his papers at the San Francisco Public Library, James C. Hormel LGBTQIA Center, Hay mentions several Guthrie songs in his copious notes for a class he taught for People's Songs, "Music: A Barometer of Class Struggle" (box 21, folder 9). He also discusses trying to raise money for the singer when his family arrived in LA and they were, according to Hay, sleeping in their car (box 21, folder 12).

CHAPTER NINE: *"Sick in His Own Healthy Way"*

1. WGA, manuscripts series 5, box 7, item 40.
2. WGA, manuscripts series 5, box 7, item 40.
3. WGA, manuscripts series 5, box 7, item 40.
4. WGA, manuscripts series 5, box 7, item 74.
5. WGA, manuscripts series 5, box 7, item 40.
6. Aaron J. Leonard, "Newly Released FBI Files Expose Red-Baiting of Woody Guthrie," *Truthout*, August 14, 2018, https://truthout.org/articles/newly-released-fbi-files-expose-red-baiting-of-woody-guthrie.
7. Cray, *Ramblin' Man*, 337.
8. According to Cray, he lost the Decca contract in early 1952 because of McCarthyism and, possibly, because of direct HUAC testimony. *Ramblin' Man*, 346–47.
9. WGA, Stetson Kennedy Papers, WG to SK, August 19, 1951, box 1.
10. A 1949 performance was released in 2011 as *The Live Wire* (Rounder Records).
11. James W. Mavor Jr. tape in American Folklife Center, Library of Congress, AFC 1991/003.
12. Quoted in Klein, *Woody Guthrie: A Life*, 385.
13. Quoted in Klein, *Woody Guthrie: A Life*, 390.
14. Quoted in Klein, *Woody Guthrie: A Life*, 392–93. My italics.
15. "Dr. C. H. Bellinger, Hospital Director," *New York Times*, August 14, 1952, 23.
16. *Annual Report of the Board of Visitors of Brooklyn State Hospital*, 1953.
17. WGA, notebooks series 1, item 74.
18. WGA, notebooks series 1, item 74.
19. WGA, notebooks series 1, item 74.
20. WGA, notebooks series 1, item 74.
21. WGA, notebooks series 1, item 74.
22. Sharon L. Snyder and David J. Mitchell, *Cultural Locations of Disability* (Chicago: University of Chicago Press, 2006), 8. Sandy Sulaiman, author of a 2007 memoir about living with Huntington's, describes her ongoing battle to get doctors "to realize you are a human being, not a lab rat." See her *Learning to Live with Huntington's Disease: One Family's Story* (London: Jessica Kingsley Publishers, 2007), 19.
23. Talcott Parsons, *The Social System* (orig. 1951; New York: Free Press, 1964).
24. WGA, notebooks series 1, item 74.
25. WGA, correspondence series 1, box 3, folder 3.
26. WGA, notebooks series 1, item 74.

27. Albert Deutsch, *The Shame of the States* (New York: Harcourt, Brace, 1948), 161.
28. WGA, manuscripts series 5, box 7, folder 40.
29. WGA, notebooks series 1, item 74.
30. WGA, notebooks series 1, item 74.
31. WGA, notebooks series 1, item 74.
32. WGA, notebooks series 1, item 74.
33. WGA, notebooks series 1, item 74.
34. WGA, notebooks series 1, item 74. My italics.
35. WGA, notebooks series 1, item 74.
36. WGA, notebooks series 1, item 74.

CHAPTER TEN: *Look Away*

1. Quoted in Cray, *Ramblin' Man*, 353.
2. Quoted in Cray, *Ramblin' Man*, 357.
3. WG to MMG, October 13, 1952, WGA, correspondence series 1, box 3, folder 4.
4. WGA, notebooks series 2, item 11.
5. Most of the images discussed in this chapter are reproduced in high quality in Steven Brower and Nora Guthrie, eds., *Woody Guthrie Artworks* (New York: Rizzoli, 2005).
6. Glenda Elizabeth Gilmore, *Defying Dixie: The Radical Roots of Civil Rights* (New York: Norton, 2009), 9.
7. Gilmore, *Defying Dixie*, 7.
8. Guthrie, "The Blinding of Isaac Woodward," RRFAC, WG-1-01-31. Guthrie's title misspells the surname of the song's subject; it was, in fact, *Woodard*.
9. On these cases and the tensions between radicals and liberals that arose in the left's attempt to address them, see Martha Biondi, *To Stand and Fight: The Struggle for Civil Rights in Postwar New York City* (Cambridge, MA: Harvard University Press, 2003).
10. WG to MMG, December 8, 1945, WGA, correspondence series 1, box 2, folder 11.
11. WGA, notebooks series 1, item 62.
12. WGA, notebooks series 1, item 52.
13. Quoted in Seth Archer, "Reading the Riot Acts," *Southwest Review* 91, no. 4 (2006): 509.
14. Susan Sontag, *On Photography* (New York: Farrar, Straus and Giroux, 1973), 23.
15. "Lynchers Avenge the Murder of Geo. Loney," *Okemah Ledger*, May 25, 1911.
16. Quoted in Quintard Taylor, *In Search of the Racial Frontier: African Americans in the American West, 1528–1990* (New York: Norton, 1998), 145. See, also, Russell Cobb, "Dreams of a Black Oklahoma," in *This Land Race Reader* (Tulsa: This Land Publishing, 2017), 15–21.
17. Booker T. Washington, "Boley, A Negro Town in the West," in *Booker T. Washington Papers*, vol. 9, *1906–08*, ed. Louis Harlan (orig. 1908; Urbana: University of Illinois Press, 1980), 430.

18. James Loewen, *Sundown Towns: A Hidden Dimension of Segregation in America* (New York: New Press, 2005), 82–84.
19. Department of Commerce and Labor—Bureau of the Census, Thirteenth Census of the United States, 1910—Population, available at http://laura nelsonlynching.weebly.com, accessed November 22, 2019.
20. "Negro Female Prisoner Gets Unruly," *Okemah Ledger*, May 18, 1911.
21. "Lynchers Avenge the Murder of Geo. Loney."
22. Guthrie, *Pastures of Plenty*, 37.
23. Woody Guthrie, Alan Lomax, and Pete Seeger, *Hard Hitting Songs for Hard-Hit People* (orig. 1946; Lincoln: University of Nebraska Press, 2012), 334–35.
24. Guthrie, Lomax, and Seeger, *Hard Hitting Songs for Hard-Hit People*, 335.
25. Earl Conrad, *Harriet Tubman: Negro Soldier and Abolitionist* (New York: International Publishers, 1942), 5, 7. Italics in original.
26. Howard Fast, *Peekskill, USA: Inside the Infamous 1949 Riots* (New York: Civil Rights Congress, 1951), 29. Other details from Martin Duberman, *Paul Robeson* (New York: Knopf, 1988).
27. Hays, "On Woody," Lee Hays Papers, RRFAC online, http://edan.si.edu /slideshow/slideshowViewer.htm?damspath=/Public_Sets/CFCH/CFCH -RRFAC/CFCH-SOVA/CFCH-HAYS/Interviews/HAYS_05_05_049, accessed July 19, 2018.
28. Kaufman, *Woody Guthrie, American Radical*, 160. Kaufman's book features the best account of the Peekskill riots.
29. The song appears on Billy Bragg and Wilco's *Mermaid Avenue, Vol. III* (Nonesuch, 2012).
30. Civil Rights Congress, *We Charge Genocide: The Historic Petition to the United Nations for Relief from a Crime of the United States Government against the Negro People* (orig. 1951; New York: International Publishers, 1970), 8–9.
31. The 2,253 figure is from Alden Whitman, "A Builder Looks Back—and Moves Forward," *New York Times*, January 28, 1973, https://www.nytimes .com/1973/01/28/archives/a-builder-looks-backand-moves-forward-builder -looks-back-but-moves.html.
32. WG to SK, November 5, 1951, WGA, Stetson Kennedy Papers, box 1.
33. Compare with Guthrie, "Houses to Houses," WGA, manuscripts series 9, box 4, folder 55.
34. Biondi, *To Stand and Fight*, 132.
35. For a full account of this work, see Will Kaufman, "Woody Guthrie, 'Old Man Trump,' and a Real Estate Empire's Racist Foundations," *The Conversation*, http://theconversation.com/woody-guthrie-old-man-trump-and-a -real-estate-empires-racist-foundations-53026, and "Trump Made a Tramp Out of Me," *The Conversation*, https://theconversation.com/in-another -newly-discovered-song-woody-guthrie-continues-his-assault-on-old-man -trump-64221.
36. WGA, manuscripts series 1, box 8, folder 10.
37. WGA, manuscripts series 6, box 8, folder 9.
38. WGA, notebooks series 2, item 11.

39. See the ten compact discs collected in *Songs for Political Action*, Bear Family Records, 1996.
40. Shawn Michelle Smith, *Photography on the Color Line: W. E. B. Du Bois, Race, and Visual Culture* (Durham, NC: Duke University Press, 2004), 134.

CHAPTER ELEVEN: *"Exactly How My Own Mother Saw and Felt"*

1. AVK to MMG September 30, 1953, WGA, correspondence series 3, box 1, folder 17.
2. MMG to WG, undated, WGA, correspondence series 3, box 3, folder 35.
3. MMG to WG, March 17, 1953, WGA, correspondence series 3, box 3, folder 36. She also maintained a correspondence with Anneke; Anneke wrote letters to Nora, Joady, and Arlo.
4. WGA, manuscripts series 6, box 8, folder 34.
5. Cray, *Ramblin' Man*, 374.
6. WG to Ken Lindsay, September 30, 1952, Woody Guthrie Manuscript Collection (AFC 1940/004), American Folklife Center, Library of Congress.
7. September 1953 letter to Ken Lindsay from Beluthahatchee, quoted in Cohen, *Woody Guthrie: Writing America's Songs*, 44.
8. WGA, notebooks series 1, item 74.
9. WGA, notebooks series 1, item 74.
10. WGA, manuscripts series 5, box 1, folder 21.
11. WGA, correspondence series 1, box 3, folder 12.
12. WGA, correspondence series 1, box 3, folder 10.
13. WGA, correspondence series 1, box 3, folder 10.
14. WG to MMG, October 25, 1956, WGA, correspondence series 1, box 3, folder 10.
15. *The Collected Poems of Allen Ginsberg, 1947–1997* (New York: Harper Collins, 2006), 141.
16. WGA, manuscripts series 5, box 8.
17. The song "New Multitudes" appears on Jay Farrar, Will Johnson, Anders Parker, and Yim Yames, *New Multitudes* (Rounder Records, 2012).

INDEX

to World War II, 10–11; and
racism, 24, 168, 169, 178, 179;
and Seventh World Congress of
the Committee, 24; and sexual-
ity, 76–77; tactics of, 37; after
World War II, 104; during World
War II, 48, 60, 71
Communist Political Association, 93,
104
Comstock, Anthony, 127
Comstock Act, 123
Coney Island: life in, 90–94; move to,
88–89
Coney Island Hospital, 147
confusion, 142
Congress of Industrial Organizations
(CIO), 68
Conrad, Earl, 178, 179
"consciousness of guilt," 111–13,
116–17
Cooper, James Fenimore, 7
Counterattack (magazine), 144
Country Gentleman (magazine), 25
CPUSA. See Communist Party of the
United States (CPUSA)
Cray, Ed, 21, 113, 190
Creedmoor Hospital, 188
Crissman, Mary Ruth, 123, 126,
127, 129, 136, 137
Crissman, Maxine, 22, 121, 126
Cunningham, Merce, 36, 159

Daily Worker (newspaper): on communist tactics, 37; on domesticity, 76; Guthrie's column and
articles in, 42, 47, 62, 93, 145;
on racism, 168;
Daily World (newspaper), 145
Dalcroze, Émile Jaques-, 96
dance: Woody Guthrie's writings on,
38–42, 48; and politics, 34–35;
priorities of modern, 50
Dance-A-Long (album), 99
"Dance Around" (song), 98
Dance Observer (magazine), 40, 41,
42, 62, 66, 67
Davenport, Charles B., 19

Davis, Lennard, 25–26
"Dear Mrs. Roosevelt" (song), 106
Debs, Eugene, 22, 33
"The Debt I Owe" (article), 103–4
Decca Records, 146, 213n8
"degradation ceremonies," 118, 144
de Kooning, Willem, 209n11
Denby, Edwin, 37
Denning, Michael, 9, 10, 52, 68
"Deportee (Plane Wreck at Los Ga-
tos)" (song), 170
the Depression, 46
Deutsch, Albert, 149–50, 155
Disc Records, 96, 101, 103, 107
Distler, Marian, 103, 110
diversity, 196
"Dixie" (song), 172, 183
"Doctors, Nurses, Hospitals" note-
book, 151, 162–63
"Dodgers" (song), 43
Doerflinger, Joy, 47
domesticity: after birth of Cathy,
90–93, 103; leftist politics and,
76–77; meeting of Marjorie and,
38, 43–44
"Don't Kill My Baby and My Son"
(song), 177
"Do Re Mi" (song), 24, 28
Dos Passos, John, 107, 108
"Drain the Swamp" (song), 182
drinking. See alcoholism
Du Bois, W. E. B., 174
Duncan, Isadora, 34
Dust Bowl, 3, 12, 21, 28, 46, 80–81
Dust Bowl Ballads (album), 1, 2–3,
29, 32, 38, 108
Dust Bowl migrants, 25
"Dust Can't Kill Me" (song), 4
"Dust Pneumonia Blues" (song), 4
"Dusty Old Dust" (song), 21, 145
E. P. Dutton & Company, 47, 57
Dylan, Bob, 7, 49, 135
dyskinesia: and alcoholism, 148,
151–52; and sense of body, 158;
as symptom of Huntington's dis-
ease, 18, 100, 146; and writing,
193

keeping tempo and prompting by, 2, 6, 92, 97, 101, 142, 146; letters on sexuality to, 72–73, 74, 77–78, 79; marriage to, 89; as mother figure, 54, 57; and move to Coney Island, 88–89; organizational skills of, 66; and politics of intimacy, 26, 49–50, 58–59, 60, 62; separation and divorce from, 147–48, 151–52, 165–66, 189; union with, 60, 66–70; and *Work Songs to Grow On*, 97–99
McCabe, Edwin, 175
McCarthyism, 105, 213n8
McGhee, Brownie, 105, 185
Melville, Herman, 7
Merchant Marine, 62, 71–74, 102
Mermaid Avenue (album), 9
Metropolitan Life Insurance, 180
Mickenberg, Julia, 95
midwifery and intimacy, 85–86
Millay, Edna St. Vincent, 107
Mishler, Paul, 10, 94, 209n18
"Miss Pavlichenko" (song), 71
Miss Stackabones, 92–93, 97
Mitchell, David, 153
mobility, 45–46
Mooney, Tom, 102
Mother (Gorky), 52
mothering, 50, 51, 52, 54, 86–87
multiculturalism, 170
Mussolini, Benito, 66, 105
"My Best Songs" (essay), 127, 130–35, 139
"My Voices" (poem), 155
"My Whore" (play), 192

nakedness, 131–32, 183, 184
"Name Wanted" (poem), 170
National Association for the Advancement of Colored People (NAACP), 169
Navasky, Victor, 118, 144
Neighborhood Playhouse, 34, 35, 36, 90
Nelson, Austin, 175–76
Nelson, Carry, 176

Nelson, L.D., 4–5, 168, 174, 175–78, 183, 185–86
Nelson, Laura, 4–5, 168, 174, 175–78, 183, 185–86
Neuhaus, Jessamyn, 84
Neumann, Natanya (Tanya), 101, 126, 128–29, 135
New Dance Group, 35, 38
New Deal, 7, 11, 24, 39, 56, 105–6, 130
New Deal Democrats, 24, 56, 102
New Left, 9–11, 49
New Masses (magazine), 106, 107, 114, 148, 155
"New Multitudes" (song), 195–96
New York: growing reputation in, 29–30; move to, 27
Niagara (poem), 86
"No Help Known" (article), 189–90
nudity, 131–32, 183, 184
nursing and intimacy, 85–86

obscenity charges, arrest on, 122–25, 127–28, 129–30, 133–36
"Okies," 25, 80, 108, 135
Oklahoma: early life in, 4–6; racism in, 175; sterilization in, 26
"Old Judge Thayer" (song), 101
Old Left, 9–10, 12
"Old Man Trump" (song), 180
"One Big Union," 67
On the Road (Kerouac), 49
organization, 66, 70
outlaws, 124

Parsons, Talcott, 153
passive resistance, 181
Pay Day (Asch), 108
Pearl Harbor bombing, 48
The People, Yes (poem), 36
"People as Words" (essay), 42–43
"People Dancing" (essay), 41, 42
People's Artists, 105
People's Songs, 104–5, 106, 131, 138, 145
People's World (newspaper), 23, 42
"permissive" parenting, 95

rhythm, 2, 6, 92, 97, 101, 142
The Rhythm Book (Waterman), 96
Ribble, Margaret, 95
Richmond, Howie, 146
The Rights of Infants (Ribble), 95
Robbin, Ed, 22–23, 75
Robeson, Paul, 11, 179
Robinson, Earl, 27, 39, 40, 145, 148, 190
Rogers, Will, 21
Roosevelt, Franklin Delano (FDR), 39, 58, 105, 106
"Round and Round Hitler's Grave" (song), 71
"Rug Wearing Out," 92
"Run, Nigger, Run" (song), 24
Russian Jewish intelligentsia, 33–34

Sacco, Nicola, 35, 102–3, 106–18
Sacco, Rosa, 109, 110, 115–16
Sacco-Vanzetti Defense Committee, 111–12
Sandburg, Carl, 1, 36, 37, 67
Sayler, Oliver, 34
schizophrenia, 148, 156
scientific socialism, 60–61
Scottsboro Nine, 35, 102
"Scrodging Around," 92
Sea Porpoise (ship), 72–73, 74
Seeds of Man (novel), 79, 146
Seeger, Pete: blacklisting of, 145; on death of Cathy, 120; and *Hard Hitting Songs for Hard-Hit People*, 177; letters to, 151, 156; and Alan Lomax, 27, 30; and People's Songs, 104–5; plays mailed to, 192; on Sacco and Vanzetti songs, 113; songwriting with, 71; in tribute concert, 190; in the Weavers, 122
segregation, 24, 138, 168, 169, 175
"sentimental maternalism," 52–53
Servicemen's Readjustment Act (1944), 212n29
Seventh World Congress of the Comintern, 24
"Sex Bureau," 135

sexuality, 74–87; defense of Guthrie's writings about, 75; in erotic letters to other women, 75, 125–26, 128–29; and eugenics, 80; homo-, 127, 133–34, 138–39, 159–61; in *House of Earth*, 79–87, 128; and Huntington's disease, 75, 125, 129; and infidelity, 14; and leftist politics, 69, 76–78; in letters to Marjorie, 72–73, 74, 77–78, 79; and lynchings, 183–84; and masturbation, 72, 74, 78, 95, 126, 160; as political struggle, 69, 130; and *Seeds of Man*, 79; and sex manuals, 78, 84; and sexual deviance, 122–25, 127–28, 129–30, 133–36; and sexual repression, 126–27; and songwriting, 79; and union, 77; utopian view of, 77; of Walt Whitman, 130–35; and womanizing, 76
Shachtman, Max, 112
Shahn, Ben, 107
Shakespeare in Harlem (Hughes), 52
shame and shaming: in *Bound for Glory*, 66; and collective solidarity, 144; and consciousness of guilt, 113, 117; about Guthrie's white Southern past, 167–68, 171–72; and homosexuality, 159; about Huntington's disease, 53–55, 56; and intimacy, 65; in "My Best Songs," 132–33; of own kind, 129; as political problem, 78; transformation of, 122
The Shame of the States (Deutsch), 150
Shaw, George Bernard, 52
Shelton, Robert, 113
Ship Story (unfinished novel), 81
shock treatment, 155–58
Short, Elizabeth, 123
sickness, 161
"sick role," 153
Siegel, Frederick, 105–6
Sinclair, Upton, 107, 108